Information Access in Digital Libraries

NIPA® GENX ELECTRONIC RESOURCES & SOLUTIONS P. LTD.
New Delhi-110 034

Information Access in Digital Libraries

(A Festschrift Volume in Honour of Dr. M.S Pathania)

Editors

Stanley Madan Kumar

Rabindra K. Mahapatra

K.Veeranjaneyulu

Associate Editors

G.Rathinasabapathy

Rajive K. Pateria

N.P.Ravi Kumar

nipa®

NIPA® GENX ELECTRONIC RESOURCES & SOLUTIONS P. LTD.

New Delhi-110 034

NIPA® GENX ELECTRONIC
RESOURCES & SOLUTIONS P. LTD.

101,103, Vikas Surya Plaza, CU Block
L.S.C. Market, Pitam Pura, New Delhi-110 034
Ph : +91 11 27341616, 27341717, 27341718
E-mail: newindiapublishingagency@gmail.com
web: www.nipabooks.com

For customer assistance, please contact
Phone: + 91-11-27 34 17 17
Fax: + 91-11- 27 34 16 16
E-Mail: feedbacks@nipabooks.com

ISBN: 978-81-19215-20-1

Composed and Designed by NIPA®.

In Honour of
Dr. M.S. Pathania

Dr. M. S. Pathania: A Man of Vision and Action

Introduction

Dr. M.S. Pathania was born at Shimla on April 14, 1953. He had his school education upto class IV at Shimla. Thereafter with the transfer of his father to Chandigarh he shifted there. He had his school education upto Hr. Secondary Part II at D.A.V. Higher Secondary School, Chandigarh. He did his B.Sc. in 1971 from Govt. College, Chandigarh and M.Sc. in Chemistry in 1973 from Panjab University, Chandigarh. He did Bachelor of Library Science in 1975 and Master of Library Science in 1976 from Panjab University, Chandigarh. He did his Ph.D. in Library & Information Science as an in-service candidate from Panjab University, Chandigarh in 1997. He served as an Asstt. Librarian from 1975 to 1977 at Punjab Vidhan Sabha, Chandigarh. In 1978 he joined as Lecturer in Library Science at Govt. Polytechnic for Women, Jalandhar City and served there up to 1983. In 1985 he joined as an Asstt. Librarian in the Central Library of Panjab University, Chandigarh and served there upto 1987. Thereafter he joined as an Asstt. Librarian in 1987 at Dr.Y.S. Parmar University of Horticulture and Forestry, Nauni, Solan (HP). He was promoted to Deputy Librarian under CAS in 1998. He was selected as University Librarian in 2008. He retired from the university services on April 2013 on superannuation, but the university authorities have honored him by reappointing him as librarian keeping in view of the development of university library.

Yashodha Negi
Assistant Librarian
Dr Y S Parmar University of Horticulture and Forestry, Solan
E-mail : yashodha_40@rediffmail.com
and
Sudhir Gupta
Assistant Librarian
Dr Y S Parmar University of Horticulture and Forestry, Solan
Email : gupta_sud@rediffmail.com

Contribution to Satyanand Stokes Library

Dr. Pathania is instrumental in organizing the Satyanand Stokes Library keeping in view the changing IT scenario of the users. In April, 1989 he submitted the proposal for the computerization of the library to the Founder Vice-Chancellor and started work in this direction. He outsourced Photocopying Service (First outsourcing of UHF in 2003) at reasonable rates in the central library of the university as well as in the Institute of Biotechnology & Environmental Science, Neri, Hamirpur. He is responsible for initiating modernization of the library making it one of the best libraries in the country. Under his guidance all the records have been digitized and bar-coded. He has contributed significantly in the development of in-house databases on Horticulture and Forestry. He has been responsible for introducing the Wi-Fi Technology in Satyanand Stokes Library which is the first SAU Library in the country that has been converted into Wi-Fi Library. He has been responsible for enhancing the information retrieval and disseminating capabilities of the library by putting the OPAC on the web. Besides this he is responsible for installing the 3 M Tattle Tap Electromagnetic Security System in the library. He has contributed significantly in the establishment of the Multimedia Center in the library at a cost of Rs. 60 lakhs in 2007 which was inaugurated on May 15, 2007 by the Director General, ICAR. He utilized this occasion to discuss in detail for the establishment E-Journals Consortium by the ICAR and submitted proposal in this regard to the DG, ICAR which was duly accepted/implemented at national level as CeRA. He is also responsible for linking the library with the Regional Research Stations and Krishi Vigyan Kendras of the University by creating connectivity facilities so that the scientists/staff working there can access the latest information and be in a position to communicate fast through E-Mail.

He is a Member of University Senate & Academic Council and has contributed significantly in the under mentioned committees of the University:

a. Member, Technical Committee on Computerization.

b. Member, Campus Purchase Committee.

c. Member, Central Purchase Committee.

d. Chairman, Committee for recommending/ installation of Audio visuals, Interactive Boards, etc. in COH.

e. Member, Space Allotment Committee.

f. Inquiry Officer for Departmental Inquiries.

Author/Editor of Books/Research Papers

Dr. M.S. Pathania has two books to his credit, besides chapters in books and 20 research papers in journals to his credit. He has contributed a number of papers in IUFRO World Conferences besides being a Resource Person in a number of Conferences/ Trainings/Seminars. He has edited two books listed as under:-

1. Pathania, M.S. ...[*et al.*], eds. 2011. Transformation of Agricultural Libraries in Collaborative Era. Hyderabad : B S Publications. 552 p.
2. Mahapatra, R.K., Pathania, M.S. & others, eds. 2012. Innovative practices in Management of Agricultural Libraries in the ICT Environment. Bhubaneswar: Reproprint. 374 p.

He has also been the Advisor and Editor of the College Magazine, Poly-voice.

Conferences Organized

He has organized the National Conference on the theme, "Transformation of Agricultural Libraries in Collaborative Era," during November 17-19, 2011 in collaborative with the Association of Agricultural Librarians and Documentalists of India (AALDI).

Organisation of Computer Training Programmes

He has organized six Computer Training Programmes in collaboration with INFLIBNET, Deptt. Of Higher Education to Govt. of Himachal Pradesh and Raja Ram Mohun Roy Foundation, Kolkatta for the benefit of working Librarians. This has helped the State and the region in upgrading the skills of Librarians in the area of application of modern information technology in Libraries.

Development of Phoenix Schedule in Forestry Classification

He has developed a phoenix schedule for classifying the forestry documents. An examination made over a period of years of the principles of classifying the 'Forests and Forestry' documents for use in the libraries and their treatment in DDC convinced him that there is an utmost necessity for expanding and modifying the forestry schedule. In India, majority of Agricultural Universities are imparting forestry education, Dr. Y.S. Parmar University of Horticulture & Forestry, Library, Solan and many Forest Institute Libraries arrange their documents by DDC Scheme find forestry class unsatisfactory. While working at Dr. Y.S.Parmar University of Horticulture & Forestry, Library where he is heading the Technical Section of the University Library, he had the invaluable opportunity of testing the existing schedules of DDC against the rapidly growing collection of forestry documents. His interest in developing the Forestry Schedule was first aroused there. The phoenix schedule on forestry has been prepared for the aid of those librarians, bibliographers who are interested in classifying and tabulating the forestry documents in their respective libraries and bibliographical tools, and use or desire to use DDC but find the scheme inadequate.

Honours

For his services and contributions in the field of Library & Information Science, the Association of Agricultural Librarians and Documentalists of India (AALDI) honoured him on December 5, 2012 for developing the most modern library in the country during the National Conference of Agricultural Librarians held at Orissa University of Agricultural Technology (OUAT), Bhubaneshwar. The honour was bestowed on him by the Vice-Chancellor of OUAT.

Dr. Pathania as a Person & Family

He is an able administrator, innovator, good planner and a friend indeed. He is a man of vision and action. He never loses his cool even at the time of crisis. He never hesitatates to take bold decisions in the interest of the library. He is very passionate about library profession and he has chosen it knowingly. The development of libraries during his tenure tells the story of his success in librarianship.

Above all he is a good human being too.

DR VIJAY SINGH THAKUR
Vice Chancellor

Dr YS Parmar University of Horticulture and Forestry
Nauni, Solan-173 230
Himachal Pradesh (INDIA)

December 26, 2013

Foreword

The Librarianship has been in practice ever since ancient times. The scholars and philosophers used to perform the roles of librarians as additional duties. Callimachus—a noted Greek poet, critic and scholar—is an example to cite who was entrusted with the responsibility to run the Library of Alexandria around 250 B.C. The emergence of Librarianship as a subject is of recent origin—it dates back to mid-20th century. The advent of Information and Communication Technologies (ICT) and its adoption by libraries over the last two decades has transformed the library techniques and services of the previous century. In fact, the introduction of new technologies in libraries is a great leap forward towards the achievement of the library objectives embedded in Ranganathan's Five Laws of Library Science.

The use of ICT as a tool has empowered the librarians to re-invent their roles and re-shape library services to meet the demands of library users. The role of the librarian has changed from that of a custodian to an information provider. They have to be technology savvy and good information managers to take full advantage of ICT potential. Libraries are now centres of information and knowledge, playing a vital role to achieve the literacy goals of a country, spread of education, accomplishment of the research, empowerment of women, upliftment of

Phone: +91-1792-252363 & 252357 (O), 252343 (R); +91-98160-82048 (M)
FAX: +91-1792-252242
E-mail: vcuhf@yahoo.com; thakurvs@satyam.net.in
Website: www.yspuniversity.ac.in

disadvantaged sections of society, social transformation and national development.

Revolutionary changes are taking place in the libraries in their methods of collection, organization, archiving, and dissemination of knowledge. There is an ostensible shift from the print to the paperless media in terms of number and variety. The electronic information offers numerous advantages like exhaustive, pin-pointed and instantaneous access to up-to-date information, economical storage and maintenance, ease of usability, provision of information to the information seekers at ail places (office, home, park, bus, train, aeroplane, etc.), and round the clock access to information.

I am immensely happy to pen down the foreword of the book entitled, "Information Access in Digital Libraries," which is being published to felicitate Dr. M.S.Pathania, Librarian, Satyanand Stokes Library, Dr. Y.S. Parmar University of Horticulture and Forestry, Nauni, Solan, Himachal Pradesh to acknowledge his contributions to the discipline of Librarianship. There is a perfect match between the person chosen and the contents of the book which focus on the use of ICT and its impact on library services, as Dr. Pathania is a technology savvy professional, a crusader for implementation of new technologies in the libraries, an enviable leader and service-oriented library professional who places service to the user before self. The book will undoubtedly be of great value to ail those who need to keep themselves abreast with the latest trends in ICT in general and electronic resources in particular.

(Vijay Singh Thakur)

Phone: +91-1792-252363 & 252357 (O), 252343 (R); +91-98160-82048 (M)
FAX: +91-1792-252242
E-mail: vcuhf@yahoo.com; thakurvs@satyam.net.in
Website: www.yspuniversity.ac.in

Preface

With the breakthroughs in S & T we see a greater demand for application-based learning and a decreasing need for old and basic knowledge. Libraries are shifting their role from custodian of traditional information resources to the provider of service-oriented digital information resources. For information dissemination, the electronic media offers unique advantages such as flexibility, rapid delivery, low cost, compact storage and interactivity. Traditional manual operations and services of libraries are being replaced by automated system which is leading to a 'Paperless Society'. Extensive use of computers, increased reliance on networks, rapid growth and expansion of Internet, information explosion have compelled libraries to adopt new innovative methods for storage, access, retrieval and dissemination of information. As a result of rapid developments in telecommunication and networking technologies the world has turned into a 'Global Village'. Internet, computers and digital technology have become an integral part of our social life. Challenges facing the library profession have never been more demanding than they are in the present Information Age.

ICT has produced voluminous quantity of information, innovative ways of packaging information and new user friendly tools for managing and accessing information, 24x7. Changing user's information needs, information handling and management in distributed environment are posing tremendous challenges for librarians to provide easy access to reliable information resources, quickly and economically. Sheer abundance of information and unprecedented advances in ICT applications have ushered in radical changes such as blogging, tweeting and other social net work media transforming the way information is accessed and disseminated.

The degree of knowledge and skill level required for effective library service is decided by the users' information requirements and the information sources. Three factors viz. accessibility, ease of use and perceived utility have profound effect on the use of an information service. Librarians need to be able to help users navigate and choose right information source. The current digital era has thrown several challenges for library profession to compete with Google, to provide effective information services to the user community. Net savvy individuals are taking full advantage of internet and web facilities to get information without visiting a library and also which saves their time. In order to survive this competition libraries have to develop innovative methods to provide improved services to the user community. 'Service' is the core of library profession. The emergence of web-based ICT, globalization of networks and internet all have deeply influenced the library profession and has provided new opportunities and challenges for library professionals. Digital technology has even affected the printing world. E-publishing is gaining prominence as it provides fast and easy multi-access to information. As a result, the present day libraries are over-loaded with information in various print and non-print formats.

World Wide Web (WWW) and digital technology have revolutionized the way people access, retrieve and communicate information. Using web 2.0 technologies authors are now able to publish liberally with ease and promptness. It must be remembered that digital objects are more easily altered and corrupted than their print-counterparts. Ensuring authenticity and integrity of e-content is given low priority when compared to increased access and content preservation. To carry out information analysis, evaluation and identifying authentic information is a challenge for present day library professionals. The users need to be educated to handle digitized library resources. Information literacy has gained importance. The rise of celebrated knowledge worker is a reflection of changing skill requirements and the need for up-skilling.

Contribution of Thirty one articles in the volume reflects various facets of accessing information in digital libraries. This volume is brought out in honour of Dr. M.S. Pathania, University Librarian, Dr. Y.S. Parmar University of Horticulture and Forestry, Solan for his valuable service and contribution to the field of library service.

Editors

Contents

Dr M S Pathania: A Man of Vision and Action .... *vi*

Yashodha Negi and Sudhir Gupta

Foreword .... *xi*

Preface .... *xiii*

1. **Useful Online Resources in the Field of Veterinary and Animal Sciences** **1**

   Balwan Singh

2. **University Library Automation and Network Services in Chhattisgarh: A Study** **15**

   Brajesh Tiwari and Uaday Kumar Watti

3. **Management of Open Access Resources: An Overview** **25**

   D.Ravinder

4. **Role of the Libraries in 2020** **33**

   Dev Walia

5. **Role of Cloud Computing in Library Services and Bioinformatics** **39**

   K. N. Kandpal, S.S.Rawat and Faheem Khan

6. **Tools and Techniques of Knowledge Management (KM) and Knowledge Sharing (KS) For Library Profession** **47**

   Khaisar Muneebulla Khan

7. **Web Based Library Services** **59**

   Minhaj Fatima

8. **Role of Web Applications in Modern Libraries** **67**

   N.S.Rohila, B.P. Singh and B.R. Yadav

9. **Emergence of Electronic Resources in Present Academic Libraries** 73

Nidhi Srivastava, Ramnivas Sharma and Manoj Tiwari

10. **Problems of E-Resources in Digital Libraries** 81

M. Papegowda, R. H. Walmiki, R.M. Shivakumar and V. Srinivasa

11. **Digitization of Central Potato Research Institute Library, Shimla** 93

Prem Lata, Yashodha Negi and Sudhir Gupta

12. **Digital Libraries: Whither thou Goest?** 99

R.D. Dabhi and Ushabala

13. **The Role of Librarian's in the Electronic Information Environment** 107

Rajkumar Singh

14. **Bibliometric Monitoring of Research Performance in the field of Dairy Science with Special Reference to Krishiprabha** 117

Ramnivas Sharma, Nidhi S Tiwari and Manoj Tiwari

15. **Digital Library: Development of Digital Library** ... 129

Rishabh Kumar Jain

16. **Library Consortia** 139

Saurabh Nagariya and Barsha Gupta

17. **Cloud Computing: Issues and Concern with the Libraries** 145

Seema Parmar, Rajive Pateria and Bhanu Partap

18. **Information Literacy Competency For Higher Education and the Role of Librarians** 161

Stanley Madan Kumar and Subramani, M.K

19. **Social Media and Academic Libraries: Trends and Challenges** 169

Stanley Madan Kumar and Devraj

20. **Role of E-Books as Important Electronic Resources in Digital Environment** 177

Subarna K. Das

21. **Open Source Software for Modern Libraries: A Comparative Study of ABCD, Koha and Newgenlib** 187

Surendra Kumar Pal and Bharat Praveen Sonker

22. **Implementing RFID Technology for Enhanced Library Services** 197

Tarvinder Singh Handa and Arvind Mittal

23. **Use of Electronic Resources by the Faculty Members of Indira Gandhi Krishi Vishwavidyalaya, Raipur (C.G.)** 207

Uaday Kumar Watti and Brajesh Tiwari

24. **Use of E-journals in A Engineering College Library with Special Reference to Gates Institute of Technololgy (GIT) Gooty, A.P : A Study** 217

Y.Ch.Venkateswarlu

25. **Digital Preservation in the Context of Institutional Repositories in Academic Libraries of India** 227

Sunil Kumar Satpathy

26. **Electronic Resource Management: Opportunities and Challenges** 237

Kamal Lochan Jena

27. **Marketing and Promotion of Library & Information Products and Services in Digital Era** 247

Chandresh A. Shah and Rabindra K. Mahapatra

28. **ICT among State Agricultural University and ICAR Institutes Libraries in India: An Overview of E-Granth** 255

Jadhav U.S.

29. Innovative Practices in Management of Agricultural Libraries of Chhattisgarh 267

Dr. Madhav Pandey

30. Harnessing Access to Information and Knowledge in Digital Libraries 277

Rabindra K. Mahapatra and Yadunath Prasad

Author Index 287

1

Useful Online Resources in the Field of Veterinary and Animal Sciences

Balwan Singh
Asstt. Librarian
Nehru Library, CCSHAU, Hisar
Email: balwanss@rediffmail.com

Introduction

While tracing the history of veterinary medicine, we come across the Chinese writings about the diseases of horses, oxen and buffalos in the past about 2500 B. C. Similarly we can find about 4000 years old. Indian art showing the people caring the horses and elephants. Even we can find in the art about ancient Egypt how they cared for their cattle and dogs health. The Ancient Romans had a word for the people that are doctors for animals, which is, veterinarius. In about A.D. 500 a Roman wrote a book on what veterinarians do. In 1598, Carlo Ruini, an Italian author wrote a book named as, "Anatomy of the Horse". The first school that taught people about scientific veterinary was in Europe in the mid-eighteenth century. By the end of the nineteenth century excellent veterinary schools were established in the United States. When Cornell University opened in Ithaca, New York, it had only two classrooms and one professor, Dr. James Law. Hc taught in Scotland. Dr. Law was the first professor who taught veterinary medicine in the United States.

Today veterinary education has been spread all over the world and the Veterinary doctors enjoy the same status as of the human doctors. Further, as Internet has become life blood for whole of the society especially for the educationists and researchers we can find online resources available on Internet in the field of Veterinary and Animal Sciences also. Having adequate knowledge of useful online resources, the scholars can save their valuable time.

Online Resources

Following types of online resources have been mentioned in this article, which are of immense use in the field of Veterinary Medicine:

A. Full Text Online Journals

B. Journals with Contents and Abstracts

C. Online Theses

D. Online Useful Informational Websites

A. Full Text Online Journals

There are a number of open access journals available on the Internet for the use of veterinary medical students, researchers, scientists and doctors. We can find 126 journals relating to animal sciences and 22 journals on Aquaculture and Fisheries subjects from the Directory of Open Access journals (DOAJ) http://www.doaj.org/doaj?func=subject&cpId=115&uiLanguage=en). Following is the list of some of the Full Text Online Open Access Journals:

1. Acta Veterinaria Scandinavica [http://www.actavetscand. com]

Acta Veterinaria Scandinavica is an open access, peer-reviewed journal published by BioMed Central Ltd. Acta Veterinaria Scandinavica is the official journal of the Veterinary Associations of the Nordic Countries, and it publishes articles on all aspects of veterinary researches and medicine of domestic and wild animals. Free full-text articles are available and information is provided about the journal editorial board, instructions for authors, and the peer-review process.

2. BMC Veterinary Research [http://www.biomedcentral.com bmcvetres]

BMC Veterinary Research is an open access, peer-reviewed journal published by BioMed Central Ltd. BMC Veterinary Research is an electronic-only journal and it publishes articles on all aspects of veterinary science and medicine, including epidemiology, diagnosis, prevention and treatment of medical conditions of domestic, companion, farm and wild animals. Full-text articles are freely available and information is provided about the journal editorial board, instructions for authors, and the peer-review process.

3. Iraqi Journal of Veterinary Sciences [http://www.vetmedmosul.org/ijvs/]

It is an open access peer reviewed scientific journal published biannually in Arabic and English by the College of Veterinary Medicine, University of Mosul, Iraq.

4. Journal of Equine Veterinary Science [http://www.j-evs.com]

Published monthly by Elsevier, each issue includes original scientific research, review articles, case reports, short communications and clinical techniques from leaders in the equine veterinary field. Full text from the year 2000 is available to the subscribers of the print version of the journal.

5. Journal of Swine Health and Production [http://www.aasv.org/shap/issues/]

It is a peer-refereed journal on applied swine medicine. The full text of the *Journal of Swine Health and Production* is online and is searchable.

6. Open Veterinary Science Journal [http://www.bentham.org/open/tovsj/]

The 'Open Veterinary Science Journal' is an open access peer-reviewed online journal made available through the Bentham Open initiative of the Bentham Science Publishers Ltd. The Open Veterinary Science Journal publishes research articles, reviews, and letters in all areas of experimental and clinical research in veterinary science and medicine. Full-text articles are available from Volume 1 (2007) to the present. Information is provided about instructions for authors, manuscript submissions, and the Editorial Board.

7. Veterinarian, The [http://www.theveterinarian.com.au/]

'The Veterinarian' is an independently-produced Australian veterinary publication. Aimed at veterinarians and veterinary nurses, this publication covers small, large and exotic animal cases. It provides current product and industry news, practice management features, and clinical reviews. There is an online forum, an events calendar, and a collection of full-text articles related to veterinary and animal health research topics. The Veterinarian is published by Sydney Magazine Publishers Pty Ltd.

8. Veterinary World [http://www.veterinaryworld.org/]

It is an International open access journal which aims to disseminate scientific knowledge related to veterinary medicine, animal husbandry and allied sciences. It provides information about submitting manuscripts, subscriptions and advertising.

B. Journals with Contents and Abstracts

In this category the publishers provide abstracts and contents free of cost and if the full text is required, then it could be made available through payments. Some of such journals are described as under:

1. American Journal of Veterinary Research (AJVR) [http://avmajournals.avma.org/loi/ajvr]

Published by the American Veterinary Medical Association (AVMA), the American Journal of Veterinary Research (AJVR) is a peer-reviewed veterinary medical journal which provides access to the contents and abstracts of original research articles that have the clear potential to enhance the health, welfare, and performance of animals and humans. The scope of the journal covers the general field of applied biomedical research with applications to veterinary medicine. Access to tables of contents and abstracts is freely available from 2000 onwards. Full-text access to journal content is available to personal and institutional subscribers only.

2. Journal of the South African Veterinary Association [http://www.journals.co.za/savet/]

The Journal of the South African Veterinary Association (known as the Journal of the SAVA) is the official journal of the South African Veterinary Association and it publishes articles of general and particularly of South African veterinary interest. Tables of contents and abstracts are available from Volume 68 (1) 1997 through to the present. Information is provided on the Editorial Committee, subscription charges for the print version of the journal, and instructions for authors. This journal is made available on the Web by Sabinet Online Ltd.

3. Medical and Veterinary Entomology [http://www.wiley.com/bw/journal.asp?ref=0269-283x]

Medical and Veterinary Entomology is published by Wiley-Blackwell on behalf of the Royal Entomological Society. This journal covers "all aspects of the biology and control of insects, ticks, mites and other arthropods of medical and veterinary importance." Tables of contents and article abstracts are freely available, and access to full-text articles requires a personal or institutional subscription. Instructions for authors and subscription information are available.

4. Nigerian Veterinary Journal [http://www.ajol.info/journal_index. php?jid=19&ab=nvj]

The Nigerian Veterinary Journal is the official journal of the Nigerian Veterinary Medical Association (NVMA). It publishes articles covering topical issues on animal health and diseases. Tables of contents and abstracts are available from Volume 23 (1) 2002 through to the present. Information is provided on the Editorial Board and instructions for authors. This journal is made available on the Web through the African Journals OnLine project (AJOL).

5. Preventive Veterinary Medicine [http://www.elsevier.com/wps/find/journaldescription.cws_home/503315/descript]

Preventive Veterinary Medicine is an international journal on research and development in veterinary epidemiology, animal disease prevention and control, and animal health economics. Aimed at research workers in veterinary epidemiology and animal health, the online version of Preventive Veterinary Medicine provides access to full-text articles for those readers whose library has subscribed to Preventive Veterinary Medicine through Science Direct. Abstracts are freely provided for all the back issues starting from Volume 1 (1) Aug 1982. This journal can be searched by keyword and author and there is information for authors, online manuscript tracking information for authors, and ordering information available from this site. Preventive Veterinary Medicine is published by Elsevier Science

6. Research in Veterinary Science [http://www.journals.elsevier. com/research-in-veterinary-science/]

Research in Veterinary Science is an International journal publishing original articles, reviews and short communications of a high scientific and ethical standard in the veterinary sciences.

7. Veterinarski Arhiv [http://www.vef.hr/vetarhiv/]

Veterinarski Arhiv is the official journal of the Faculty of Veterinary Medicine, University of Zagreb. This journal publishes results of original research and observations in veterinary sciences and medicine. All articles are available in English, and information is provided on institutional and personal subscriptions. Much of the journal content is freely available, and archives are available from Volume 68 (1) 1998 to the present. Instructions for authors and details of the editorial and advisory board are available. Journal content is searchable by the keyword, author, article title.

C. Online Theses

The under mention websites provide free full text dissertations/ theses in the field of agriculture and animal sciences:

1. Epsilon Dissertations and Graduate Theses Archive [http://epsilon.slu.se/eindex.html]

This is part of the English language site of Sveriges lantbruksuniversitet - Swedish University of Agricultural Sciences. All graduate dissertations and theses from the university are accessible online from this site via the Epsilon archive, which is searchable by author, department, year or keyword. Topics cover all aspects of animal science, agriculture, forestry, horticulture and rural development. Over 700 publications issued since 1998 are listed here, with full bibliographic data, abstract and downloadable full text files freely available.

2. Krishiprabha [http://192.168.1.22:8080/HAU/thesis.html]

KrishiPrabha is a full-text electronic database of Indian Agricultural Doctoral Dissertations submitted by research scholars to the 45 State/Deemed Agricultural Universities during the period from 1.1.2000 to 31.12.2007. This database, listing about 7500 Doctoral Dissertations with a full text of about 6000 Dissertations has been created by the Nehru Library, Ch. Charan Singh Haryana Agricultural University, Hisar with financial support from Indian Council of Agricultural Research, New Delhi under its National Agricultural Innovation Project. A number of theses on Veterinary Medicine are also available on this website through which scholars of State Agricultural Universities and ICAR Research Institutes can access full text theses and the scholars of rest of the world can access only abstracts of the theses.

D. Online Useful Informational Websites

There are number of useful websites which provide important information for the students and researchers and veterinary medical professionals and doctors. Some of these websites are given below:

1. Animalscience.com [http://www.animalscience.com/]

Animal science.com is an Internet subscription based service published by CABI publishing, available for researchers, practitioners and information specialists in animal and veterinary science. This resource contains information resources tailored to meet the needs of the animal science community and these include free access to the CAB Abstracts database, current news items on public health, animal production and welfare, genetics and biotechnology, equines, pets and exotics, animal diseases and product news. The journal section provides links to core journals in animal science and veterinary medicine, and tables of contents and chapters from animal health books are available. Additional resources available to subscribed users include published reviews, spotlight on hot topics in animal science, an events calendar, conference proceedings, job adverts and community areas that provide facilities for discussion groups. Presently a free 24 hour trial is available after a brief registration.

2. AVMA Media Library [http://www.avmamedia.org/]

The American Veterinary Medical Association (AVMA) Media Library provides free and open use of all its audio and video content contained within the media library. Downloading, viewing, and audio instructions are provided and resources available include podcasts, videos, audio news releases, and public service announcements, on a collection of animal health/veterinary topics.

3. Axiom Veterinary Laboratories [http://www.axiomvetlab.com/]

Axiom Veterinary Laboratories Ltd provides an extensive range of in - house clinical pathology diagnostics for multiple veterinary species to veterinary surgeons of the United Kingdom (UK), Ireland and Europe. Information and clinical advice is offered through the team of eleven clinical pathologists/internal medicine diplomats. This site contains an extensive library of images, fact sheets and case studies. Axiom is an ISO 9001 registered company and an ECVCP approved training facility.

4. Ectoparasites and Endoparasites [http://www.soton.ac.uk/~ceb/]

This site hosts a categorized directory of links in medical and veterinary parasitology, developed and maintained by Dr Clive Bennett at the University of Southampton. In addition, details of the author's teaching modules and research is provided. This site is hosted by the University of Southampton.

5. Eudrapharm [http://eudrapharm.eu/eudrapharm/welcome.do]

EudraPharm is a source of information on medicinal products for human or veterinary use that have been authorized for use in the European Union (EU) and the European Economic Area (EEA). The EudraPharm database can be searched by keyword under human products, veterinary products and human or veterinary products. Results have a simple or extended view that includes product information and presentation that gives labeling, packaging information and a summary of product characteristics. You can also view an A-Z product list and an advanced search facility is available. The database is available in 24 different languages.

6. European School for Advanced Veterinary Studies [http://www.esavs.net/]

The European School for Advanced Veterinary Studies (ESAVS) was established in 1991 as a pilot-project of the European Union's COMETT II program. The ESAVS is a non-profit organization that runs training courses and continuing education courses in veterinary medicine. This site contains detailed information on all the training programs provided by ESAVS and covers the intensive and distance learning programs. Biographical information is also provided about the trainers and their areas of interest.

7. European Veterinary Diagnostic Imaging (EVDI) [http://cheval.vet.gla.ac.uk/EVDI/]

This site represents the two groups that promote veterinary diagnostic imaging in Europe; the European College of Veterinary Diagnostic Imaging (ECVDI), and European Association of Veterinary Diagnostic Imaging (EAVDI). News and events from divisions and related associations can be found on this site. Details of office bearers, conferences and meetings of both ECVDI and EAVDI are provided. Links to other Web resources on veterinary radiology are provided. This site is hosted on the Web by the Faculty of Veterinary Medicine, University of Glasgow.

8. European Veterinary Libraries Group : EVLG [http://elib.tiho-hannover.de/virtlib/evlg/]

Formed in 1994 the European Veterinary Libraries Group (EVLG) acts as a section of the European Association for Health Information and Libraries (EAHIL). The group aims to unite all those who are interested and or employed in the animal health information field and facilitates cooperation and discussion between veterinary medical libraries. The website provides details of EVLG organised conferences, access to the newsletter, news and information about membership and the office bearers of the group.

9. Faculty of Veterinary Science, University of Melbourne [http://www.vet.unimelb.edu.au]

The website for the Faculty of Veterinary Science at the University of Melbourne provides information for prospective undergraduate, postgraduate and international students. The veterinary science research clusters currently focus on four main areas, namely, animal production, performance and welfare; animal biotechnology; cell biology and morphology; and infectious diseases, public health and biosecurity. The site includes material relevant for the local community, including details of the vet clinic and hospital.

10. GisVet [http://www.gisvet.org/]

The GisVet Project is an initiative, started in 1999, by the Department of Epidemiology of the Veterinary Laboratories Agency.

GIS (Geographical Information Science) is defined as software/ hardware which allows geo-referenced data to be sorted, stored, manipulated and displayed in a number of ways. The GISVET project provides general GIS information, as well as GIS information specifically relevant to veterinary use. Details on GIS, spatial statistics, data and metadata, related literature, remote sensing, and veterinary related case studies are provided. Papers presented at GisVet Conferences are available for viewing (2001-2004).

11. LIVE (Lifelong and Independent Veterinary Education) [http://www.live.ac.uk/]

LIVE (Lifelong and Independent Veterinary Education) is the only Centre for Excellence in Teaching and Learning (CETL) educational program specifically focused on veterinary education. The LIVE centre opened in February 2007 and is located at the Royal Veterinary College (RVC). This site provides information on the aims and activities of the program, projects and academic fellowships, and an event listing (for both past and future conferences). Brief biographical information is provided on LIVE core, clinical and advisory staff. LIVE is funded by HEFCE (Higher Education Funding Council for England).

12. Martindale's Health Science G : Virtual Veterinary Center [http://www.martindalecenter.com/Vet.html]

Martindale's Health Science Guide: Virtual Veterinary Center provides annotated links to Web resources under the following categories: veterinary journals, veterinary bioscience and genetics, veterinary clinical sciences, veterinary dictionaries, animal drugs and veterinary pharmacology, animal diseases and viruses, vaccination schedules and injection techniques, clinical medicine by species, veterinary histology, microbiology, parasitology, entomology, pathology and veterinary resources and indexes.

13. Med-Vet-Net [http://www.medvetnet.org/cms/]

Med-Vet-Net is the European Network of Excellence for Zoonoses research. Med-Vet-Net aims to be a network of excellence for the integration of veterinary, medical and food scientists, in the field of food safety, at the European Level, in order to improve research on the prevention and control of zoonoses, including food-borne diseases. This website provides information on partner institutes, the four main thematic research areas (risk research, detection and control, host-microbe interactions, epidemiology), publications (including research papers and policy reports), training and workshops, and an event calendar. The Med-Vet-Net Newsletter is available for downloading.

14. One Health Initiative [http://www.onehealthinitiative.com/]

The 'One Health Initiative' is collaboration between veterinarians, physicians, and other scientific-health related disciplines supporting the concept of 'One Health' which is "a worldwide strategy for expanding interdisciplinary collaborations and communications in all aspects of health care for humans and animals." This site provides details of professional organisations supporting this initiative, an archive of news items, ProMED disease outbreak reports, and an events calendar. The quarterly newsletter is available for viewing and downloading and is archived from Volume 1 (1) winter 2008. A range of publications (including the One Health AVMA Task Force Report) are all available from this site.

15. Vaccine & Infectious Disease Organization : VIDO [http://www.vido.org/]

The Vaccine & Infectious Disease Organization (VIDO) was formed in 1975 and is an organization dedicated to research on disease problems and production barriers facing the livestock and poultry industries (particularly in Canada). VIDO is based at the University of Saskatchewan and this site provides information on current research activities, disease specific information on beef, dairy, swine, poultry and other species, and educational publications produced by VIDO. This site is made available on the Web by the University of Saskatchewan.

16. Veterinary Education Worldwide (ViEW) [http://www.vet education.org/]

Established in 2004, Veterinary Education Worldwide (ViEW) is an international association for veterinary education. ViEW aims to "promote and support excellence in veterinary education at an international level." The site provides information on membership, the ViEW constitution, and a listing of current members. Information on the international annual meetings from 2004 to the present and any relevant recent news items are available. Links to further sources of information are provided.

17. Veterinarians without Borders [http://www.vsf-belgium.org/dzf/view/en/214]

This is the homepage of Vétérinaires Sans Frontières (Veterinarians without Borders). Their aim is to develop livestock keeping and improve veterinary medicine to improve living conditions in developing countries. The website gives information on current projects and education information. Press releases are available as well as information on making a donation and volunteering.

18. Virtuelle Fachbibliothek Veterinarmedizin - ViFaVet [http://elib.tiho-hannover.de/virtlib/index-e.html]

ViFaVet is a virtual library providing access to resources in veterinary medicine and general parasitology. Created and hosted on the Web by the TiHo Hannover Library, Germany, this resource is available in both English and German. Access is provided to evaluated Internet resources, including databases; documents; congress proceedings; electronic journals; teaching materials and CAL packages. Access is also provided to the OPAC of the TiHo Library (in German).

19. Wellcome Trust [http://www.wellcome.ac.uk/index.htm]

Wellcome Trust is a global charitable foundation dedicated to achieving extraordinary improvements in human and animal health. It supports the brightest minds in biomedical research and the medical humanities. The main support includes public engagement, education and the application of research to improve health.

20. World Veterinary Association (WVA) [http://www.worldvet.org/]

The World Veterinary Association (WVA) represents the veterinary profession at the global international level. This site provides information on the structure of the WVA, its history, membership requirements, and its aims and activities. Additional resources available include a calendar of events, an archive of news items, technical articles and reports, and the WVA newsletter (archived from January 2006).

Conclusion

There are number of online resources available on Internet which are of immense use for the veterinary and animal science professionals. The professionals who are doing research or practice can save lot of time by using these resources. Though it is tough to get related information from the Internet but if the persons already have some knowledge of these websites then they can use these resources effectively in their pursuits of study and research.

References

(http://www.doaj.org/doaj?func=subject&cpId=115&uiLanguage=en
http://192.168.1.22:8080/HAU/thesis.html
http://avmajournals.avma.org/loi/ajvr
http://cheval.vet.gla.ac.uk/EVDI/
http://elib.tiho-hannover.de/virtlib/evlg/
http://elib.tiho-hannover.de/virtlib/index-e.html
http://epsilon.slu.se/eindex.html
http://eudrapharm.eu/eudrapharm/welcome.do
http://library.thinkquest.org/03oct/00176/history.html
http://www.actavetscand.com/
http://www.ajol.info/journal_index.php?jid=19&ab=nvj
http://www.animalscience.com/
http://www.avmamedia.org/
http://www.axiomvetlab.com/
http://www.bentham.org/open/tovsj
http://www.biomedcentral.com/bmcvetres
http://www.elsevier.com/wps/find/journaldescription.cws_home/503315/descript
http://www.esavs.net/
http://www.gisvet.org/
http://www.insipub.com/rjavs.html
http://www.martindalecenter.com/Vet.html
http://www.medvetnet.org/cms/
http://www.soton.ac.uk/~ceb/
http://www.theveterinarian.com.au/
http://www.vef.hr/vetarhiv/
http://www.vet.unimelb.edu.au
http://www.vsf-belgium.org/dzf/view/en/214
http://www.wiley.com/bw/journal.asp?ref=0269-283x
http://www.onehealthinitiative.com
http://www.live.ac.uk
http://www.vido.org
http://www.wellcome.ac.uk/index.htm
http://www.veteducation.org

2

University Library Automation and Network Services in Chhattisgarh: A Study

Brajesh Tiwari
Associate Professor
Dept. of Library and Information Science
Guru Ghasidas Vishwavidyalaya, Bilaspur(C.G.)
and
Uaday Kumar Watti
Asst. Librarian, Indira Gandhi Krishi Vishwavidyalaya
Raipur (C.G.)

Introduction

Libraries are universally recognized as important social institutions for diffusion of knowledge and information. The modern and highly equipped libraries are found in the universities since they are the centers of higher education, training and research. The universities libraries are essential to achieve the objective of university education and research.

The concept of library is changing very fast due to impact of ICT. Today we are at the beginning of 21st century and entering in the period of change. We can see the impact of ICT in every walk of life such Banking, Insurance, Railway, Mobile Technology etc. The current digital revolution of ICT is biggest change to have a merged in the field of library science. According to an estimate about 12-15 million documents are added annually in the world on various subjects and fields. The libraries and information centers have to generate and popularize their services for proper utilization of information, and also have to promote their resources in this changing environment. With the introduction of computers and ICT tools, libraries are on the threshold of library automation which will enhance standard library services.

Objectives

An investigation was carried out to review the status of automation and implementation of networked services in these libraries with the following objectives:

1. To identify library functions and services been or being automated
2. To identify the software packages being used
3. To identify automated and networked services being provided

History of Library Automation

The phrase library automation has been used almost synonymously with library mechanization in the context of computerization; machines with appropriate capabilities and software that has been properly written are the basic pre- requisites to any successful venture into library automation. It is as much a human process as a technological one. Library automation is perceived in a simple sense as a process of mechanization of library operations, which are of a routine and repetitive nature. This covers usually house keeping operations such as acquisition, cataloguing, circulation and serial control, however today it has expanded to the library management systems to incorporate OPAC, CD-Rom, Networks and desktop publishing, office automation etc.

D.S.Harder in 1936 defined that the automatic handling of parts between progressive production processes in relation to engineering industries. Since the term has applied to a wide variety of automatic machinery and automatic system.

The Punch card invented by Hollerith in 1880 was used for tabulating the census data. Later the Punch card has been used for automation in many fields. The University of Texas was the first university to use this punch card in 1936 for circulation control and later for serial control in mid 1940's

The Punch card was installed for book charging machines for recording individual transaction automatically by the Montclair Public Library in New Jersey in 1942 .

The unit record machine are invented for the production of catalogues for the first time in 1950 by the Library of congress, USA, since than many libraries in USA used the unit record machine for automating their several activities.

Library automation was entered in to its second era with the introduction of computers in 1960.The MEDLARS projects, Serial Control Work by Southern Illinois University of California, A Circulation System by the Southern Illinois University at Carbondale, Computerized Book Catalogues by Ontario New Universities and MARC Projects by The Library of congress are some of the important developments for automation of Libraries.

On-line Library systems was implemented at MIT under its technical information projects (OCLC and BALLOTS) in 1967 for the purpose of speedy access of cataloguing records of very large data bases.

The Bell Telephone Laboratories and Eastern University had On-line Serial Control Systems and the Washington State University had On-line Acquisition System in the early 1970s. Library automation package and Mini-computers were developed in 1980; which helped in easier automation of day to day work of library operations.

Status of Library Automation in India

The Indian Statistical Institute, Calcutta was the first in India to install a computer system in 1955, and to develop in indigenous computer in 1964. As far as use of computer for library work is concerned, computer were used in library work for the first time possibly by INSDOC, when they computerized the author and subject indexes of 'Indian Science Abstract" in 1965. In 1967, the INSDOC brought out the Roster of Indian Scientific and Technical Translators and the Regional Union Catalogue of Scientific Serials, Bombay and Poona in 1973. In 1978, INSDOC initiated SDI services as a NISSAT Project with Chemical Abstract and INSDOC databases utilizing CAN/SDI software of IIT, Madras. In 1970, many libraries ventured in preparing computerized databases through the initiative and financial support of NISSAT, many library networks were initiated and operative. Notables of these networks are CALIBNET, DELNET, INFLIBNET, PUNENET etc. Now a days, many institution such as, INFLIBNET, INSDOC, DESIDOC, NISSAT etc. are engaged in importing training for computer application in library work through regular sponsored and adhoc courses. INFLIBNET was established in 1991 at Ahmadabad with objectives to increase networking of Universities libraries and form database. This institute also developed SOUL software package for computerizing and interlinking between universities.

Need of Library Automation

Automation helps libraries to improve their operation and accelerating their working and saves the effort, time and resources than processing manually. The automation of the library is needed for the following purposes:

1. Improve control over collection.
2. Effective control over the entire house keeping operations.
3. Share the resources through network among various libraries in a region, effectively.
4. Avoid duplication of work
5. Use the services of the existing staff more effectively.

Areas of Library Automation

1. Automation of library functions;
2. Accessing remote electronic resources
3. Use of electronic resources within the library e.g. CD-ROM
4. Office automation (e.g. Word processing)
5. Patron services

Methodology

The present study was based on a comprehensive survey carried out with specific intension to assess the present status of library automation and networking services of the universities in Chhattisgarh State. The questionnaires for this survey were achieved from the websites and from the Librarians of respective libraries of universities of Chhattisgarh State.

Analysis and Discussion

Universities of Chhattisgarh State: The libraries of universities play in important role in Research and Education in the Universities. In Chhattisgarh, there are 15 Universities. 4 Universities, namely Indira Kala Sangit Vishwavidyalayam, Khairagarh, Pt. Ravishankar Shukla University, Raipur, Guru Ghasidas Vishwavidyalaya, Bilaspur, Indira Gandhi Krishi Vishwavidyalaya, Raipur were formed before the formation of this state in 2000 and rest 11 Universities were formed after the formation of this state. The list of Universities is shown below in chronological order.

S. No.	Name of University		Year of establishment
1	Indira Kala Sangit Vishwavidyalayam, Khairagarh	IKSV	1956
2	Pt. Ravishankar Shukla University, Raipur	RSU	1964
3	Guru Ghasidas Vishwavidyalaya, Bilaspur	GGV	1983
4	Indira Gandhi Krishi Vishwavidyalaya, Raipur	IGKV	1987
5	Hidaytulla Law University, Raipur	HLU	2003
6	Kushabhau Thakre Patrakarita Vishwavidyalaya, Raipur	KTPV	2004
7	Swami Vivekanand Technical University, Bhilai	SVTU	2005
8	Pt. Sunderlal Sharma Mukat Vishwavidyalaya, Bilaspur	SSMVV	2005
9	Dr.C.V.Raman Vishwavidyalaya, Bilaspur	CVRVV	2006
10	Baster Vishwavidyalaya, Jagdalpur	BV	2008
11	Sarguja Vishwavidyalaya, Sarguja	SV	2008
12	MATS University, Raipur	MATS	2008
13	Aayush avam Sawasthya Vigyan Vishwavidyalaya, Raipur Chhattisgarh	ASVV	2009
14	Kamdhenu Vishwavidyalaya, Durg	CKV	2012
15	ITM University, Raipur	ITM	2012

The various status of libraries of the state are described below in the different tables with various parameters:

Table 2.1: Library Automation Packages

S.No.	Name of the University	Integrated Library Automation Software	
		Installed	In progress
1	IKSV	-	SOUL
2	RSU	SOUL	
3	GGV	-	SOUL
4	IGKV	LIBSYS & KOHA	
5	HLU	-	
6	KTPV	-	
7	SVTU	-	
8	SSMVV	-	
9	CVRVV	-	
10	BV	-	
11	SV	-	
12	MATS	New GenLib	
13	ASVV	-	
14	CKV	-	
15	ITM	-	

Table 2.1 clearly indicates that out of 15 Universities only 1 University Library uses SOUL software, another one University uses LIBSYS software, and one Law department of MATS University uses NewGenLib software. The establishment of SOUL software is in progress in 2 Universities (1 KSV and GGV).

Table 2.2: Section Automated

S.No.	Name of University	Acquisi -tion	Catalo -guing	Circu -lation	Serial management	Barcode Printing
1	RSU	Y	Y	Y	Y	Y
2	IGKV	N	Y	Y	Y	Y
3	MATS	N	Y	Y	N	N
4	IKSVV	N	Y	Y	Y	Y
5	GGV	N	Y	N	N	Y

Y = Yes N = No

Table 2.2 indicates that only one university libraries (RSU) are being completely automated. This clearly reveals that out of 5 automated libraries, less than 20 % response Acquisition section, 100% response Cataloguing and Circulation section and less than 60 % response Serial management section and Barcode Printing.

Table 2.3: OPAC Services

S.No.	Name of University	OPAC	Web OPAC
1	RSU	Y	Y
2	IGKV	Y	Y
3	MATS	Y	Y
4	IKSVV	Y	N
5	GGV	N	N

Y=Yes N=No

Table 2.3 shows the library access status of above universities. Four libraries avail Online Public Access Catalogue (OPAC) and only three avail the Web Online Public Access Catalogue (Web OPAC).

Table 2.4: Online Databases

S.No.	Name of University	Database
1	RSU	MATHSCINET, ISID
2	GGV	Sciencedirect, Academic Search Complete, CMIE Prowess & Alpha
3	HLU	West Law, Manupatra
4	MATS	IND Law, West Law

Table - 2.4 reveals that only four libraries provide Online Database Access.

Table 2.5: Memberships of Consortia

S.No.	Name of University	Name of Consortia
1	RSU	UGC Infonet
2	GGV	UGC Infonet
3	IGKV	CeRa
4	IKSVV	UGC Infonet

Table - 2.5 reveals the study of libraries in respect of Membership of Consortia. RSU,GGV and IKSVV are the members of UGC Infonet consortia and IGKV is the member of CeRA Consortia.

Table 2.6: Offline Database

S.No.	Name of University	Offline Database
1	IGKV	CAB, AGRIS, AGRICOLA, CROP CD, SOILCD, PLANT PROTECTION CD, HORT CD, etc.
2	HLU	Grand Jurix

Table - 2.6 reveals that only two libraries provide the offline database access.

Suggestion

Based on the finding of the study, the following suggestions are made to automate and networked services in the library:

1. Adequate Budget should be provided to computerize the library system,
2. The in-charge of the library should have strong will power to establish the automated systems in the library.
3. The authorities of the Institute should be convinced about the importance of the automated systems in the library.
4. Required no. of Technical and supporting staff should be provided to the library.
5. A PG Degree holder in Computer Science should be provided.

Conclusion

The study concludes that very less number of libraries have been automated in Chhattisgarh state. This reveals that the process of automation and networking of libraries is very slow. Automation of the libraries services plays very important role for efficient and effective working of the library and information centers. The automation of the libraries provides facilities of easy handling, retrieval and dissemination of information efficiently and effectively. It is very important to avail the automation and networking services in the library in this modern era to save the time and work load of library authorities as well as of library users.

References

Chinnasamy, K. and Durga, K. Kanaga. 2010. Why need to automate libraries. Library Progress (International). 30(1): 33-38.

Jose, Bino; Panda, K.C. and Rao, J.S. Giri. 2005. State of Automation in major newspaper libraries in Delhi city: A study. Library Progress International. 25(1): 23-35.

Lohar, M.S. and Nayak, M. Nagaraj. 2009. Planning of Library Automation in Kannada University, Hampi (Karnataka): A Study. SRELS Journal of Information Management. 46(3): 305-320.

Pandey, S.K. Sharma. 1993. Library Computerization: Theory and Practices, New Delhi. Ess Ess Publication. p:89-100.

Rao, I.K. Ravichandra. 1996. Library Automation, New Delhi. New Age International. p:1-7.

Samantaray, Moorttimatee. 2007. Automate your library. Library Herald. 45(1): 31-40.

Thapa, Neelam and Sahoo, K.C. 2005. Problems and Prospects of Automation: a survey of special libraries in Bhopal. Library Progress International. 25(1): 71-83.

Vasishta, Seema. 2007. Library automation and networked services: a case study of the technical deemed university libraries in North India. Iaslic Bulletin. 52(2): 120-126.

www.IKSVV.com/lib.htm retrieve date 05.05.2013

www.RSU.ac.in/centrallibrary.htm retrieve date 05.05.2013

www.ggu.ac.in/facility_computer%20centre.html retrieve date 05.05.2013

www.igau.edu.in retrieve date 10.05.2013

www.hnlu.ac.in/Home/index.php retrieve date 28.04.2013

www.ktujm.ac.in retrieve date 10.05.2013

www.csvtu.ac.in retrieve date 10.05.2013

www.pssou.ac.in retrieve date 10.05.2013

www.cvru.ac.in retrieve date 28.04.2013

www.bvvjdp.ac.in retrieve date 05.05.2013

www.sua.nic.in retrieve date 10.05.2013

www.matsuniversity.ac.in retrieve 10.05.2013

3

Management of Open Access Resources: An Overview

D.Ravinder
Head & Associate Professor
Dept. of Library and Information Science
S.K.University, Anantapuram (AP)

Introduction

Modern libraries have evolved from paper-based storehouse of books and journals into network of digitized information and knowledge, now known as digital libraries. Libraries these days have consortia, and use electronic resources and databases so that they can provide better services to the users. Librarianship has shifted from use of printed and manually operated system to world wide access to information. Modern academic library is a conglomeration of printed books and journals as well as electronic resources where both forms of the documents can be stored, retrieved and delivered as and when required. The diversified hunt for information and knowledge, the innumerable books and other printed materials together with endless and ever increasing scholarly e-resources makes the traditional management of academic library a difficult task. Access of information is no longer restricted to what is physically available in a particular library. Information is accessible from a wide variety of globally distributed commercial repositories such as electronic publishers and aggregators with access charge. However it is also accessible from open access journals, open access archives, few websites and institutional repositories free of charge.

The library and information services of the 21st century are fast changing. With the rapid development of electronic publishing, libraries are not only acquiring reading materials such as printed books and journals but also arranging for providing access to various learning resources in electronic form. In the new situation, the role of library professional is playing the new role of access manager of e-resources rather than acquisition manager and custodian of scholarly resources in print form.

Mission of Open Access

The goal or the mission of the libraries is to provide continuous access to books and knowledge in order to support educational and research activities of the parent institution.

Types of open access information resources

The libraries with their traditional holdings in print format are now being added with electronic information resources in various formats like CD-ROM and DVD-ROM databases, online data bases, e-books, e-journals and plenty of internet and web resources. The content of these sources varies from bibliographic or factual to full text.

i. **CD-ROM Databases:** CD-ROM Databases are increasing day by day in almost all fields due to their many advantages in information storage and retrieval. Majority of publishers of books and journals, online vendors and various learned societies are bringing out new titles in CD format with powerful retrieval software. Electronic information resources in CD format include abstracting and indexing services, encyclopedias, dictionaries, directories, yearbooks, back volumes, standards, patents and many other reference works.

ii. **DVD-ROM Databases:** The advent of DVD, with its 17 GB of high data storage capacity, has made it possible to include more multimedia elements like video and sound and to integrate many reference sources on single disc. The other features like higher quality of sound and video, higher rate of data transfer, data security etc. are making DVD more viable option to CD-ROM.

iii. **Recent growth of internet:** The recent growth of internet and the popularity and ease in use of web are making libraries to subscribe to online information services. An e-database is an organized collection of information, of a particular subject or multi-disciplinary subject areas; information within an e-database can be searched and retrieved electronically. There are two types full-text databases containing the whole content of an article such as citation information, text illustrations, diagrams and tables and the other bibliographic databases which contain only citation information of an article, such as author name, newspaper articles, book reviews and conference proceedings.

iv. **E-Books:** According to Encyclopedia of Library and Information Science, electronic book is "a term used to describe a text analogous to a book that is in digital form to be displayed on the computer screen". Electronic books, or e-books, are books in computer file format and read on all types of computers, including handheld devices designed specifically for reading e-books.

v. **E-Journal:** E-journals or electronic journals are gaining more importance with the emergence of internet. The publishing world is undergoing a revolutionary change as more and more publications are becoming WEB centric. Online journals, whose full text articles are available in the web for viewing and downloading free of charge, called open access journals. Open access to articles can be achieved in two ways by publishing fast article in repositories. The later is often referred to as self archiving. Open archiving or self-archiving initiative is an ambitious effort to free online full-text articles from the clutches of the commercial publishers. The use of these articles is more important to libraries in developing countries such as India as most libraries in this region are facing financial crunch.

vi. **The Institute of Management Development and Research (IMDR):** The IMDR caters to management education mainly conducting fulltime courses in management, international trade and human resource management with a few other areas like diplomas in human resource management, financial management international trade and masters diploma in business administration etc. The need is felt to have open access e-resource websites listed at a place and have a library portal so that the faculty and students of this organization can access the same on the intranet.

The author first identified the websites of management organizations and institutions worldwide with the help of Google and then went to these websites and picked up open key-words like e-resources open access e-resources, etc. the searched e-resources described in the following paragraphs with their features.

Open Access Resources on Management

a. **Gateways:** This is a internet service for business and economics students and teachers consisting of a catalogue of websites in field, learning materials, economic, business, finance and demographic datasets, and factual information about leading companies to be used in case studies. Includes online models where students apply business and economic theory to the real world such as the virtual factory, and the virtual economy an online model of the economy based on the treasury model.

b. **Intute: Business and Management:** Searchable database of business and management internet resources selected by university librarians for students, staff and researchers in higher and further education.

c. **Open J-Gate:** Open J-Gate is an electronic gateway to global journal literature in open access domain. Launched in 2006, open J-Gate is the contribution of Informatics Ltd. To promote OAI. Open J-Gate is also a database of journal literature, indexed from 6082 open access journals, with links to full text at publisher sites.

d. **Directory of Open Access Journals (DOAJ):** The result of the Budapest Open Access Initiative, it provides information on open access journals, including some social science journals. This service covers free, full text, quality controlled scientific and scholarly journals. It aims to cover all subjects and languages. There are now 4459 journals in the directory. Currently 1711 journals are searchable at article level. As of today 328524 articles are included in the DOAJ service.

e. **Electronic Journal Libraries:** Developed by the university library of Regensburg in cooperation with the university library of the Technical University of Munich, the service covers academic and scholarly journals, veering all subject. Full text of some of the journals are available free of charge, others are restricted to member institutes of the initiative. The service also lists journals for which full text is not available, but table of contents and abstracts may be available. The search function allows you to narrow your search to free full text journals.

Repositories

- **BS Ahmedabad Institutional Knowledge Repository:** This repository is a collection of articles published, conference papers presented journal/research papers, cases, the intellectual capital of the faculty & research fellows of ICFAI Business School, Ahmedabad.
- **DSpace at Indian Institute of Management, Kozhikode:** This service facilitates the institute researchers in self archiving and long-term preservation of their scholarly publications and provides easy access to these publications worldwide and improves impact of their research.
- **RePEC Research Papers in Economics:** Database of working papers and journal articles on economics. The website links to IDEAS, the largest bibliographic database on economics available on the internet.

Advantages of Open Access

- **Easy Access:** Access e-resources are easier for the users. They can access the desired material within minutes, or even seconds, on their desktops, provided equipment is available. Large collections of material can be searched and retrieved simultaneously and instantly. There is an active dissemination of information by alerting the readers at their desktops about the new e-resource that are accepted into the database. In other words, e resources allow intelligent full text retrieval based on past use and interests.
- **Speed:** High speed and efficiency benefits the publishing and distributing electronically. Authoring and publishing systems can be integrated easily by computer readable text.

Also, electronic transmission, especially in the review process, saves valuable time.

- **Linkages:** Linkages can be enabled by hypertext and hypermedia formats among sections within an electronic resources. E-Mail contacts would be easier among users, publishers and suppliers. Users have more creative ways to have their information queries answered.
- **Costs:** The e-resources are published electronically rather than on paper and no new costs are introduced.
- **Multimedia:** Innovative ways of presenting research results can be supported by electronic page layout. Integrative three dimensional models, motion video and sound are a few possibilities.

Disadvantages of Open Access

- **Financial Constraints:** The infrastructure required the displaying storing or printing electronic resources are expensive. Downloading and printing will be a costly affair. This means a net increase in economic and ecological costs and it becomes a relatively expensive way to acquire a single copy.
- **Social Constraints:** Electronic interfaces can take as long time to master. Electronic searching, downloading and printing replace the traditional activities of physically browsing scanning and photocopying. The intricate steps to accomplish the previously simple or habitual tasks might frustrate users. People read up to 25 to 30 percent more slowly on a computer screen than on paper.
- **Technological Constraints:** The academic community can be divided into "haves" and "have-notes" because of access to equipment and network. The network or connection speed can be too slow. Screen quality graphics and dots is still primitive when compared to print.

Other Issues

- **Stability and Storage:** The volatility of e-resources makes preservation a major concern. In case of the benefits of access are enhanced, the ability of electronic resources to transmit information through time is not completely confirmed. Offline storage methods suggested are magnetic media, such as tape, hard disks, and floppy disks, and optical media such as CD-ROM's. There are issues of preservation of storage media, hardware and software dependency and dynamic versions of electronic resources that also need to be dealt with.

- **IPR Issues:** There are certain issues like, protection of the intellectual property of the author in order to preserve the originality and integrity of the work, warrant for the attachment of the author and the work in pubic protection of the author's ideal and economic interest and benefits, including publication and reproduction of his/her work. This is usually accomplished through the publishers, who disseminate the work in an appropriate, protected and retraceable manner. Electronic resources presently emphasize information access instead of ownership.
- **Selection and Acquisition:** The selection criterion for e-resources resembles the selecting of other media. The library selection policies can be applied to electronic resources; there are considerations unique to electronic resources that should be addressed by libraries, such as standards, effectiveness of the search engine, ability to limit to local holdings and hardware and software compatibility.
- **Cataloguing:** E-resources can be classified according to the ordinary guidelines such as LC call numbers. Libraries should be alert to emerging standards for cataloguing electronic publications.

Conclusion

It is said that e-resources can't replace print formats yet because only a fraction of scholarly materials is available electronically. What is available varies in quality, accessibility and price. But e-resources provide many opportunities and potentials for academic libraries. Out of the advantages and disadvantages of e-resources librarians' need to identify and balance the factors that would make e-resources librarian success or failure in their libraries. Certain bottlenecks still arise with such as users expertise in frustration and difficulty in their first efforts to use e-resource. If they lack proper infrastructure they may oppose efforts by libraries to replace printed formats by electronic ones. Librarians facing financial pressure identify journal price rise as a significant contributing factor. Library users want the advantages of the digital format, but until archive issues have been satisfactorily addressed, many librarians consider it necessary to acquire the print format as well, specially in case of journals. Developing a common vision of the future of IT can consolidate efforts to tap into the evolving telecommunication infrastructure.

References

Creation & management of Digital Resources – Caliber 2001, Ed Naidu, M.K.R. Jambhekar, Ashok, Sagar, S.M.Kumhar, TS., INFLIBNET Centre, Ahmedabad. 2001.

E-Resources for Acadmeic Community in Indian Scenario" J.Sridevi N.R.Sathyanarayana T.A.V. Murthy, 3rd convention PLANNER-2005, Assam Univ.Silchar, 10-11 Nov.2005, pp 317-321.

Moving Beyond library automation: Role of E-resources in Academic Libraries. Sharma, Hari Prasad. University News, 46 (34), August 25-31-2008.

Open Access, open source and digital libraries: A current trend in university libraries around the world" Krishnamurthy, M. Aslib Proceedings, vol.42, No.1 2008, pp 48-55.

http://library.osu.edu/sites/techservices/ERMpolicies.php

http://www.gdnet.org

http://library.ust.hk/info/databases/science

http://www.bu.edu/library/management/ref/ebooks.html

4

Role of the Libraries in 2020

Dev Walia
Professional Assistant & CCPI (e-Granth Project)
University Library, CSK HPKV,
Palampur – 176 062, H.P.

Introduction

The libraries of 2020 become multi-media centres of information resources, leaving behind their dull and drab image of repositories of old dusty books materials like micro-films, audio and video cassettes. Various electronic products for use both off line and on line representing the special type of materials need special equipments of different makes for their effective use.

Library Development & Management

ICT based phase of library development has resulted in not only extended access of library users to the documents extensively but also quick retrieval of bibliographical and textual information. The erstwhile concepts of storage, various sections based on the types of library materials, technical processes and reader services, work flow and staffing pattern all are in fresh look. The 21st century libraries' management becoming more integrated. In modernization of libraries Ranganathan's Five Laws in the changing situations are :

1. Libraries serve humanity
2. Respect all forms by which knowledge is communicated
3. Use technology intelligently to enhance service
4. Protect free access to knowledge.

5. Honour the past and create the future

Libraries and Librarianship towards 2020 is well reflected in these.

Information Technologies

Information technologies and knowledge based societie's requirements have not only changed but also increased manifold. The libraries are now changing their old patterns to new system of procuring the libraries collection, documents in e-forms. All the knowledge can not be incorporated in a single library. Digitization helps to overcome the space problem. In 2020, most of the libraries will be equipped with e-Books and in spite of many challenges progress has been made in the production and distribution of e-Books. The benefit of e-Books are as under:

1. Easy access to content
2. On demand availability
3. Prevention from being lost, stolen or damaged
4. Capability to search within a book
5. Absence of physical space management
6. Easy transportation
7. Access from anywhere and any time

Libraries Vision in 2020

The Library will be leader in integration of information services and technologies that are essential to learning, research and creation of knowledge. The library will promote a sense of place both physical and virtual to support advance research, exploration and exchange of ideas and creation of new knowledge.

Integrated Libraries System

It will enable the users to communicate with the computers for visualized searching and multi-media resources. The system will recognize the users' new questions needs and quick response to them.

Information Available

Collections will undergo dramatic transformations. They will be largely users selected, featuring multi-media resources and data bases, mostly provided collaboratively through extensive consortia arrangements with other libraries and information providers.

Access to Information

Schemes like print on demand will be developed providing mechanisms by which the readers can obtain the information so that the collection like books, manuscripts and journals remain undamaged. Out of print/rare collections will also be used for similar type of utilization.

Study Space

Space for work and study will be adaptable, with easy reconfigured physical and virtual spaces.

Organizational Aspects

The library staff will be imparted training on latest technologies adopted for library and information sciences for providing best and quality services to the users.

Computer Access

Library system should adopt wireless technologies so that the users can use library e-Resources at anywhere at any time.

Consortia

Library consortia will be deeply involved by 2020 in collaborating to create and publish academic journals and resources, particularly e-Journals, e-Books and collections of visual resources in various media.

Radio Frequency Identification (RFID)

In the 21st century most of the libraries will be in position to RFID. (Radio frequency identification) providing/enhancing self services of operations. There are two main reasons for this. Firstly, self service is seen as the "quickest win" available and offers significant cost saving in circulating stock. Secondly, the methodology employed by RFID self services is identical to that used for bar-coded for over 25 years. It is consequently very stable and well understood.

CCTV Cameras

In 2020 most of the libraries for security purpose covered under closed circuit television. This facility helps to monitor libraries system successfully.

Mission

To facilitate advance research by providing information resource and users centered services of the highest possible quality. The mission of the library is to provide access to high quality information resources in all forms to the users. With a commitment to excellence in services, the library offers information resources and innovative services to the readers.

Objectives of the Libraries in 21st Century

1. To develop, maintain and promote the library as an inviting comfortable place where the readers read, study and do their research.
2. To develop, maintain and promote high quality print and electronic collection that are readily accessible.
3. To promote user-centered services that anticipate and respond to the needs of the users.
4. To develop and provide quality collection, resources, users facilities and library staff to maintain an environment conducive to study and research.
5. Network information and document delivery services can be created .
6. To create library consortia to optimize the access to knowledge base, etc.

Role of the Librarians in 2020

Traditionally the Librarians have acted as the mediator between the reader and the book. The main duties were associated with acquiring and making the resources available in the library. Librarian was a messenger between the learner and the knowledge sought. The role of the Librarians was Select – Display –Evaluate and Improve. Now in 2020 the Librarian's role has become much more diverse.

1. Continues to acquire resources in many formats and media on line.
2. Works closely in partnership on joint projects.
3. According to plan or strategy i.e. evaluated for outcomes and impacts.
4. Reaches outwards to inform attract and respond to priority audiences
5. Researchers innovation are test products and services with users
6. Evaluates through user survey and user benefit analysis or cost benefit analysis.

Advocacy for Library in the 21st Century

A strong advocacy for Libraries must :-

1. Networking and relationship
2. Building friendships creating allies, securing influence
3. Building partnerships and collaborating working relationships
4. Leading to collective project
5. Research and evidence, building the use for the library to be recognized and engaged.
6. Fund raising and bidding for grants and sponsorship.
7. Evaluating and demonstrating results and outcomes

Library Consortia

In the 21st Century there is much more need for library consortia. Library consortia consist of number of libraries preferably by some common features by subject institutional affiliation, unit of libraries with common interest and objectives for certain jobs collectively. The consortia for library can be considered in 2020 as major step towards library cooperation in sharing electronic resources. In 21st Century library consortia can be considered as major steps towards library cooperation for information. Some important library consortia are :

1. CeRA by IARI

2. Sodhganga and Sodhgangotri a repository of Indian electronic theses and dissertation and repository of research in progress.
3. E-Granth – Agricat-Krishi Kosh

Conclusion

New advances of ICT have brought about great opportunities for libraries so they can fulfill their mission of providing the community with relevant timely and up-to-date information in 2020. The main problem is how to manage and balance the traditional and digital resources. Future libraries must be hybrid libraries which are users centered and expert –assisted.

References

John, Dolan: Transformation through Action : Making the case for libraries in the knowledge economy. In Delhi University Library System, University of Delhi (Ed) Globalizing Academic Libraries Vision 2020 (28-36).

Pandey, S.N. : New Challenges in the Transformation of Traditional Libraries into Digital Environment and their Preservation : A critical analysis. In M.S.Pathania, et al. (Eds) National Conference on Agricultural Libraries and User Community NCALUC-2011 (17-19 November, 2011) Transformation of Agricultural Libraries in Collaborative Era (179-184).

Walia, Dev. : Library network and consortia. In : K Veeranjanajulu, et al. (Eds) Library services in the knowledge web (198-204).

http://www.iias.org.

5

Role of Cloud Computing in Library Services and Bioinformatics

K.N.Kandpal
National Library of Veterinary Sciences
Indian Veterinary Research Institute,
Izatnagar (U.P.) – 243 122
and
S.S.Rawat
National Library of Veterinary Sciences
Indian Veterinary Research Institute,
Izatnagar (U.P.) – 243 122
and
Faheem Khan
Bioinformatics Centre
Indian Veterinary Research Institute,
Izatnagar (U.P.) – 243 122

Introduction

Cloud computing is now evolving like never before, with all types of establishments irrespective of shapes and sizes adapting to this new technology. The experts believe that this trend will continue to grow and develop even further in the coming years. While cloud computing is undoubtedly beneficial for mid-size to large establishments, it is not without its downsides, especially for smaller establishment.

Major Cloud Computing Advantages

The cloud computing can benefit all types of establishments and government organizations. The advantages of cloud computing are:

- **Cost Efficient :** Cloud computing is the most cost efficient, maintain and upgrade. In case of traditional desktop and software cost is more than cloud computing. Adding up the licensing fees for multiple users can prove to be very expensive for the establishment concerned. The cloud, on the other hand, is available at much cheaper rates.
- **Almost Unlimited Storage :** In the cloud there is no limit for storage capacity. It is unlimited storage capacity. No more need to worry about running out of storage space or increasing current storage space availability.
- **Easy Access to Information :** Once one registers in the cloud, if one has Internet connection, he can access the information from anywhere. There is no geographic boundary for access to information.
- **Backup and Recovery :** Since all the data is stored in the cloud, backing it up and restoring the same is relatively much easier than storing the same on a physical device. This makes the entire process of backup and recovery much simpler than other traditional methods of data storage.
- **Automatic Software Integration :** In the cloud, software integration is usually something that occurs automatically. So one do not need to make additional efforts to customize and integrate applications as per preferences.
- **Quick Deployment :** Cloud computing gives the advantage of quick deployment. Once opt for this method of functioning, the entire system can be fully functional in a matter of a few minutes.

Limitations of Cloud Computing

In spite of its many benefits, as mentioned above, cloud computing also has few limitations.

- **More elasticity means less control** - While public clouds are great for quickly scaling up and down your resources, companies that require complete and total control over their data and applications will need to avoid the public cloud. Alternative solutions include hybrid clouds, private clouds, and collocation.

- **Not everything fits into the cloud -** Depending on the cloud provider, one may face restrictions on available applications, operating systems, and infrastructure options. Complicating matters more is the simple fact that not all platforms can live in the cloud.

Global Scenario of Cloud Computing

Cloud computing services were first offered by Amazon Web services in 2006. Initially most of the potential clients were not convinced to accept this shift. But gradually it has started picking up the market looking at its primary features viz. storage space, efficiency, easy accessibility, strong security, longevity, cheaper investment and maintenance, interoperability, ease of shifting base, quality support etc.

Bhagwan Nath (2012), describing the current global market scenario mentions that cloud computing is considered to be one of the most revolutionary tools that has already started showing its impact in the international market. It is treated as a paradigm shift of ICT services from the traditional way of owning the whole organization based ICT setup to hiring the set-up and delegating the most difficult parts of it to the service providers.

Some of the key facts that are the most prominent ones in uplifting cloud computing globally, according to a study done by one of the cloud service providers, *"cloudhypermartket.com"*, are given below:

- Almost 70% of the users believe that it has simplified the IT management process.
- 72% users have experienced improved end-user assistance.
- 63% users consider that it has brought down the IT performance challenges.
- 73% users believe that it has reduced the cost of infrastructure.
- According to 74% of the users, it has alleviated internal resource pressures.

Application of Cloud Computing

The Cloud Computing presents a new approach to permit the development of dynamic, scattered and highly significant software. Cloud Computing offers services, software and computing infrastructure autonomously throughout the network. To achieve a system that supports these features, Service- Oriented Architectures and requiring framework which provide tools for developing distributed computational systems that can be used for the establishment of Cloud Computing environments.

Cloud Computing in Library Services

Libraries may soon be developing and managing their own data centres. This model would let libraries manage and maintain more control over the applications and data stores that contain susceptible, confidential information about patrons. Provisioning and maintenance of infrastructure for Web based digital library present several challenges. In this paper we discuss problems faced with digital library and development efforts to overcome that problem. Infrastructure virtualization and cloud computing are particularly attractive choices which is challenged by both growth in the size of the indexed document collection, new features and most significantly usage. With the purpose of applying Cloud Computing to university library, the paper describes the current status of user service models in university libraries. Then it proposed to enhance to improve the current user service model with Cloud Computing. This paper explores some of the security issues surrounding data location, mobility and accessibility (Sanchati *et al.*, 2011).

Digital library is a development-oriented hardware and software integration platform through technical and the product integration. Each kind of digitization is carried on the effective deposit and the organization of documents, provides effective services through network. After Digital library technology popularization, high grade information services are provided to the users but simultaneously also to expose all sorts of questions unceasingly. Each one information isolated island or the resources are redundant, create the resources waste, satisfied the aggregate demand with difficulty, the cloud computing possibly provides a good plan day by day for this kind of phenomenon (Yang j *et al.*, 2012).

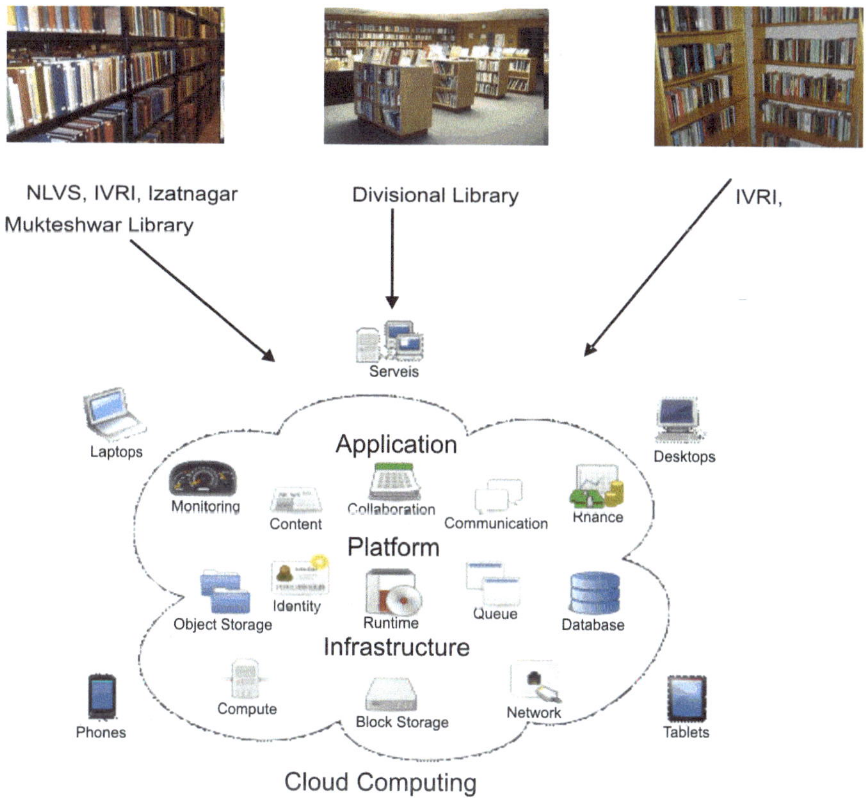

Fig.1: Cloud computing architecture in sciences (Image Source www.Lislinks.com)

Problems of Digital Library

Digital library for our study provides a suitable, along with the rising knowledge level, requirement for increasing cloud computing. But because of irregular economic development in different regions causes the digital library's assets to be relatively short. University digital library is an example for the same. Various colleges and universities while are raising the respective teaching level continuously, have established the digital libraries to purchase and to make available its own database resources to their users. But because of the teaching focus and economic conditions, library resources between universities have the differences. Data resources between various universities are relatively autonomous. Building various digitization projects possibility is high which has created the misuse of manpower, the financial resource and the resources waste as some of the colleges and universities use only part of database or insufficient use of resources or and cannot utilize the resources properly. Digital library represents one kind of new infrastructure and the environment, through the cloud computing. It may use resources more effective manner, and can resolve the errors of digital library system.

Cloud Computing in Bioinformatics

When we compare the activity of the genomic sequencing status in current time in the world through the different biological research with computer speed, the sequencing is winning this race by a huge distance. Sequencing throughput has been improving at a rate of about 5-fold per yearhttp://www.ncbi.nlm.nih.gov/pmc/articles/PMC2904649/ - R1 in recent time, while computer follows "Moore's Law". As this gap widens, the problem is existing about how to design higher-throughput analysis pipelines becomes difficult. Therefore this is the time when we have to think about the implementations of cloud computing phenomena in bio-computing or bioinformatics.

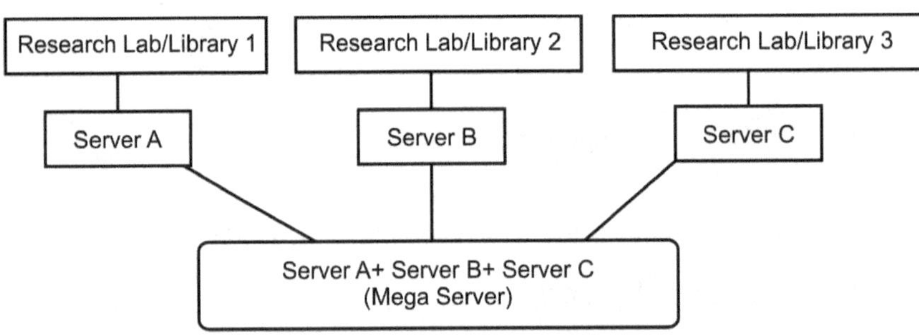

Fig.2: Server Share Plan

The invention of new algorithms make enhanced computer power. Unluckily, algorithmic breakthroughs of this type, like scientific breakthroughs, are difficult to plan or predict. For reducing the gap between the DNA sequencing and computer performance we have to make new algorithms which can be run on distributed computer network and several computer simultaneously with low time complexity and this can be possible by using cloud computing approach.

A more practical option is to concentrate on developing methods that make better use of multiple computers and processers.

Conclusion

Cloud computing facilitates the development of dynamic and clever electronic systems. It is the Cloud Computing based model approach where functionalities are implemented using Web Services. The most important characteristics cloud computing based system is to provide a robust, flexible, modular and adaptable solution for recent computational system. Therefore it is very handy to implement in bioinformatics research because bioinformatics research can be speed up using cloud computing approach.

The Cloud Computing is also very useful for Library and information services. We already knew that library is not only an unlimited universe of a knowledge, its ultimate emphasis is to provide significant and assured services for all the people. Therefore in the modern era, library should improve itself constantly by adopting many new IT technologies. And in this paper, we indicated the improved current user service model in university library by using Cloud Computing (Lixia *et al.* 2009). While the study of Cloud Computing is still in the beginning stage, impacts brought by Cloud Computing are very noticeable. With the introduction of Cloud Computing in modern sciences the approaches can be improve and speedy. It is therefore now big requirement of data analysis and management demanding a special approach to resolve mentioned problems. Cloud computing approach may be helpful to tackle this problem and make significant impact in upcoming world.

Future Perspective

Most of the activities slackly grouped together under cloud computing have already been happening and centralised computing activity is not a novel phenomena: Grid Computing was the last research-led centralised approach. However there are concerns that the mainstream adoption of cloud computing could cause many problems for users. Whether these worries are grounded or not has yet to be seen. Cloud computing technology is still relatively young in terms of maturity and adoption. The expectation is that it will undergo several changes in the future, in terms of resources, issues, risks, and ultimately best practices and standards. However, there are some sought advantages it can potentially provide value for institutions of higher education. On-demand services can reverberate positively with the current university tight budgets across the nation and other parts of the world.

References

Bhagawan Nath, Somnath Chaudhuri, International conference at Thimphu Bhutan "Application of Cloud Computing in Agricultural Sectors for Economic Development", Page no. 1-11, 2012.

Huang Fuyan. Research on the Development of Library Information Service Modelsin the Information Culture Environment. OJ. Xiangtan University, 2008(7).

http://www.cloudtweaks.com

Judith Hurwitz, Robin Bloor, Marcia Kaufman and Dr.Fern Halper. Cloud Computing For Dummies [M].Wiley Publishing, 2009.

Li Xia. Research on the CRM-based Mode of Individualized Information Service in the University Library. Journal of Modern Information, 2009(11).

Michael Miller. Cloud computing: Web-based Applications That Change the Way You Work and Collaborate Online [M].Que Publishing, 2008.

Yang Jie, Liu Wanjun, "Cloud Computing in the Application of Digital Library," icicta, vol. 1, pp.939-941, 2010 International Conference on Intelligent Computation Technology and Automation, 2010

6

Tools and Techniques of Knowledge Management (KM) and Knowledge Sharing (KS) For Library Profession

Khaisar Muneebulla Khan
Professor
Dept. of Library and Information Science
Mangalore University, Mangalagangothri - 574199
Email: khaisarmk@yahoo.com

Introduction

The Web-enabled infrastructures, practices and strategies are creating confusions disruptions for virtually every institution and enterprise. The responses to these disruptions are progressively leading to new practices, business models, and strategies in a variety of domains posing challenges to the profession of librarianship. The acquisition, assimilation, and sharing of knowledge is one such sphere that is really experiencing a revolution. The Information and communication technologies that are already developed or will be deployed over the years of information explosion and information revolution, and best practices in knowledge sharing are not only diffusing rapidly but will definitely be substantially reinvented in all areas such as education, corporations, government, associations, and nonprofit organizations including libraries and information centers and the knowledge centers. These will help individuals and organizations achieve quantum leaps in their abilities to exchange knowledge. Even the manner in which they experience knowledge will be transformed in this era of scientific and technological innovations being used in information and its communication with the librarians transforming themselves as knowledge mangers and information scientists.

Knowledge Management (KM) and Knowledge Sharing (KS) are important factors that support continuous and lifelong learning enabling people to continue developing their skills throughout their careers. There are many problems associated with traditional education and assessment including student's and employee's schedule conflicts, geographical isolation, changes in demographic and economic issues, and other obstructions that preclude employees and the users of information and knowledge from attending traditional classes and training programmes. Many organization and institutions are beginning to feel that the knowledge of their employees is their most valuable asset. However, only few have actually began to actively manage their knowledge assets on a broad scale, though the information communication technology has facilitated easy sharing of information and knowledge from any geographical location across the globe which has led to the concept of the global village.

It has been realized that it is essential to create a knowledge sharing culture as part of knowledge management initiative. An isolated KM programme looked after by a privileged few is a paradox in itself and will not survive for long. Only effective coloration and communication, which spans across the whole company structure, will give KM the boost it really needs. Employees have sphere of influence along with their own individual knowledge, and this is where one believes a knowledge sharing culture can initiate.

There have been diversified approaches in developing KM technology as a solution to promote knowledge dissemination, knowledge creation and KS in an organization or community. These approaches have strengths and weaknesses of their own with respect to technological advances, user's perception, adoptability and success rate in the actual sense of generating knowledge thereby transferring the role of librarians and information professionals on more significant and challenging ground.

Knowledge Sharing/Distribution

Knowledge sharing/distribution is required to be understood as a process of bridging organizational interdependencies inherent in on-going organizational activities. Looking at KS as a process of bridging organizational dependencies expands our understanding what type of knowledge at stake and what channels are best suited for sharing knowledge. KS or KD is the process by which individuals collectively and interactively refine a thought, an idea or suggestion in the light of experiences. The original idea may be progressively modified or gradually rejected until a shared perspective emerges. Knowledge can be shared through face to face interactions, synchronous and asynchronous communication using an electronic knowledge repository. The degree of explicitness of knowledge share is influenced by the media richness of communication channels used.

The process of knowledge management and knowledge sharing/distribution involves the empirical setting. Four types of knowledge, viz, professional knowledge (PK), coordination knowledge, object-based knowledge and know-how are identified. The type of knowledge is related to situations of interdependencies of KS. The PK basically describes knowledge that enables the operation supporter to perform the job. PK is limited to the practice of being on operation supporter and has also been ruffed to as know how. It originates from the persons formal education in combination with the experience in performing job. It is a prerequisite for being able as specialist to contribute to organizational activities, but in itself it does not reduce any organizational outcome (Ohristensen, 2007).

Knowledge sharing or distribution is referred to as the activities of transferring or disseminating knowledge from one person, group, or organization to another (Lee, 2001). In the context of information technology, involves the use of given knowledge bases or portions of knowledge bases either at sights other than those at which those knowledge bases where developed or in a context of new computer programmes at the same sight, possibly within software environments that are quite different from those in which the knowledge bases where first developed (Musen, 1992). The process of KS involves both the creation and transfer of knowledge through different artifacts such as documentary or communication, among entity. The entity may refer to individuals, groups (Weiss, 1999), organizations (Sole and Applegate, 2000), or network of organizations (Ciborra and Andreu, 2001). Knowledge is initially created by the individuals (Apostolou, Sakkas and Mentzas, 1999) but it can be produced and held collectively (Nonaka, 1994). When the sharing activity involves a larger number of individuals who are exposed to different values, environments, or interests as result of being part of different organization, the sharing may not be as straight forward.

Bartol and Srivastava (2002) define KS as the action in which employees diffuse relevant information to others across the organization. According to Bock and Kim, KS has been considered the most important part of KM. The ultimate goal of sharing employees' knowledge is its transfer to organizational assets and resources. As Inkpen puts it, "unless individual knowledge is shared throughout an organization, the knowledge will have a limited impact on organizational effect" The goal of KS can either be to create new knowledge by differently combining existing knowledge or to become better at exploiting existing knowledge. KS is defined as the process intended at exploiting existing knowledge (Yang, 2007) and hence defined as identifying existing and accessible knowledge, in order to transfer and apply this knowledge to solve specific tasks better, faster and cheaper than they would otherwise have been solved.

Significance of Knowledge Sharing

Now-a-days the creation and application of knowledge is essential for the survival of all most all businesses. There are many reasons which include:

a) The intangible products – the ideas, processes and information are taking a growing share of global trade from the traditional, tangible goods of the manufacturing economy. This has led to the increasingly sustainable competitive advantage continuous innovation. In other words, it is the application of new knowledge.

b) The increasing turnover of staff. People don't take a job for life anymore. When someone leaves an organization, his/her knowledge walks out of the door with him/her. Further, the problem in an organization is that we don't know what we know. Large global or even small geographically dispersed organizations do not know what they know. Expertise developed and applied in one part of the organization is not leveraged in another.

c) Accelerating change-technology business and social change. As things change so does our knowledge base erode. In some business as much of fifty percent of knowledge known five years ago becomes obsolete today.

d) The KS is to help an organization as a whole to meet its business objectives. Learning to make knowledge productive is as important, if not more important, than sharing knowledge.

e) Sharing knowledge is not just about giving but it is about soliciting feedback, asking questions, telling people what you plan to do before you doing it and more importantly why you are doing it. By sharing knowledge, you gain more than you lose. Sharing knowledge is synergistic process- you get more out than you put in. if I share product idea with another person, then just the act of putting my idea in words or writing will help me shape and improve that idea. If I get into a dialogue with other persons then I will benefit from their knowledge, their unique insights, and improve my idea further.

f) To get most things done in an organization requires a collaborative effort. If you try to work alone you are likely to fail- you need input not only from other people but their support and buy-in. Being open with them, sharing with them helps you achieve your objectives.

g) There are three key knowledge sharing behaviors which are also the means of KS. Firstly, seeking ways the documents and share your own knowledge. Secondly, taking advantage of other peoples experience when starting a new activity, and finally, reusing and building on previous work from within our organization or other sources.

Technology Support and Knowledge Sharing

Technology plays an important transformational role in changing corporate culture to knowledge sharing. In many ways, technology has made knowledge sharing a reality. In the past it was if not impossible very difficult to share knowledge or work collaboratively with coworkers around the globe. But now it is a reality thanks to the technology support. However, there are a few who argue that you do not need technology to implement KM and KS programmes. To an extant they may prove to be right but then KM and KS is fundamentally about people and not technology. However, there is absolutely no way that one can share knowledge effectively within an organization or a larger geographically dispersed one, without using technology. Information technology, communication technology can be classified into the use of proper repository for storing and sharing knowledge and the use of a communication medium for communicating and transporting knowledge among individuals.

The first approach is the use of proper repository or the repository model of knowledge management system, which is related to database management and organizational memory. IT can be used to capture knowledge, categorized, search, subscribe relevant content or information and present it in more meaningful formats across multiple contexts of use. IT can be used successfully to convert tacit knowledge into an explicit form.

The second approach is the use a communication medium or the network model of KM system, which is an extension of the stream of computer-mediated communication methods. It is used to support interactions, direct communication and contact among individuals. The facilitative IT tools support for knowledge management and knowledge sharing are shown in the figure given below:

IT Tools in KM

Knowledge Management - Intellectual Capital

- Tacit/Implicit Knowledge
- Explicit Knowledge

Information "Resources" Mgmt **Information Mgmt** (lifecycle mgmt)

Content Mgmt

Technology Mgmt (Infrastructure) **Data Mgmt** **Record Mgmt** (respondents)

Document Mgmt
- Versions
- Workflow

Application Mgmt

Social Capital
- Communities/Networks
- Collaboration
- Culture

Human Capital
- Organizational Learning
- Succession Planning
- Business Processes

Information Services
- Library
- Research
- Knowledge repositories

Static——————CONTENT——————Dynamic

Taxonomies / Metadata

Facilitative IT Tool

Barriers to Knowledge Sharing

The barriers in knowledge sharing can be divided into three categories (Ramesh Babu and Gopalakrishnan, 2008). They are;

a) Individual KS barriers

b) Organizational KS barriers and

c) Technological KS barriers

a) Individual KS barriers

The individual KS barriers comprises of general lack of time to share knowledge, and time to identify colleagues in need of specific knowledge. The apprehensions that sharing may reduce or jeopardize people's job security. Low awareness and realization of value and benefits possessed knowledge to others and the dominance in sharing explicit knowledge such know how and experience that requires hands on learning, observation, dialogue and interactive problem solving. The use of strong hierarchy, position based status, and formal power is also a barrier. The insufficient capture, evaluation, feedback, communication, and tolerance of past mistakes that would enhance individual and organizational learning effects also come in the way of knowledge sharing. The differences in experience levels, lack of convenient time and interaction between knowledge sources and recipients. Poor verbal/written communication and inter personal skills, age differences, gender differences, lack of social networks and the differences in educational level hinders KS. Besides, taking ownership of intellectual property due to fear of not receiving just recognition and accreditation from managers and colleagues, lack of trust in people because they may misuse knowledge and take unjust credit of it, and the lack of trust in the accuracy and credibility of knowledge due to the source, and also finally the differences in national culture or ethnic background and values and beliefs associated with it contribute to the hindrance of individual knowledge sharing.

b) Organizational KS barriers

The organizational KS barriers comprise of integration of KM strategy and sharing initiatives into the company's goals and strategic approach are missing or unclear. The lack of leadership, managerial directions for the benefits and values of knowledge sharing practices are unclear. The shortage of formal and informal spaces to share, reflect and generate (new) knowledge, the lack of transparent reward and recognition systems that would motivate people to share more of their knowledge. The existing corporate culture does not provide sufficient support for sharing practices and also the deficiency of company resources that would provide inadequate sharing opportunities. Communication and knowledge flows into certain areas are restricted. The internal competitiveness within business units, functional areas and subsidiaries can be high. Further, the hierarchical organization structure inhibits or slows down most sharing practices and that the size of business units often is small enough and unmanageable to enhance contact and facilitate ease of sharing.

c) Technical KS barriers

The technical KS barriers are the lack of integration of IT systems and processes which impede the way people do things. The lack of technical support (internal and external) and immediate maintenance of integrated IT system obstructs work routines and communication flows, unrealistic expectations of employees as to what technology can do and can not do also the technical KS barriers . The lack of compatibility between diverse IT systems and processes, mismatch between individual requirements and integrated IT system and processes restricts sharing practices. Further, reluctance to use IT system due to lack of familiarity and experience and also the lack of communication and demonstration of advantages of any new systems over existing ones also do act as a technical barrier.

Practical Approaches to KS

The principle approach used in traditional intra-organizational KM is the process approach. The process approach is characterized as a formal and technologically based process of gathering and storing explicit knowledge within the organization. The alternative approach to managing knowledge is the practice approach. This approach is more effective in gathering tacit knowledge through informal networks with moderate use of information technology. The same is represented below (Ramesh Babu and Gopalakrishnan, 2008):

Category	Process Approach	Practice Approach
Type of knowledge supported	Explicit knowledge: codified in rules, tools, and processes	Mostly tacit knowledge: unarticulated knowledge not easily captured or codified.
Means of transmission	Formal controls, procedures and standard operating procedures with heavy emphasis on information technologies to support knowledge creation, codification, and transfer of knowledge	Informal social groups that engage in story telling and improvisation (Wenger and Snyder, 2000).
Benefits	Provides structure to harness generated ideas and knowledge Achieves scale in knowledge reuse	Provides an environment to generate and transfer high –value tacit knowledge Provides spark for fresh ideas and responsiveness to changing environment.
Disadvantages	Fails to tap into knowledge. May limit innovation and forces participants into fixed patterns of thinking	Can result in inefficiency. Abundance of ideas with no structure to implement them.
Role of information technology	Heavy investment in IT to connect people with reusable codified knowledge	Moderate investment in IT to facilitate conversations and transfer of tacit knowledge.

Conclusion

The concept of knowledge management and knowledge sharing/distribution effort is a consortium to develop convention facilitating sharing and reuse of knowledge bases and knowledge based systems. The goal of the effort is to define, develop and test infrastructure and supporting technology to enable participants to build much bigger and more broadly functional systems than could be achieved working alone. KS should be incorporated into daily procedures and routines, thus making it part of the work and not an extra curricular, time consuming activity where one feed reports into some systems and never know if someone else makes use of it. If companies are to practice KS/KD, they must accept that getting started on sharing knowledge requires through analysis of the problems that KS/KD are supposed to be solved. This analysis has to start with identifying organizational inter dependencies, and the flaws in bridging these interdependencies. Different forms of interdependencies involved different types of knowledge, and sharing of these types of knowledge is to be facilitated differently. However, the evolution towards KM and KS/KD tool implies more than state of the art technology. Expert knowledge need to be pooled and shared thorough the web based networks. The global networking and web based services are catalyst for addressing today's challenges of knowledge management and knowledge sharing which are in turn the challenges to the profession of librarianship.

It can be thus concluded that, there is no doubt that information technology, information and communication technology is essential to enable the full potentials of knowledge sharing/ distribution and knowledge management. However it is important not to get carried away by the technology alone if it does not improve the basic process of KS/KD and KM. In fact more importantly people have to be motivated to share information and knowledge, The challenge to the library profession is being taken seriously by library profession by fully changing its role from the traditional librarianship to modern librarianship as a significant and indispensible partner as Knowledge manager and knowledge distributor in this era of knowledge society.

References

Apostolou, D., Sakkas, N. & Mentzas G., (1999), Knowledge networking in supply chins: A case study in the wood/furniture sector, J. Inf. Know. Syst. Manag., 1, 267-81.

Bartol, K.M., & Srivastava A., (2002). Encouraging knowledge sharing: The role of organizational reward systems, J. Leadership & Organis, Studies, 9(1), 64-76.

Brown, J.S. & Duguid, P., (1998), Organizing knowledge, California Nanag. Tev., 40(3), 90-111.

Ciborra, C.U. & Andreu R., (2001), Sharing knowledge across boundaries, J. Inf. Tehnol.,, 16, 73-81.

Christensen, Peter Holdt., (2007), Knowledge sharing: Moving away from the obsession with best practices, J. Knowl Manage, 11(1), 36-47.

Hansen, M.; Nohria, N. & Tierney, T., (1999), what's your strategy for managing knowledge? Harvard Business Rev., 77(2), 106-16.

Lee, J.N., (2001), The impact of knowledge sharing, organizational capability and partnership quality on IS outsourcing success, Inf. & Manage., 38(5), 323-35.

Musen, M.A., (1992), Dimensions of knowledge sharing and re-use. Comput. Biomed. Res., 25, 435-67.

Neches, Robert, et al. (1991), Enabling technology for knowledge sharing. Al Magaz., 12(3), Fall.

Nonaka, I., (1994), A dynamic theory of organizational knowledge creation. Organization Science, 5, 14-37.

Nonaka, I., (1991), The knowledge creating company, Harvard Business Rev., 69(6), 96-104.

Ramesh Babu B. & Gopalakrishnan, (2008), Knowledge sharing tools & technology: In overview, DESIDOC J., Lib. Inf. Technol., 28(5), 19-25.

Riege, A., (2005), Three-dozen knowledge-sharing barriers managers must consider. J. Knowl. Manag., 9(3), 18-35.

Rowley, J., (2000). From learning organization to knowledge entrepreneur, J. Knowl, Manage, 4(1), 7-15.

Sole, D. & Applegate, L., (2000), Knowledge sharing practices and technology use norms in dispersed development teams. In Proceedings of the 21st International Conference on Information Systems, Brisbane, Australia.

Weiss, L., (1999), Collection and connection: The anatomy of knowledge sharing in professional service firms., Organ. Develop. J., 17(4), 61-77.

Yang, ken-Te, (2007), Knowledge sharing: Investigating appropriate leadership roles and collaborative culture, Tourism Manage, 28, 530-43.

7

Web Based Library Services

Minhaj Fatima
Information Scientist
Maulana Azad National Urdu University
Gachibowli, Hyderabad -32

Introduction

The innovative use of web technologies enables us to reach both local and distant users much more easily and effectively. Technologies such as email and Web provide tremendous opportunities for library & Information Scientists to deliver the information to the desktops of users. Web offers significant advantage by integrating different library & information services with a common user interface offered by Web browsers.

Web provides library users with a vast array of services and accurate information. Users will not only need to learn how to best access information, they will also need to be taught to critically evaluate web resources to determine their validity. Librarians need to provide this guidance. There is a lot of information sources available on the Web, for example, wikipedias, social networking sites, blogs, wikis, video sharing sites, hosted services, web applications, mashups and folksonomies etc where everyone can create or upload the information but we have to differentiate valid, accurate useful, reliable, and appropriate information. Library professionals have to embrace the changes confronting them, and remain flexible and open to the potentials of the web and its impact on library services. Internet access should be seen as a means to augment information access to users.

History of Internet

J.C.R. Licklider of MIT was the first to suggest a network of computers in the US Defense Advanced Research Projects Agency (DARPA). In the year 1962 for the first time in the history of mankind Internet was invented. Lawrence Roberts of MIT connected a Massachusetts computer with a California computer in 1965 over dial-up telephone lines. The Internet, then known as ARPANET was brought online in 1969. Charley Kline at UCLA was the first to send the first packets on ARPANET as he tried to connect to Stanford Research Institute on Oct 29, 1969.

In the early days Internet was used only by computer experts, engineers, scientists, and librarians. There was nothing friendly about it. There were no home or office personal computers in those days, and anyone who used it, whether a computer professional or an engineer or scientist or librarian, had to learn to use a very complex system. E-mail was adapted for ARPANET by Ray Tomlinson of BBN in 1972.

As the Internet has become faster, and increasingly accessible to common man, social networking and other related services have grown rapidly, enabling people to communicate and share. Sites like Facebook, Orkut, Twitter, You Tube, blogs, wikis, and many more, let people of all ages rapidly share their interests with others all over the world.

Web-based Library Services

Web based library services are nothing but use of web/internet in providing library services. These services are available 24/7 days from anywhere on the globe. Web offers various services such as Email, Telnet - (Remote login), File Transfer Protocol (FTP), World Wide Web (WWW) and HTTP, HTTPS Hyperlinks/ Hyper text/ Hypermedia based, Text, Graphics, Programs, Audio, Video, Gopher, WAIS, Archie, Veronica, Usenet, bulletin Board Services, Podcast, vodcast, social networking sites, blogs, wikis, video sharing sites, hosted services, web applications, mashups and folksonomies etc. In order to keep pace with the changing technology and developments, libraries began automating and networking their catalogs in the late 1960s. Frederick G. Kilgour of the Ohio College Library Center (OCLC) began networking of Ohio libraries and in the mid 1970s more regional consortia from England and other states joined with Ohio to form an international network. Automated catalogs became available through Telnet and the IBM and then through the web though they were not very user-friendly at first but were very useful. Tim Berners-Lee and others at the European Laboratory for Particle Physics, CERN invented a new protocol i.e. World Wide Web in 1991 for information distribution. It was based on hypertext (linking one text to another text).

Web has given a vast scope for resource sharing among libraries. The libraries of today have undergone a rapid change and have adopted the web services in all the housekeeping operations of the library. Now every Librarian has access to advanced features like MARC21, Z3950, Live web OPAC, Acquisition, Cataloguing, Customized Report Generation and many more without spending much on procurement of expensive hardware and software.

Acquisition

The Acquisitions Module enables the library to fully manage the ordering process. It broadly includes fund management and control, and multiple orders.

1. Book order requests can be placed to new titles suggested through web by faculty and students by filling out the Request Form. Users can enquire about ordering status or availability of a title in the Online Catalog, or to be notified when the title has been received.
2. Web-based ordering and billing of books can be done by Acquisition staff with vendors.
3. Lists of booksellers, publishers and booksellers indexes, book meta sites, lists of libraries and book fairs, reviews, awards are available online.
4. Lists which are available on the Web aid in book selection.
5. Maintain and provide Web access to On-order and In-process files
6. Exchange information, ideas, and to find solutions to any problem pertaining to Acquisition FAQ's relating to acquisition, Reminders, Price verification, Bookshops are on-line e.g. amazon.com, flip cart etc.

Accessioning

Accessioning of books is not a tedious process as in the manual method. Now the books can be accessioned just by downloading of bibliographic records from Library of Congress or OCLC, World cat etc.

Classification

Now the classification has become very easy. No need to go through the lengthy four volumes of Dewey Decimal Classification Scheme. It is available online for example Library of Congress or OCLC world cat etc. as well as in the CD form.

Collection Development

The whole scenario of collection development has changed and now the concept of ownership has been replaced by Pay-per-use Access, subscription to e-resources, and Consortium approach.

Cataloging

The web based Cataloging module has a graphical text editor, authorities and thesaurus management, bibliographic file management and powerful tools to handle bibliographic descriptions. It supports a range of standard data formats and protocols, such as MARC21, Dublin Core, Getty, XML, Unicode and Z39.50. In the module's data dictionary the library can also define other formats in order to provide access to multiple databases.

Web OPAC

Web OPAC is nothing but online public access catalog available on the web which enables speedy searching of library books, journals, periodicals and manuscripts. Users can access the library on the move, from anywhere in the world and they are constantly updated about New Arrivals, Resources of Interest, Due Status, Reminders etc. The reading materials are arranged according to the subject content that is given a call number. The web OPAC uses international standard format to search the database. Users can query the database and make necessary reservations for the required resources. They can create their own virtual shelf and share them with their colleagues / friends. Most searched keywords are indexed in TAGs which facilitate users to execute a quick search. Search results can be published on Readers Blog or website using RSS feeds. Local language books can be searched using phonetic keyboard. Advanced Search enables users to find the required resource accurately and quickly saving the time and energy.

Circulation

Web based circulation module offers the users to remote login, enables the library to control its inventory, manage user information, payments, and circulation transactions. It includes customizable menus and mnemonic keys for quick access to frequently used functions. The Circulation Module also interfaces with third-party systems to extend the library's services. External systems may include card readers, self-check machines and voice response systems.

Resource Sharing

Resource sharing is possible in the areas of cataloging, classification and e-books & e-journals by uploading and downloading of bibliographic records from databases of other libraries available on the internet ex. Library of Congress, OCLC World cat etc. and accessing the e- resources through consortium. RSS module enables libraries to share their data across various blogs, social networks, official sites and more

Reference Service

Internet for reference work in the library is gaining popularity. It can be successfully utilized for providing short-range as well as long-range reference service because various primary and secondary sources of information are available online. More than 1200 digital/e- newspapers from across the world are available on the web. E-Paper module enables libraries to provide users with an easy-to-use interface to access the most current editions of international and local newspapers and magazines. They can search any newspaper, use instant translation, select articles in a table of contents and share them with others. E-Paper does not require installation of any software or plug-in and saves delivery costs of print subscriptions, staff resources and shelving space, and it is environmentally friendly.

User Education

User Orientation is no longer restricted to the four walls of a library it can be done through Email and online.

Retrieval of Information

Directories, Search Engines, Meta Search Engines and Information Gateways/Virtual Libraries etc are widely used to retrieve relevant information from Internet.

Conclusion

The Internet has given the libraries numerous easy-to-use and inexpensive research tools. The advent of IT and other communication technologies changed all means of information services and sources. Internet is changing the way we view information sources. The shift in publication process has taken place as individuals, institutions, publishers, professional associations, business houses and many others are publishing information on Internet which is known as Electronic Publishing. Electronic publishing is considered as the speedy, accurate and effective way of communication among academic and research community. The library and information professionals have a vital role to play in organizing the information and bridging the information gap. Internet has become an essential part of library environment today; we cannot imagine a library without internet. There is a tremendous increase in the number of reference sources on the Web, making Internet a suitable media for libraries to provide a timely, convenient and direct way to get answers to users' queries. The biggest challenge before the library professionals is to arrange the relevant sources of information available on the internet in a classified or structured manner to suit the changing needs of the users.

References

Hobbes' Internet Timeline 1993-2010: Robert H Zakon, Significant dates in the history of the internet

Impact of Internet on Library and Information Services p. 49- 56 INFLIBNET Regional Training Program on Library Automation (IRTPLA) 2004

Information Security: a source book for Librarians, (2001). C. R. Ramamurthy, Author Press, New Delhi, 29-31

Internet for Library House Keeping Operations and Management: K. Thulasi National Centre for Science Information (NCSI), Indian Institute of Science, Bangalore

Libraries and Learning Resource Centers (UK) Edwards, B., Fisher, B., Woburn, 2001, 288 pp

Library building projects: tips for survival Floor plan and elevations included by Susan B. Hag loch.

People places: public library buildings for the new millennium: Jones, D.J. Australasian Public Libraries and Information Services 14, no. 3 (2001): 81-89

Planning Academic and research library buildings. 3rd Ed. By Philip D. Leighton and David C. Weber.

Planning public library buildings: Concepts and issues for the librarian by Michael Dewey.

The physical library in a virtual age: library building in the year 2001: Sigurd, S. Scandinavian, Public Library Quarterly 34, no.1 (2001): 8-9

www.wikipedia.org

8

Role of Web Applications in Modern Libraries

N.S.Rohila
National Library in Dairying
National Dairy Research Institute
Karnal, Haryana
and
B.P. Singh
National Library in Dairying
National Dairy Research Institute
Karnal, Haryana
and
B.R. Yadav
National Library in Dairying
National Dairy Research Institute
Karnal, Haryana

Introduction

The library and information centre is an important component of any educational institution. It is a hub of specific information where the end users can explore the vast resources of information. In the era of old age libraries users had to spend more time for searching a small piece of information and for that had to depend on library professionals. But now we are living in the age of information and communication technology, computers are being used for day-to-day work of library which saves the time of users and avoid the redundancy work of library staff.

Web Applications

The web applications are those software applications which are accessed by the user over the network like internet or intranet. The web applications are created by the programming languages which supported to web browsers such as Java script and HTML. User can access the applications with the help of browser anywhere and everywhere on internet.

Benefits of a Web Application

In web application the developer feels easiness because he does not care about the client for specific type of computer or a specific operating system. Since the client runs in a web browser, the user could be using an HP or HCL machines. They can be running Windows 7 or Windows 8. They can even be using Internet Explorer or Firefox, though some applications require a specific web browser. Web applications commonly use a combination of server-side script (ASP, PHP, etc) and client-side script (HTML, Javascript, etc.) to develop the application. The client-side script deals with the presentation of the information while the server-side script deals with all the hard stuff like storing and retrieving the information.

Web Applications - Need for Library

Before the introduction of computer in the library, there was card catalogue system. This was time consuming and chance to do repeated work. Users had to come in library to access the book. They had to read and write their requirements which was laborious and boring work.

With the development of information technology, a drastic change came in every field. The storm of information technology (IT) also affected the library. The computer based softwares were started to generate for different activities like accessing, cataloguing and circulations. But these were standalone systems. Nobody could share the data with each other. Then came different types of networks like LAN and WAN. Where the data could be shared on the same network. For wide area network the web applications were created which can be open on browser over the internet anywhere. Most web applications are based on the client-server architecture where the client enters information while the server stores and retrieves information. This technology made the library 24x7 and without the boundaries.

Web Based Library Services

There are different types of web services in library services and some of these are described here:

Web OPAC – as name itself described that OPAC which is web based. OPAC is used by the library users to search the bibliographic data of books, journals, proceedings, annual reports etc. Being based on web application it is accessed by the browser anywhere and anytime on internet. Web OPACs have provision of boolean operators. While searching library collection using OPAC, we can use operators like AND, OR, NOT and make our query more specific.

Koha- is a web based open sources software for integrated library management with back end of SQL database. It comprises various aspects to handle the library. It has some features as given below:

1. Simple interface for library staff and users.
2. Web 2.0 facilities like tagging, social sharing, comment and RSS
3. Union catalogue facility
4. Customizable search
5. Circulation and borrower management
6. Full acquisitions system including budgets and pricing information
7. Periodicals management
8. Reporting, etc.

Consortium for e-Resources - Due to the less financial assistance to the libraries and increase in the cost of the information sources, it has been very difficult for the libraries to procure all the information sources needed by their users. The solution to the above problem is library consortia especially in relation to electronic resources. Many initiatives have been initiated in India for the formation of library consortia. Many library consortia in India are doing well and many libraries are benefited. Various issues related to consortia like uninterrupted online access, perpetual access to back issues, pricing, licensing, copyright and archival solutions etc are pinpointed and need to be strategically tackled and well addressed to get the best out of the consortia.

e-Granth- 'Strengthening of Digital Library and Information Management under NARS (e-GRANTH)' is a subproject under component-1 of National Agricultural Innovation Project (NAIP), Indian Council of Agricultural Research (ICAR). National Agricultural Research System (NARS) in India comprises of Agricultural Research Institutions and Agricultural Universities.

It provides digital access to library resources of 12 different research institutes and agricultural universities which include OPAC, important institutional repositories, rare books and old journals and makes them publically accessible over internet under NARS with Online Computer Library Center (OCLC) partnership.

e-Books – an electronic book which is published in digital form and readable on computer and other electronic devices. It can have numbered pages, table of contents, pictures and graphics, exactly like a printed book. An e-book collection is usually set up in an e-database, which supports full-text searching within and across titles, advanced search and bookmark functions.

It is very simple and easy to purchase and download e-books through the Internet. It is like purchasing any other product. The only difference is that after payment we can download page or receive the download link in an email. Users have to click on the link and the ebook will automatically download to your computer, to a folder of your own choice. Users can view fulll text of e-books in HTML or PDF format online.

E-database- An e-database is an organized collection of information, of a particular subject or multi-disciplinary subject areas.The information of an e-database can be searched and retrieved electronically.

Coverage: Contents include journal articles, newspaper articles, book reviews and conference proceedings, etc.

Update frequency: Usually updated on a daily, weekly, monthly or quarterly basis.

Types of e-databases: Full-text vs. Bibliographic

Full-text databases contain the whole content of an article such as citation information, text, illustrations, diagrams and tables. Bibliographic databases only contain citation information of an article, such as author name, journal title, publication date and page numbers.

Virtual Reference Services- Technological developments have affected not only the format and sources of the information the libraries use to provide reference service, but also where we provide reference service. Libraries and their resources have partially moved to the virtual world of the Internet. As a result, library patrons can access our resources from outside of the physical library. In an effort to reach patrons accessing the library via their computers, many libraries and library consortia are extending their reference service to include virtual reference. Technology now allows users to submit their queries to the library at any time from any place in the world. Virtual reference is responsive to patrons' need for convenient access to reference service.

OCLC- It connects libraries in a global network to manage and share the world's knowledge and to form a community dedicated to the values of librarianship: cooperation, resource sharing and universal access. The network links members to a powerful, cloud-based infrastructure that provides the system wide intelligence and cooperative platform needed to collectively innovate and drive operational efficiencies in metadata creation, interlibrary loan, digitization, discovery and delivery. It also provides opportunities for cooperation and resource sharing built around a worldwide community of users—working together at the scale of the Web.

The OCLC cooperative is member-owned and member-governed. Librarians guide and shape our direction through a 16-member Board of Trustees—more than half of whom are librarians—and a global council of librarians, who are elected by librarians from regional councils of member libraries.

CABI Abstract- It is very comprehensive database of its kind, CAB Abstracts gives researchers/scholars quick access to over 7.1 million records from 1973 onwards, with over 350,000 abstracts added each year. It covers agriculture, environment, veterinary sciences, applied economics, food science and nutrition. CABI Abstracts is the leading English-language bibliographic information service providing access to the world's agricultural literature. It has a reputation for comprehensive, quality abstracting and indexing, and integrity of its data.

Web Portals for Libraries- continuous progress in technical information offers researchers an ever-increasing array of resources. Researchers are likely to find material relevant to their subject in a variety of Web-based resources: Their own library's catalogue; catalogues outside their own library, such as a national or union catalogue or a catalogue of another institution that specializes in similar subjects; reference databases, such as an abstracting and indexing database or citation database; full-text resources; digital repositories; and Web pages. Web portals can be helpful in accessing of these information as desired by the users.

Web 2.0- Web 2.0 is the term given to describe a second generation of the World Wide Web that is focused on the ability for people to collaborate and share information online. Web 2.0 basically refers to the transition from static HTML Web pages to a more dynamic Web that is more organized and is based on serving Web applications to users. Other improved functionality of Web 2.0 includes open communication with an emphasis on Web-based communities of users, and more open sharing of information. Over time Web 2.0 has been used more as a marketing term than a computer-science-based term. Blogs, wikis, and Web services are all seen as components of Web 2.0.

Conclusion- The method and media of information storage and its dissemination have undergone a sea change. The traditional print media has been acquiring the shape of multimedia and hyper media as source of information. Earlier, research scholars used to spend a lot of time in libraries, looking for books, journals, magazines and other print media to support their teaching and research. But in the recent years, the focus has shifted from print to electronic resources. The web technology has revolutionized the way end users seek information. They now spend time on the internet looking for e-books, e-journals and other relevant information sources.

References

http://www.ala.org/rusa/resources/guidelines/virtrefguidelines

http://www.oclc.org/worldcat.en.html

http://www.cabi.org/

http://www.librijournal.org/pdf/2003-2pp118-129.pdf

http://www.exlibrisgroup.com/files/Publications/Library_portals_toward_the_semantic_Web.pdf

http://www.lib.ied.edu.hk/is/tutorial/

9

Emergence of Electronic Resources in Present Academic Libraries

Nidhi Srivastava
Librarian
Rajiv Academy for Technology & Management
Mathura (U.P.)
and
Ramnivas Sharma
Assistant Librarian
Rajmata Vijyaraje Scindiya Krishi Vishvavidyalaya
Gwalior (M.P.)
and
Manoj Tiwari
Librarian
K.D. Dental College & Hospital
Mathura (U.P.)

Introduction

Electronic resources represent an increasingly important component of the library collection building. "Electronic resources" refer to those materials that require computer access, whether through a personal computer, mainframe, or handheld mobile device. They may either be accessed remotely via the Internet or locally. Some of the most frequently encountered types are:

- E-journals
- E books
- Full-text (aggregated) databases
- Indexing and abstracting databases

- Reference databases (biographies, dictionaries, directories, encyclopaedias, etc.)
- Numeric and statistical databases
- E-images
- E-audio/visual resources

Electronic resources referred here are "information packages made available in digital format." These electronic resources consist of online journals databases, CD-ROM/DVD and audio/video course materials. In this present study, the main objectives are as follows:

- To examine the strength of online journals' database at research libraries in India.
- To study the physical form of electronic resources (CD-ROM databases and audio/video cassettes) among research libraries in India.
- To evaluate zone-wise performance with respect to electronic resource facilities

Present Practices and Emerging Goals

The special libraries attached to research and higher education were lucky enough to garner resources to automate their in-house routine operations and for hosting online public access catalogues (OPACs); some of them also set up facilities to search electronic databases. The major advantage of the progress in computerization is considerable increase in the amount of information available online. We have experienced that at the start of computer applications only the surrogates (metadata) existed online, but some full-text content has been made accessible online in recent years (online access to all content in the collection will continue to be an unattainable long-cherished dream of librarians). These libraries are experiencing the virtues of electronic information in different forms such as e-journals, e-books, bibliographic/full-text electronic databases on CD-ROMs and through Web access. Due to publishers' 'electronic plus' policies, libraries are able to access electronic versions of printed sources such as journals either for free (with the print subscription) or by paying an additional fee.

Library Services: Challenges and Opportunities

E-learners require more than access to e-resources. Traditionally, a reference librarian acts as an additional type of resource, one who can be counted upon to provide expertise in making sense of library systems and research tools, and to offer a helping hand along that often slippery path known as the research process. Virtual library users face additional challenges in mining relevant information out of a computer system that "obstinately" returns zero hits in response to a query that does not match the character strings in its database files. The most common means of providing electronic reference services to remote users has been e-mail, the advantages and disadvantages of which have been well documented in the literature. The around-the-clock and around-the-world accessibility of e-mail allows users to connect with librarians beyond the walls of library buildings and outside the usual hours of operation. E-mail provides a written record of requests and responses, permits the electronic transmission of search results, and allows librarians time to reflect on requests. One of the most serious concerns about e-mail reference services is their impact on the traditional face-to-face reference interview, particularly the absence of the verbal and non-verbal cues that typically assist a librarian in effectively responding to a question. A librarian

identifies three issues related to the use of electronic communication in serving virtual patrons (e-learners): immediacy, intricacy, and interaction. Because it is so easy for a learner to send a request electronically and have it arrive at the library instantly, there is a perception that the librarian's response will be as immediate. The learner may become frustrated, not realizing that the process of locating information and developing a response takes the librarian just as long when the request is made electronically as when it is made in person or in any other way. The more intricate or complex the request, the longer it will take for the librarian to clarify it and respond appropriately: a series of e-mail messages may be required, which will further reduce the immediacy of the e-mail request. Immediacy and intricacy relate to the lack of interaction: the opportunity to discuss and clarify inquiries that occurs in person or over the telephone is not so easily accommodated by e-mail.

New Roles of Library Professionals

The role of library professionals is also changing. They have to get incorporated into this technology and help the users in guiding and locating the required information. They need to be skilful person in indexing and searching the databases. They can help readers with alerts, TOC, local mailing through intranet and other information bulletin board displays on the topics of their interests and such other information from internet. Their increased roles are like:

- Creating a helpful interface for the users to link all available resources.
- Providing proper guidance on the usage and usability of the available resources.
- Locating the resources from the internet and getting their database updated.
- Collaborating with the digital information and services.
- Improving the information usage.

Alerting the users on the technological advancement in their field and the information that is available in the library.

Use of E-resources in Libraries

The electronic resources are becoming more and more available in the libraries. The print media is now being digitized which increases the availability of books and journals in the electronic format. The electronic books are helpful because of their portability and its feature of incorporating more than one book in a single hand held device. The published material is also available on open access. This helps the people to get the information required free of cost. They need not worry for licensing and usage of the information.

The CD shelf in Digital Library

The government is also undertaking various steps to introduce this facility in academic institutions for the benefit of research scholars. UGC-INFONET is a programme that provides electronic access to scholarly literature in all areas of learning to the academic institutions in India. This programme is wholly funded by the UGC and administered and monitored by INFLIBNET. Universities/ Colleges which are always short of funds are greatly benefited by this facility.

Role of Open Access Publishing

The fee-based publishing has restricted the users from accessing scholarly literature by using their security system and access mechanism, thereby putting a restriction for the use of researcher. If this was made available freely, then the new research findings can be obtained by anyone without any restriction. This helps the libraries reduce the financial constraints as now they can own a collection of archives of different subjects. The objective of open access is to maximize research impact by maximizing research access. Open access journals are mostly used by researchers for their reference compared with other media. This also helps the researcher to find journal articles in his subject irrespective of their subscription. According to the Directory of Open Access Journals only about 15% of all journals are open access. Hence in some cases, a researcher will not get the information he requires from any of the sources. Moreover, there are some authors who could not publish their articles in any open access journals. This situation must change and the number of open access journals must increase.

Conclusion

The technology helps the reader to get the information in various other formats than the traditional means. The e-journals as well as the e-books have made changes in the way the information is delivered to the readers. They help them to get up-to-date and latest information that is updated frequently. The hardware required for the use of e-books has to be considered before creation of the content. Their licensing, pricing and standards are the usability constraints. The open access publishing help the readers with free information availability but in some cases their standards are not tested, they may have broken links, wrong mappings and server problems. This has to be taken into consideration. Although the technological advancements have helped the people, yet it has some disadvantages as well. However, the use of resources is in the hand of users. It is the expertise of users to handle this tool efficiently which helps them to get right information. The future developments should overcome the disadvantages of the technology and give a new path for its effective usage.

References

Arora, Jagdish. 2001. Indian National Digital Library in Engineering Science and Technology (INDEST): A Proposal for Strategic Co-operation for Consortiabased Access to Electronic Resources. International Information & Library Review 33: 149–165.

Arora, Jagdish and Pawan Agrawal. 2003. Indian Digital Library in Engineering Science and Technology (INDEST) Consortium: Consortia-Based Subscription to Electronic Resources for Technical Education System in India: A Government of India Initiative, International CALIBER 2003, Ahmedabad, 13–15 February 2003, Conference Volume – Mapping Technology on Libraries and People. Ahmedabad: INFLIBNET, 271–290.

P.P.Singh Ed. and Sandhir Sharma Ed., E-Publishing: Concepts and Practical Approaches, 2004.

Ravichandra Rao, I.K. (2000) Sources of Information with Emphasis on Electronic Resources. DRTC Annual Seminar on Electronic Sources of Information. 1-3 March 2000.

Subba Rao, Siriginidi. (2001). Networking of Libraries and Information Centres: Challenges In India Library Hi Tech, 19(2), 167-179.

Suber, P and Arunachalam, S. (2005). Open Access to Science in the Developing World, World-Information City. Tunis: WSIS.

10

Problems of E-Resources in Digital Libraries

M. Papegowda
Assistant Librarian, University Library
University of Agricultural Sciences
Bangalore-560065
and
R. H. Walmiki
Deputy Librarian
Kuvempu University, Shankarghatta
Shivamoga
and
R.M. Shivakumar
and
V. Srinivasa

Introduction

The basic concept of digital libraries is the sharing of information and resources globally for providing right and nascent information to the right user at the right time. It is the computing terminals having linkage to different sources of information in electronic or digital form. Digital library is a collection of information that is both digitalized and born in digital form, which offer capabilities beyond those of the agricultural and traditional libraries. Digital library is not only digitization of physical resources, but also thoughtful organization of electronic collection for better access. Such organization provides coherence to a massive amount of shared knowledge base. Essentially a digital library deals with organization and access of a large information repository. Information and communication technologies have changed the landscape of information handling activities. The proliferation of electronic resources and a paradigm shift from print to electronic format of journals, has led to another crisis due to the escalating costs of electronic resources. With the available of open source software for creating repositories, many institutes have established institutional repositories in support of open access realizing the importance and the benefits of such a repository at the institute level. In this paper, we describe the growth and evolution of repository, the problems encountered the solutions explored, the strategies formulated to add relevant content and finally lessons learnt while executing the project.

Over the recent years, modern digital libraries and information centers have been greatly affected changes in Information Technology (IT), and the changing rate of information is still accelerating in this epoch. IT is now coming up with new products, processes and machines that can be used independently, customized information packages, CD/DVDs personal computers and reprographic equipments; external dependents, online database information system; cooperative library information networks, electronic information processing system such as the electronic books, journals, magazines etc. IT has been able to abridge time and space dimension in communication. In order to cope with the present development in IT, modern libraries are now adopting various electronic resources for its collection developments to fulfill the requirements of different users in a better way. However to achieve the goals of an ideal information system there is a need to select, evaluate and organize the e-resources in the best possible way as to provide maximum ease, both to the users and the staff for its access and retrieve at all times.

Digital Library and Modern Services

Rapid revolution in information technologies has revolutionized the role of libraries. As a result, libraries face new challenges, competitors, demands, and expectations. Libraries are redesigning services and information products to add value to their services and to satisfy the changing information needs of the user community. Information seekers are no longer satisfied with only printed materials. They want to supplement the printed information with more dynamic electronic resources.

Digital Libraries in India are heading from print documented library to digital environment libraries. A library's mission is to provide information of past and present literature and help in reshaping the future by maintaining the documents either in the print or in the form of e-resources. This mission is unlikely to change in the near future. The main difference between digital libraries and traditional physical libraries is that a digital library is entirely computer-based. In many aspects of life we benefit just as much from the way one computer interacts with another as we do when a person interacts with a computer. This is equally true of digital libraries. A "software agent" is a useful general term to describe the many different ways systems can interact with digital libraries. These include:

- Other libraries: Any library that cannot service a query can easily pass that query on to other libraries and return the results of the query.
- Virtual learning environments: As the delivery of on-line courses included more and more granular material it will be essential to keep track of this dispersed material. Digital libraries will be able to keep resources in safe, searchable repositories and respond to delivery requests on demand. The resources will remain in the library at all times and be delivered dynamically from secure, accountable sources.
- Bibliography and email agents: Teachers can submit searchers to build bibliographies but these can be "active" bibliographies that will find and deliver objects or will inform the student which library has the book or journal or when it will be returned by the current borrower. Increasingly, the users of digital libraries will be software agents acting on behalf of people rather than the people themselves.

Planning for Digital Library

A digital library committee should be formed to plan for its creation and maintenance. The members must be from various library departments, and if necessary, consultants can be hired. There are at least two ways of developing a digital library: converting a traditional library into a digital library, and direct development of a digital library.

Planning includes: IT Infrastructure, Digitization, Access, Staffing, Furniture, equipment, space Services and Funding, Planning mainly involves identifying various tasks related to creating a digital library collection, developing strategies for handling these tasks, identifying required resources and formulating a timeline for accomplishing these tasks. If there is a need to have a large digital project, you may consider conducting a feasibility study to assess the viability of the project before detailed planning.

The outcome of the feasibility study could be a formal proposal for obtaining management approval or grant for the project. The important task in creating a digital library collection is the conversion of the source materials available in hardcopy into a digital format. There should be a clear cut statement about the related requirements and their processes, namely:

- How to convert the source materials into required digital format.
- What are the digitization requirements?
- The workflow involved in digitizing the source material.
- Identify the resources and money required for creating and maintaining digital collections.
- What type of information technology (IT) infrastructure is required in the establishing and maintaining the digital collections?
- What are the personnel requirements and
- What are the financial requirements for setting up and maintaining the collection.

Need for Digital Library

- Expedite the systematic development of procedures to collect, store, and organize, information in digital form.
- Promote efficient delivery of information economically to all users.
- Encourage co-operative efforts in research resource, computing, and communication networks.
- Strengthen communication and collaboration between and among educational institutions.

- Take leadership role in the generation and dissemination of knowledge.

Digital Library and Digitization

The terms digitization (for digital collections) and digital library go hand in hand and the elements that form both concepts cannot be separated. Debate rages among information and knowledge professionals as to what constitutes a digital library and what is digital collection. Digital Libraries can be considered as enabling technologies with which to create and manage collection of digital materials so that it can be found and used. In other words it is to make these materials more broadly, quickly and efficiently accessible. The term "Digital Library" is also often used to describe any multi-media management system holding digitized information, but this does not mean it will deliver true library application functionality. Thus, these digital library components must also be tailored to capture, encode, and deliver information according to the standard practices adopted by the library industry. Because of the rapid pace of technological change, some standards are concrete and others are emerging.

Problems of Digitization

There are mainly two problems involved in digitization.

- Lack of technical knowledge and support.
- Lack of sufficient funding.

Lack of technical knowledge and support

Lack of technical knowledge required in provide digital library services continues to change rapidly as researchers and commercial vendors expand the kinds of content and access services that might be included. The software to support these services is complex and dynamic. It is difficult for an average academic library, with limited technical resource to manage the development and growth of a practical, real-world, production digital library that meets its unique requirements.

Lack of sufficient funding

Building and managing digital libraries involves huge financial resources. The budget allocation of most of the university libraries is not sufficient for the digital library research and development. Hundreds of millions of dollars have already been spent on digital library research and development activities throughout the world. Digitizing the existing library materials also involves a huge expenditure.

Some Other Problems of Library Digitization are

Software development

Large academic libraries may be able to develop their own software, perhaps in collaboration with university researchers and departments. But many libraries do not have the resources to build a complete solution, and a comprehensive commercial solution is often too expensive. Moreover, due to the various and expanding content and services, no single product can meet all the requirements of even a basic function of a digital library (Lund, 2001).

Copyright issue

Access to the information in digital libraries is generally less controlled than it is in physical collections (Witten and Bainbridge, 2003), though copyright is a major issue for printed resources.

Organization of collection

Digital libraries are organized collections of information. Downloading information from the web and organizing them into focused collections and making the material more useful to others is a prime application area for digital libraries.

Illegal and harmful materials

Web information is a big portion of any digital library and some material in the web is illegal and harmful and clearly inappropriate for public presentation. Violence and pornography are two major issues in this aspect, it is difficult for our academic libraries to prevent the usages of those materials.

Cultural sensitivity

Most digital information are produced by people from European and North American backgrounds, yet the majority of people in the world live in countries that have a different culture than them (Written and Bainbridge, 2003)

Why Specialized Staff

Within a digitization project, converting materials into a digital form is the most important activity, along with metadata creation. Digitization staff need to understand technical theory and have the hands-on skills required to operate equipment.

If the digitization activity is going to be outsourced, then it is important that the Project Manager has an understanding of the digitization process, so that communication is clear regarding contracts, expectations and outcomes.

Issues that need to be understood by technical staff include:

- The functionality of digitization equipment (e.g. for audio, identifying an analogue-to-digital converter which operates at a suitable sample rate and bit depth.
- Workflow management and working as part of a team.
- Handling procedures for potentially fragile original materials and associated conservation issues.
- Techniques used to obtain an optimal digital surrogate from an original (e.g. for photographs, the calibration of monitors, scanners and cameras).
- The creation and use of different file types related to capture, archiving and delivery.
- The optimization of digital files before delivery.

Specifically, digital librarians are required for the purposes outlined below, among a host of emerging functions.

- To manage digital libraries.
- To organize the digital knowledge and information resources.
- To disseminate digital information from computer held digital information.
- To provide digital reference services and other electronic information services.
- To provide knowledge mining from the emerging knowledge warehouses.
- To handle the tasks of mass digitization, digital storage process and digital preservation.

- To provide universal access and retrieval of digital knowledge, ultimately access to all knowledge resources available in digital form.
- To catalogue and classify digital objects and digital knowledge.

E-Resources

E-resources are those electronic products that deliver a collection of data, be it text referring to full text basis, e-journals, image collection, other multimedia products and numerical, graphical or time based, as a commercially available till that has been published with an aim to being marketed. These may be delivered on CD-ROM, on tape via the internet and so on. According to Barker, there are three types of documents used in digital resources.

- Static-Static are the most basic, they contain fixed information but also able to change their outward form (such as traditional online data).
- Dynamic-Dynamic documents also contain fixed information but also able to change their outward form, the way embedded material is presented to users (such as multimedia CD-ROMs).
- Living-Living documents are able to change both their form (outward appearance) and the embedded information (such as information contain on the web).

Role of the Digital Library in E-Resources Management.

The adoption of e-resources has made great advantage over the library services. In fact, most of the users are satisfied with such facilities since one can easily retrieve the required information within a short period of time. However, libraries face a number of challenges as they seek to continue offering the high level of services that users have come to expect. Some of the challenges facing e-resource management are:

- **Preservation**: Though the e-resources are enabling information to be created, manipulated, disseminated and located with increasing ease, preserving access to this information posses a great challenge. Unless, preservation of digital information is actively taken, the informatio will become inaccessible due to changing technology platform and media instability.

- **Lack of professional skills**: The professional staff are required to constantly update their own knowledge and skill base so as to work in today's rapidly changing digital environment.
- **Inadequate library fund**: Most of the libraries have inadequate fund for acquiring e-resources and so the users do not get their needy information at the right time. Libraries are at a disadvantage when acting alone in this environment and there is need for cooperative purchasing through library consortia.
- **Technical infrastructure**: In a digital information service system, infrastructure such as software, hardware, internet facilities and other physical equipments are required to provide easier, faster and comprehensive access to information. Therefore, libraries in the digital age need to enhance and upgrade current technical architecture to accommodate e-resources.
- **Lack of cooperation of staff members**: The support and cooperation of staff members, programmers and technical staff are very essential to provide effective service in a digital environment. As such, the library staff should not only be technology competent but should also user-friendly-approach.

Problems in Accessing E-Resource

- Interviews observed that researchers' needs and expectations are driving new access arrangements. On the other hand, a few librarians identified a lack of demand as a barrier to providing access to e-resources.
- Licensing restrictions are seen by librarians as the key barrier, with 80 per cent of HE respondents saying this was a very important factor. Few libraries seem to have negotiated individual IISC additional Authorised User licences.

- Technical issues are a problem, with only 40 per cent of libraries surveyed having the IT infrastructure in place to allow walk-in-access for visiting researchers.
- Overcoming barriers Libraries believe that progress is being made providing visiting researchers with access to e-resources, but that much remains to be done. A number of suggestions made by respondents are reflected in this report's recommendations.

How Digital Library/Librarian will help in Overcoming the Problems Faced by the Users

Selection is not a new term to librarian and staff as they have been doing it since libraries started acquiring printed material. However libraries are now focusing to adopt the e-resources rather than printed materials. In fact, the emergence of internet, particularly, the www(World Wide Web) has a triggered proliferation of web based full text online resources as a new media of information delivery. As the web has grown, not just in popularity and use, but also in content, librarians are trying to meet the needs of the user and identify new resources, such as online database, web based resources, collections in digital library, e-books, e-journals etc.

Evaluation of resources assumes a greater importance due to the large e-resources such as e-journals, database, e-text, etc available on the net. Authority, currency, intended audience, ease of use accuracy etc are some responsible criteria for evaluation of e-resources. Moreover, extensiveness of the content, accessibility, quality of technical support, cost, conditions of licensing agreement are also other responsible factors which should be taken into account.

In any Library Information System (either traditional or modern library system), organization of resources is also one of the important and crucial works to function smoothly. In a modern digital library information system, the professional should have skills like computing, database management, networking, and other management skills relating to IT environment. Therefore, the system manager should keep in mind the following points while organizing the e-resources.

It is known that libraries and information centers are not able to procure, organize and disseminate vast amount of information due to lack of adequate budget. Now-a-days, consortia subscription to e-resources through consortia of libraries is a viable solution to increase the access to e-resources at a lower cost. Library consortia refer to cooperation, co-ordination and collaboration among the libraries or institution for the purpose of resource sharing. The libraries all over the world are forming consortia of all types and at all levels with an objective to take advantage of global network to promote better, faster and most cost effective ways of providing e-resources to the information seekers. The collective strength of consortia members facilitates to get the benefit of wider access to electronic resources at affordable cost and at the best terms and conditions.

Conclusion

This paper, gives emphasis mainly on the needs and requirements of the users in accessing the e-resources by using the new services of the modern libraries in the digital environment by using methods of observation and by discussing with the users as informal interview by the digital librarian and modifying the services as per the users and making the digital environment as modern libraries. Library now days with the application of technology, is enhancing delivery of its services to the desktop users. The use of the internet and electronic resources have created a great impact upon users of Digital Library. The rapid developments in information communication technology have facilitated the convergence of new electronic devices and formats. Information has been embedded in a variety of ways and forms in various kinds of electronic resources. Digital technology can, indeed prove to a valuable instrument to enhanced learning and extend the reach of information resources to those who seek them, wherever they are, but only if we develop it as an addition to an already well stocked tool kit, rather than a replacement for all those tools which generations before us have ingeniously crafted and passed on to us in trust. Lack of training among users and proper infrastructure in the libraries is a major de-motivating factor in the use of internet, e-resources and e-journals in digital Library. This study helps to improve the facilities and services related to On-line access to E-resources.

References

Arms, W. (2000), Digital libraries, Cambridge, M.A: MIT Press, p.2.

Bawden, Divid and Rowlands, lan. (1999), Understanding digital libraries: Towards a conceptual framework. (British Library Research and Innovation report No.170). London: British Library Research and Innovation Centre.

Bush, V.(1945), As we may think, Atlantic Monthly (July)

Chowdhury, G.G. and Chowdhury, Sudatta. (2003), Introduction to digital Libraries, London: Facet Publishing. P.8 and pp. 285-286.

Papegowda, M. & Walmiki, H. R. (2012), Emerging Information Communication Technologies to Agricultural University Libraries and College Libraries, National Conference of Agricultural Libraries and User Community – 2012 (NCALUC-2012) Role of agricultural libraries in knowledgement (AALD) 2012, Page no 232- 236.

http://unlib.unledu/LPP/trivedi-diglib.htm.

http://www.clir.org/pubs/issues/issues04.html.

http://www.clir,org/pubs/reports/pub99/section2htmlhttp://alia.org.au/publishing/alj/51.1/fulltestfuture.role.html.

http://www.jiscdigitalmedia.ac.uk/crossmedia/advice/digitisation-staff-training.

http://www.worlib.org/vol12 no2/aman-v12n2.shtml

Kemparaju T.D. et. al (2007), Management of Digital Libraries: Challenges and Opportunities Redefining the Contemporary Information Professional's Role. Retrieved December 26, 2012. from https://drtcisibang.ac.in/handle/1849/401.

Shiri. A (2003), Digital library research: Current developments and trends. Library Review 52 (5):198-202.

Sreekumar, M.G. (2012, September), Strategies on e-resources management for smart information system, Annals of Library and Information Studies, 59 (3), 155-169.

Thoudam, Suleta Devi and Keisham, Sangeeta Devi O. Management of E-Resources in the Modern Library, Information System : An Outlook, 360-364. Retrieved December 24, 2012 from http://hdl.handle.net/1944/1409

Trivedi, Mayank. (2010). Digital Libraries: Functionally, Usability and Accessibility. Library Philosophy and Practice. Retrieved December 26, 2012, from www.web pages.uidaho.edu/-mbolin/trivedi-diglib.pdf.

11

Digitization of Central Potato Research Institute Library, Shimla

Prem Lata
Assistant Librarian,
SCERT, Solan (H.P.)
and
Mrs Yashodha Negi
Assistant Librarian
Dr Y S Parmar University of Horticulture and Forestry, Solan
Email : yashodha_40@rediffmail.com
and
Sudhir Gupta
Assistant Librarian
Dr Y S Parmar University of Horticulture and Forestry, Solan
Email : gupta_sud@rediffmail.com

Introduction

The past few years have been characterized by changes in every walk of life and libraries are no exceptions. Certainly there have been profound changes in the ways we approach and manage libraries and provide basic library services such as bibliographic control, document delivery, presentation, and physical facilities for reading. The evolution of traditional interlibrary loan services into a full range of document delivery services, new avenues for document acquisions and delivery from traditional methods to "high tech" with the most efficient pathway defined by the user within desired cost and time parameters have set new standard for library resources and services management. Libraries have been the centre of learning and education and the printed information sources i.e. books, journals, maps, atlases, manuscripts etc. had been under use through centuries. Earlier, most of the library services and operations were used to be manual in nature requiring lots of time and space to locate and procure the reading material; to process, store, retrieve and serve them to users. This was not only time consuming for library users but also for library staff to perform duties in this environment. The advent of computer and communication technologies changed the entire scenario of information production, management of delivery. Libraries began to convert their catalogue card into the electronic catalogue database which eventually becomes the Online Public Access Catalogue (OPAC) available for access locally as well as remotely.

Computer based automation has been incorporated into library operation such as circulation, cataloguing, acquisions, serial management, inter library loan, indexing and abstracting, storing information on CD-ROMs and their availability via network has in the recent past popularized their acceptance and approval by many libraries. The services such as reference assistance via electronic mail, networked CD-ROM searching, full text and online database searching, citation and document delivery services have become the order of the day of any modern library system. The internet access and the web pages with the links to various online documents have become possible with application of IT and net based technologies. The proliferation of the electronic resources and increase in end users products enhanced manifold users expectations for library services. Now libraries are no more considered to be store house of information rather they have attained the status of a dynamic services institution. Advances in information technology particularly the World Wide Web have led to the evolution of the electronic and digital libraries. Dissemination of information at low cost and high speed that cannot be obtained through paper has been achieved through electronic means.

The electronic library basically consists of materials and services encompassing digital artifacts and information in digital form came to be known as digital library. It's a kind of environment where people can access information in electronic form in place of printed form. There has been drastic change during last few decades in the ways in which information is generated, distributed, accessed and used. The internet and web technologies paved the new ways of information presentation and use. One of the most important contributions of web technology has been the creation of digital libraries which allow users to access digital information resources virtually and anywhere in the world. The Association of Research Libraries (1995) one of the leaders in collaborative digitization program in US, assigns following tenets to a digital library.

- The digital library is not a single entity;
- The digital library requires technology to link the various resources of library;
- These links are transparent to end-users;
- Universal access to the library resources and information services is the goal of the digital libraries;

Digital library collections are not limited to document surrogates, they also include digital artifacts that cannot be represented or distributed in printed format. As per Arms definition, digital library is a "managed collection of information with associated services, where the information is stored in digital formats and accessible over a network."

Objective and Scope of Paper

The main objective of the present paper is to suggest the pathways for developing CPRI Library as a digital library.

SWOT is the acronym that stands for Strength, Weakness, Opportunities and Threats. These four attributes are called SWOT parameters which have been used to assess the feasibility of converting CPRI (Central Potato Research Institute) Library into potato digital library. In the present paper an attempt has been made to develop CPRI library into potato digital library.

Pathways for Digitization

Digitization is the process of converting the content of physical media in to digital format. In most libraries digitization normally result in making document accessible from the web sites of the libraries. Optical scanners and digital cameras are used to digitize images by translating them into bit maps. Since it is highly labor and cost-intensive process involving several complex issues like copyright and intellectual property right, the selection of documents for digitization must be made carefully considering all the factors of utility, quality, security and cost. Rare and much-indemand documents and images must be the first priority item for digitization. There are basically three major phases in the digitization project.

1. Preparation for digitization and selection of materials to be digitized.
2. Processing required making the digitized material easily accessible to users.
3. Preservation and maintenance of the digitized collection and services.

To begin the process of digitization the following steps must be taken into consideration.

- Get adequate information about the image to ensure retrieval from a database.
- Get the copyright situation clear.
- Find out the various images modalities that are available in the collection.
- Determine whether it is technically feasible to capture the information.
- Determine who will use the images and how.

At CPRI following kinds of document have been identified for digitization:

- Documents
- Photographs
- OPAC(Online Public Access Catalogue)
- Journal Articles

Processing of Digitization

The processing of digitization involves four steps viz. scanning, indexing, compression and storage and retrieval.

SCANNING: Electronic scanners are used for acquisition of an electronic image into a computer from its original that may be photograph, text, manuscript. Once the printed pages are scanned they may be saved in following formats.

- TIFF (Tag Image File Format).
- GIF (Graphic Interchange Format).
- JPEG (Joint Photographic Experts Group).

- PDF (Portable Documents Format).
- HTML (Hypertext Markup Language).
- SGML (Standard Generalized Markup Language).

Indexing: While converting a document into an image or text, file is the first step in the process of digitization, imaging and indexing these files is the second step.

Compression and Storage: Since the image files are generally lager than textual files, it is necessary to compress image files so as to achieve economic storage, processing and transmission over a network.

Retrieval: To make the image file searchable the scanned image has to be OCRed. The OCR refers to the process of scanning text using a scanning device from a printed page into an image and translates it into a computer proccesible format, i.e. an ASCII file. Once scanned images and OCRed text documents have been saved as a file, a database is needed for selective retrieval of data contained in one or more fields within each record in the data. Typically, a document imaging system uses at least two files to store and retrieve documents. The first is traditional file that has a text description of the image along with a key to the second file. The second file contains the document location.

Preservation and Maintenance of Digitized Collection and Services

Preservation and maintenance of digitized material and services is the third phase in developing digital library.

Preservation: There are two main aspects to ensure the long-term preservation of digital data. The first relates to life- span of digital storage media such as computer hard- disk drives and removable media such as CDs. The second concerns obsolescence of digital data. Therefore precautions should be taken into the preservation and maintenance of digital data as failure or success of digital library is very much dependent up on it.

Tools of Digitization: Digital imaging is an inter-linked system of hardware, software, image database and access sub-system with each having their own components. Tools used for digitization include several core and peripheral system. The major tools of digitization are:

- Hardware (Scanners, Digital camera, Computers, Data storage and data output peripherals).
- Software (Image capturing and image editing software like Xerox TexBridge and Caeres OmoniPage).
- Network (Data transmission).
- Display and Printing technologies.

Conclusion

The library resources and services at CPRI is the combination of printed and digital formats. All the documents are bar-coded, catalogue is computerized and web enabled. The library has its own webpage where all library resources and services are integrated to provide online access and web enabled services. Library has subscribed online and CDROM databases in agriculture like CABI, AGRIS, AGRICOLA and Current Contents.

Being member of CeRA (Consortia for E-Resources in Agriculture) consortia and Delnet, this library provides full text access to more than 2000 international journals published by renowned publishers like Springer, Annual Reviews Inc, CSRIO, Open J-Gate and resources of more than 1000 national/international libraries. Besides these, this library provides access to open source journals, e-books and other e-resources available at the internet under public domain. Therefore keeping in view its library resources and services it is concluded that this library as of now is a hybrid library having good combination of printed and digital resources and services.

However to convert this library into a fully digital library some of its resources and services viz. submission and publication of potato research journal articles, photographs, institute publications, acquisition and circulation etc. must be digitized using appropriate hardware and software under sound planning, execution and evaluation.

References

Association of Research Libraries,(Arl) Proceeding126: Annual Meeting, (http:arl.cni.org/arl/proceeding/126/2-defn.html)(1995),pp17-19.

Chowdhury, (G.G) and Chowdhary, (Sudatta). Digital Libraries: Definition and Characteristic, Introduction to Digital Libraries; Facet Publishing. London WC1E7AE. (2003),pp5.

12

Digital Libraries: Whither thou Goest?

R.D. Dabhi
Asstt. Librarian
and
Ushabala
Associate Professor
M.D. Patel Regional e-Library, AAU, Anand, Gujarat.

Paperless to Paperless Libraries

Ancient Gurus in ancient *Gurukulas* used to impart knowledge to their pupils through oral teaching. The Gurus themselves were treasure troves of knowledge, without the need to refer to hard and soft copies, and online resources. How interesting it is to note we are right now in a nostalgic phase, that takes us back to those ages, when disciples were taught, learned and accumulated oceans of knowledge through oral and moving libraries, which were in the form of their revered Gurus. It is truly fascinating how history has flair to repeat itself. The long-driven transition from paperless back to paperless, that is, from oral instruction through palm leaves through copper plates through virtual paper through electronic to digital libraries is as arduous as it is fascinating. Hence the million dollars question ... where to from here – Digital Library, *whither thou goest*?

Existing Features of Electronic Libraries

It is common knowledge that we use the term "Electronic Library" to describe the situation in which documents are stored in electronic form, rather than on paper or other localized media.

Fredrick Gridley Kilgour, the founding Director of OCLC has characterized the evolution of electronic publishing as being in four stages[1]:

1. Preparation of text in machine-readable form for the production of paper copies with subsequent discard of the machine-readable version
2. Publication of paper copies and also in machine-readable form,
3. Publication in machine-readable form only, and
4. Publication of information in machine-readable form in an encyclopedia-like database.

The advent and advantages of electronic documents are so much discussed so far that a reiteration means only repetition. Yet, we need to analyze why electronic form is the best as compared to paper:

1. As documents are highly volatile.
2. As manipulation of the document is desired.
3. As scanning for names or for particular words or phrases in a lengthy document.
4. As light use of remote material is needed, and
5. As rapid communication is desired, especially within a dispersed group that is not conveniently available at the same time and place.

Taking into consideration the above factors, if the library administration still chooses to retain an exclusive concentration on paper, microfilm, and other localized media, it means only partial rendering of library services, depriving the users of the oceans of material available out there in the form of e-resources. The e-era has provided the facility to the user to access information right on his desktop from any remote source, has literally zeroed the global distances, and made global interaction possible within fractions of seconds. In addition, library users can now obtain their own interlibrary loans, or technically speaking, copies or excerpts, on a self-service basis, requiring the tolerance but not the time or energy of the staff of the library from which it is obtained. For instance, the ILL service can be obtained just with a click with online services like Consortium of e-Resources in Agriculture, and it makes the Document Delivery Service so prompt that it is immensely being useful in expanding the academic and research frontiers of SAUs all over the country.

To be precise, the transition from the Automated Library to the Electronic Library is an extension of the same changes that have characterized the shift from the Paper Library to the Automated Library, as the automation was limited to local features like standardization of data, remote access to files, the linking and combining of files, access to numerous different files from the same terminal, increased cooperative use of shared files and discontinuation of numerous, more-or-less duplicative local files, while the electronic pattern attains global dimensions, spreading its wings all over the world and above to squeeze out information.

The Architecture of Electronic Library

With electronic documents, adherence to standards is important for progress. Electronic documents should themselves be in standard formats. Standards are needed for cataloging electronic documents. Communications formats are needed for conveying electronic documents. Substantial and compatible telecommunications protocols are of great importance. Much work needs to be done in developing and adopting compatible national and international standards for characters, images, documents, telecommunications, and so on. Also, of course, the concept of an Electronic Library assumes a substantial and expensive infrastructure of computing capacity, data storage, and telecommunications, which in turn, requires expertise for successful use.

Electronic Library vs. Digital Library

Generally, Digital Library is being used synonymously with Electronic Library, or vice versa, which may almost be true to a large extent. Still, we must take into account those features, which may distinguish both the versions. It is common knowledge that an Electronic Library consists of electronic materials in digital as well as analog format, for instance, Video tape, Audio materials etc. and it requires Electronic equipment for accessing that type of materials.

In Digital Library, the library consists mostly of Digital Materials and services. Digital materials are those materials which can be accessed by computers or networks (i.e. digital equipment).

These materials are stored, processed and retrieved through digital devices. To explain further, Digital Library is a repository of information in digital form, ie. stored as data files on a computer. It is also the tool-set provided to enable search and retrieval of the repository. An Electronic Library is the same thing — but the term should be deprecated, because the term "electronic" is less precise. It might include analogue data formats, or it might even refer to the subject of "electronics" to laymen.

The digital library in the present sense is an organization including staff, computers, networks, and all other resources necessary to organize, store provide access to, subsidize, preserve, and retrieve selected digital documents where, when, and how needed by users. The term "Digital documents" is used in the widest sense of the word, and includes, but is not limited to one or more computer usable files and can include everything from text, multimedia, database, motion pictures or any other type of digital document. The electronic library on the other hand is a term that has become outdated. It is ancient enough to define a library as an electronic library that uses fax machines. The term digital library is today's preferred vocab.

To put it in a nut shell, the difference between an Electronic Library and a Digital Library can be described as a prolonged journey from a **Digitized Library** to a **Digital Library.**

Infrastructure of Present Digital Library System

The purpose of the information infrastructure is to represent the riches and variety of library information, using the building blocks of the digital library system. From a computing view, the digital library is built up from simple components, notably **digital objects**. A digital object is a way of structuring information in digital form, some of which may be **metadata**, and includes a unique identifier, called a **handle**. However, the information in the digital library is far from simple. A single work may have many parts, a complex internal structure, and one or more arbitrary relationships to other works. To represent the complexity of information in the digital library, several digital objects may be grouped together. This is called a **set of digital objects**. All digital objects have the same basic form, but the structure of a set of digital objects depends upon the information it represents.

The different types of material in a digital library, information can be divided into **categories**, e.g.: text with SGML mark-up,

World Wide Web objects, computer programs, or digitized radio programs. Within each category, rules and conventions describe how to organize the information assets of digital objects. For example, specific rules will describe how to represent a digitized radio program. For each category, the rules describe the digital objects that are used to represent material in the library, how each is represented, how they are grouped as a set of digital objects, the internal structure of each digital object, the associated metadata, and the conventions for naming the digital objects.

A user interface that is aware of the rules and conventions applying to certain categories of information is able to interpret the structure of the set of digital objects. Complex information can be presented without the user having any knowledge of the complexity. Since the user interface recognizes how material is represented, it can provide unsophisticated users with flexible access to rich and complicated information.

The present digital library framework permits many different computer systems to coexist like User Interface, Search System, Handle System and Repository. These components support a user's query through Search, Selection, Retrieval and Display. Where the information architecture is concerned, it is motivated by basic principles like:

- Users and their applications programs are being given flexibility in the sense that taking all levels of users' computer literacy into consideration (as mentioned above), the organizational structure of information is to a large extent user-friendly.
- Collections are straightforward to manage, not making it a hectic task for the managerial staff.
- The information architecture generally reflects the economic, social, and legal frameworks developing in the information infrastructure. In particular it is able to recognize that information is valuable, subject to terms and conditions, and is transmitted over insecure networks that cross national boundaries and encompass global ranges.

Metamorphosis of Electronic Library into Digital Library

During the movement of library system, developmental changes such as closed access to open access, the role of library from a store-house to active information service organization and reading place to center of recreation have been seen. Now digital media is being used to store, process and retrieve information that causes Metamorphosis in the very form and function of library. Metamorphism of library means that the library has passed through certain amount of pressure and environmental change to be addressed, in today's electronic age, as digital library. For instance, Media wise, Electronic storage forms have changed through magnetic tapes and floppies to CDROM and now to DVDs in addition to influencing other factors like cost, access and publication. The foremost aspect to come under the impact of digital library is the cataloguing system, the catalogue being created either in HTML format or by using the OPAC module. On the other hand, the current approach is to store information in databases. These databases are made accessible through web-browsers or any other interface depending on the library. Any user can search these information using search techniques and a search engine. In such databases search can be done on a specific field and it removes the need of catalogue.

With all its benefits, the Digital Libraries carry their own challenges like IPR, economic issues, operating cost, revenue, monitoring and communication, which may be overcome with a little bit of exercise in the nearest future.

Here to where...?

We are already seeing a transformation in the world of libraries. Libraries are becoming less important for the materials they collect or house, and more important for the kind of material they can obtain in response to user requests. This movement from collecting material "just in case" someone will need it, to delivering material from elsewhere "just in time" to answer a user's needs, is a profound shift for the library as an institution. This shift is a direct result of the recent proliferation of digital networking in an environment where standards for description were already well established.

In the mid-nineties, the Digital Library was originally conceived as repositories of digital texts accessible through a search service which was operating by indexing information stored in a centralized metadata catalogue. According to the most recent understanding, the DLs of the future will be able to operate over a large variety of information object types - far wider than those maintained today in physical libraries and archives. These information objects will be composed of several multi-type and multimedia components aggregated in an unlimited number of formats. These, for example, can mix text, tables of scientific data and images obtained by processing earth observation data, or they can integrate 3D images, annotations and videos. These new information objects will offer innovative and more powerful means to researchers for sharing and discussing the results of their work. In order to be able to support these objects, the DL functionality has to be appropriately extended far beyond that required to manipulate the simple digital surrogates of the physical objects. In order to support these objects the DL may need considerable resources. For example, the creation and handling of the new documents may require access to many different, large, heterogeneous information sources, the use of specialized services that process the objects stored in these sources for producing new information, and the exploitation of large processing capabilities for performing these tasks. The emerging Digital Libraries can be specifically beneficial to the researchers in the sense that they must support the activities of their users by providing functionalities that may range from general utilities, like annotation, summarization or co-operative work support, to very audience-specific functions, like map processing, semantic analysis of images, or simulation. The availability of this new DL functionality can, in principle, change the way in which research is conducted.

Now, where the users of the avant-garde Digital Libraries are concerned, they would not only be consumers but also producers of information. By elaborating information gathered through the DL they can create new information objects that are published in the DL, thus enriching its content. The new DLs are thus required to offer services that support the authoring of these new objects and the workflows that lead to their publication.

In a Nutshell

Research and academics today are often a collaborative effort carried out by groups belonging to different organizations spread worldwide. Motivated by a common goal and funding opportunities, these groups dynamically aggregate into virtual research organizations that share their resources, e.g. knowledge, experimentation results, or instruments, for the duration of their collaboration, creating new and more powerful virtual research environments. These virtual research organizations set up by individuals that do not necessarily have great economic power or technical expertise, more and more frequently require DLs as tools for accelerating the achievement of their research results. This new potential audience demands less expensive and more dynamic DL development models. They want to be able to set up new DLs that serve their needs for the duration of their collaborations in an acceptable timeframe and with an acceptable cost. The current DL development model cannot satisfy this large demand; a radical change is needed if we want to be able to address these new emerging requirements.

It is as Alan Kay says, " The best way to predict future is to invent it." Following catch words best express future Digital Libraries:

- More Digital, Less Paper.
- More Searching, Less Organizing.
- Bigger, Fewer.
- Universities, Libraries, Society.
- More Options, ... or Fewer???????

References

Aditya Tripathi. Metamorphosis of Libraries. http://ir.inflibnet.ac.in.

Donatella Castelli. Digital libraries of the future – and the role of libraries. ISTI-CNR, Pisa, Italy.

Frederick G. Kilgour. Beyond Bibliography. (London: British Library, 1985).

Neil Jefferies. Future Directions for Digital Libraries. SERS, Bodleian Libraries, Oxford University Publication.

13

The Role of Librarian's in the Electronic Information Environment

Rajkumar Singh
Librarian, College of Horticulture and Forestry,
Central Agricultural University, Pasighat - 791102

Introduction

There are a growing number of academics and publishers who believe quite firmly that once the transition from print to electronic journals has been made — particularly within the scientific, medical and technical (STM) sector of the journals market — there will be no role for libraries in the scholarly communication chain. Electronic journals can be delivered directly from the publisher to the user's desktop. Such a scenario is certainly possible, but it is unlikely for a number of reasons. Even assuming that all academics and researchers had the technical expertise to deal with the range of hardware and software required to access a variety of relevant electronic products, individuals will not wish to purchase, out of their own pockets, the range of titles required for their research, and therefore some form of departmental/ faculty or central purchasing will be required. Moreover, an individual academic will have scant regard that the titles they are interested in having delivered to their desktop may be of interest to other colleagues on campus. They will not want to read and sign a complex license agreement so that the title can be networked across the campus. Currently librarians perform a valuable service to the academic and research colleagues by facilitating quick and easy access to information. What really matters is that relevant information is quickly and easily available to support research, teaching and learning. And librarians are currently playing a pivotal role in this process.

Librarians have traditionally been concerned with certain functions, and most of these have their parallels in the electronic publishing era.

1. *Collection development and acquisitions*: deciding what materials to obtain for their user community, finding out how to get hold of the chosen materials, and buying them.
2. *Cataloguing and classification*: Arranging the collection in such a way that users can find items within it, with search tools such as indexes and catalogues.
3. *Circulation*: Lending items to users, reserving items for users, and getting them back again and reshelving them.
4. *Reference work*: Discussing users' information needs with them, and advising them how best to use the library's resources to find the information that they need.
5. *Preservation, conservation and archiving*: ensuring that materials remain available to users in perpetuity.

It is often suggested that some or all of these functions become redundant in an era when increasing amount of information are available directly to users via the Internet. This argument is contradicted by an often-heard complaint that the Internet is completely chaotic, and that people waste much time in fruitless searching for the precise information that they need.

Selection and Acquisition

Selection

In academic and research libraries librarians have always taken guidance from subject experts on purchases: for teaching materials, academic staff provide reading lists for research journals, departments are often asked to prioritise journals in their field for purchase (or more often nowadays for cancellation). The library budget may be allocated, notionally or even totally, to different departments in order to ensure equity between subject fields in purchasing. Nevertheless, the role of the librarian is not negligible. Academic librarians usually control the purchases of general reference resources that cannot sensibly be allocated to one department. They will also know, as departmental staff necessarily cannot, whether several departments wish to purchase the same items.

Acquisition

While monographs may be purchased by libraries directly from publishers, through booksellers, or through library supply companies, journals have traditionally been purchased by libraries through subscription agents. The agents provide a valuable "sorting" function, allowing each library to submit a single order and each publisher to receive orders conveniently batched. This service — now almost totally computerised — is provided by the agents for a charge averaging about 12% of the subscription price, split approximately 6% paid by the publishers and 6% by the libraries. It would cost both parties a lot more than this to maintain all their bilateral links without the middleman.

Selection and Acquisition in the Electronic era

Selection and acquisition in the electronic medium, on the other hand, are far less straightforward and currently require much higher levels of professional involvement and administrative labour. Those freely available on the Internet have little or no marketing budget and rarely find their way in traditional bibliographic sources. Even titles emanating from commercial publishers are currently notoriously difficult to track down. The best and most comprehensive source is the Association of Research Libraries, Directory of Electronic Journals and Newsletters backed up by the NewJour electronic announcement service and web site. Individual publishers' web sites can sometimes be a useful source and the major subscription agents are slowly beginning to provide electronic journal information to libraries. Once relevant titles have been identified, selection criteria should follow the principles established for printed subscriptions, such as quality/peer-review, and relevance to research, teaching and learning. Freely available electronic journals have a zero subscription cost but they do have an upkeep cost once added to an electronic journal service, and they are more likely to move WWW site without notice than their commercial counterparts.

Payment Structures for Electronic Journals

Except for those published free of charge, electronic journals have to be paid for and, in contrast with the print versions, there is a wide range of payment structures, often involving restrictions on use imposed by the publishers that go well beyond any constraints that exist with print publications. Subscription models include: free with a print subscription; a surcharge on the cost of the print subscription (typically between 10% and 25%); available as part of a regional/national consortium deal; available through a local/regional/national site licence agreement. The whole question of libraries signing licenses for electronic products - whether they be electronic journals, CD-ROMs or networked databases - is fraught with difficulty. The terms of each licence vary considerably and the small print has to be read thoroughly to ensure that institutions are not committed to terms which are unenforceable.

Cataloguing, Classification, Information Retrieval System

Traditional library catalogues included the content of books, but not the content of journals for the content of journals, one had to use the bibliographical databases which are now generally provided in electronic form either online or on CD-ROM. The electronic medium offers the possibility of linking the library's own catalogue directly (with a single interface) to the bibliographical databases and from there in principle to the electronic full text of the articles.

Reference Work and Access

Probably the most intellectually rigorous part of the work of a librarian is the reference interview, the occasion when a user tries to explain to a librarian what their information need is, and the librarian tries to find the best available strategy for assisting the user. The overall task contains many layers. It requires an understanding of human communication problems — what people say they need initially is not necessarily a complete or an accurate description of their real need. It requires knowledge of the subject-matter: it is difficult to advise on information sources on a subject which one does not understand. It requires, quite clearly, a good knowledge of what information resources exist in a particular subject field. And it requires a knowledge of the internal structure of the sources — it will not be sufficient to say "Use Beilstein" without explaining how this complex tool can be used.

Librarian as Electronic-Resources Expert

The contribution of library and information professionals to reference work has increased, rather than the reverse, as electronic information sources have proliferated. It was probably never true that users could use all of the resources of a library unaided, but many thought that they could. With the great variety of bibliographic databases, numerical databanks, electronic journals, and general Internet resources that exist today, few users can make optimal use of them all. The software needed to search in these files, the command languages, and the facilities available for output or transfer of "hits" to other files for further processing are so complex and varied that professional help is very often needed.

Teaching Role of Libraries

It is often forgotten that students as well as staff in higher education use the journal literature: the belief that the books constitute the teaching library and the journals the research library is at best an oversimplification. It is often the case that students are directed to read particular journal articles by lecturers, and are expected to search the journal literature themselves Students, too, need to be assisted to use the journal literature, It is fair for them to assume that all the resources of the university library, printed or electronic, will be available to them without difficulty or charge.

Document Delivery and Interlibrary Loans

In the print medium, either the required item was held by the library or it could be obtained by interlibrary loan, for which well-established procedures existed. With electronic resources, access is more complex. First, and most obviously, an appropriate infrastructure must exist within the institution for delivery of electronic information services. The internal network and its outside links to the Internet must have adequate capacity for the traffic, and users need sufficient numbers of machines of adequate specification to retrieve information with convenience. Access needs to be freely available in open-access student PC laboratories as well as on the desks of staff. Many libraries have set up electronic journal web sites to provide one starting place for access to a range of different titles — and also to provide information on passwords etc. Freely available Internet titles are, superficially, the easiest titles to access. They do not require passwords (although some do require registration) and a hypertext link can be set up to the title page. However, such titles tend to be unstable in that they move sites without notice and it is advisable to instigate some system of URL monitoring to prevent the frustration of repeated error messages.

Access to Electronic Journals

Electronic journals from commercial publishers can be tedious to access. Although most publishers are moving away from password authorisation to IP address checking, it is still the case that for many publishers, access to their titles is via their web pages. This means that not only must the user know who the publisher of a title is but they must also work their way down a series of web pages before they actually find the title they wish to consult. Librarians would like to provide access to the content of electronic journals via an interface that their users are familiar with — particularly, through the online public access catalogue (OPAC) system of their choice. Unfortunately, most publishers insist that one searches all the journals that they publish through their own site, with whatever interface and software they have chosen to provide — which will most likely be quite different from those provided by other publishers.

Loss and Damage

With print materials the major concern has been environmental control of temperature and humidity to preserve books, and the repair and restoration of ones that have been damaged. The quality of paper and bindings has also been an issue. Concern has been expressed more recently about the physical lifespan of CD-ROMs. Perhaps a more serious problem with electronic media is the obsolescence of hardware and software. Files written on (for example) one-inch magnetic tape or eight-inch floppy disks, on some now-obsolete computer using non-standard software are now likely to be unreadable. Projects such as the Knowledge Warehouse have sought to address the issue of preservation, but it is acknowledged that there would be cost involved in that data in large amounts would need periodically to be ported forward on to a new software platform before the old one became unusable.

Training of Users

In the context of research institutes and commercial and industrial organisations, librarians and information officers often carry out information searches on behalf of research and managerial staff. In the electronic era this will undoubtedly continue to be the case, as many members of other professions have neither the time nor the inclination to carry out searches themselves. These areas (sometimes referred to as the "emerging market" for information and library professionals) continue to show growth in employment as the electronic revolution proceeds. The academic world is slightly different, since a relatively small number of library staff have to serve very large numbers of staff and students, and it has clearly never been feasible for them to undertake all the searching on users' behalf. It is necessary for users to do the work themselves, and academic staff indeed have often wished to do so, not being very willing to delegate their "keeping up with the literature" to someone else.

Learning to use Electronic Resources

Over the last decade, however, the number and variety of information sources available, whether locally or remotely via the WWW have increased greatly, and users in many cases have not been able to keep up with all of the choices now open to them. In addition to the classical "reference interview" mentioned earlier, therefore, librarians in most institutions of higher education have greatly enhanced their provision of user education, especially as regards electronic sources of information, to the point where this is now perhaps the dominant activity for professional staff in academic libraries — circulation duties, for example, being delegated to paraprofessionals. This must be seen as an enhancement of the status of library staff, since it renders them more equal partners with teaching staff in the educational activity of the university. They now have contact in a training role with both academic staff and students. The areas in which training is given would include not only the use of electronic primary journals from many different publishers, but also the use of abstracts and indexes databases, databanks, CD-ROM publications, document delivery services, and electronic short-loan facilities for reading-list materials. Training may even be given to academic and research staff and research students in authoring for electronic publication.

Conclusion

An analysis of the emerging electronic publication era leads to the conclusion that it is likely to be a complex and confusing scene, in which staff and students whose major concern is necessarily their subject field, and not computer and information sciences, will not be able to look after their own information needs without assistance. Together with the perceived unfashionableness of the word "library" these misconceptions may give rise to the belief that the librarian will soon be an extinct species. The analysis given in this paper seeks to demonstrate that, on the contrary, the traditional activities of professional librarians have direct parallels in essential roles in the electronic era, and that the user-education role is a growing one which librarians are uniquely qualified to fill.

References

Al-Ansari, H 1999, 'Improving the organizational structure for an electronic environment: a case analysis of Kuwait University libraries' Library Review 48 (3) pp131-139.

Cathro, W 1999, 'Digital libraries: a National Library perspective' in Strategies for the next millennium: proceedings of the ninth Australasian Information Online & On Disc Conference and Exhibition, ALIA, Sydney. Also available online: http://www.nla.gov.au/nla/staffpaper/cathro4.html (accessed 19 March 2000)

Crawford, W & Gorman, M 1995, Future libraries: dreams madness & reality, American Library Association, Chicago.

Dewey, M 1876. 'The profession', American Library Journal, vol1, September 30, p5-6, quoted in Rice-Livey, M. & Racine, J. 1997. 'The role of academic librarians in the era of information technology' Journal of Academic Librarianship 23 (1) p32.

Dugdale, C 1999. 'Managing electronic reserves: new opportunities and new roles for academic librarians?' Librarian Career Development 7 (12) pp150-163.

Encyclopaedia Britannica at http://www.britannica.com provides a detailed history of the development and role of libraries.

Gorman, M 1991, 'The academic library in the year 2001: dream or nightmare or something in between?' Journal of Academic Librarianship 17 (1) March, pp 4-6.

Graham, P 1995. 'Requirements for the digital research library' College & Research Libraries 56, July pp 331-339.

Hawkins, BL 1998, 'The unsustainability of traditional libraries' in New thinking on higher education:

Mason, M 1998. 'The yin and yang of knowing', in Books, bricks & bytes: libraries in the twenty-first century, ed. S. Graubard & P. LeClerc, Transaction Publishers, London, pp161-171.

Paterson, A 1999, 'Ahead of the game: developing academic library staff for the twenty-first century', Librarian Career Development, 7 (12) November, pp143-149.

Rice-Livey, M & Racine, J 1997. 'The role of academic librarians in the era of information technology', Journal of Academic Librarianship, 23 (1), pp 31-41.

Schmidt-Braul, I 1999, 'Does culture create new jobs in the information society?: strategic issues and new professional profiles', Librarian Career Development, 7 (12), pp 127-142.

Schuyler, M 1999, 'Prognostications on technology unbound or, the library to come', Computers in Libraries, 19 (5), pp 30-32

Wood, PA & Walther, JH 2000, 'The future of academic libraries: changing formats and changing delivery', The Bottom Line: Managing Library Finances, 13, (4) pp173-181.

Young, P 1998. 'Librarianship: a changing profession', in Books, bricks & bytes: libraries in the twenty-first century, ed S Graubard & P LeClerc, Transaction Publishers, London, pp103-125.

14

Bibliometric Monitoring of Research Performance in the field of Dairy Science with Special Reference to Krishiprabha

Ramnivas Sharma
Assistant Librarian, V.R.S. Krishi Vishwa Vidyalaya,Gwalior (M.P.)
Email:dr.ramnivas@gmail.com
and
Nidhi S Tiwari
H.O.D. / Librarian, Rajiv Academy for Technology & Management, Mathura (U.P.)
Email: nidhiji@rediffmail.com
Manoj Tiwari
Librarian, K.D.Dental College & Hospital, Mathura (U.P.)
Email: manojtiwarikddc@rediff.com

---

1. Bibliometric

Bibliometrics is the application of quantitative techniques to analyze the volume, the movement, the frequency and the characteristics, etc of published documents and the related activities. Alan Pritchard was first to use the word "Bibliometrics" in an article "Statistical Bibliography or Bibliometrics" published in the 1969 issue of the "Journal of Documentation". He defines Bibliometrics as "the application of mathematical and statistical methods to books and other media of communication." In a later article, Pritchard explained Bibliometrics as the "metrology of the information transfer process and its purpose is analysis and control of the process". Bibliometrics is a set of methods used to study or measure texts and information (Wikipedia, 2011).

2. Electronic Thesis and Dissertation

Electronic Thesis and Dissertation (ETD) initiatives in India are at an embryonic stage. At present, access to theses and dissertations is limited, as availability of comprehensive theses bibliography database or availability of full-text theses is not available. Since the beginning of this decade, few national institutes started ETD initiatives with focus on Open Archives Initiative (OAI) repositories, thus allowing metadata harvesting. It may not be surprising that some of these institutes received funding or collaborative support from other organizations to start their digital library initiatives. The Central University of Hyderabad has collaborated with Sun Microsystems Ltd. to digitize its collection and has also received the hardware at a discounted price. IIT-Kharagpur has been awarded a project by the Aeronautics Research and Development Board for developing a digital library on aerospace and technology. ETD@IIT Delhi has received grants from the Ministry of Human Resources Development and the Department of Biotechnology for a similar initiative. On the other hand, the Information Library Network (INFLIBNET) consortium, Vidyanidhi Library of Theses and Dissertations etc. are actively involved in the development of bibliographic ETDs and digital ETDs. Last year, UGC pronounced some guidelines towards the submission of metadata and full text of doctoral theses in the electronic format, to improve creation, collection and compilation of cataloguing information, and to create the Indian National Theses Database.

3. Objectives of the Study

i) To Analyze Research Productivity.

ii) To Analyze Year-wise, Subject-Wise.

iii) To Analyze Guide-wise Research Productivity.

iv) To Analyze Research Trends in Dairy Science (Agriculture Science).

4. Scope

Scope of the present study is Limited to Dairy Science. The data required for the study was collected from the Krishi Prabha (http://192.168.1.22:8080/equestthesis/IPlogin.do). KrishiPrabha is a full-text electronic database of Indian Agricultural Doctoral Dissertations submitted by research scholars to the 45 State/ Deemed Agricultural Universities during the period from 1.1.2000 to 31.12.2006. This database, listing about 10500 Dissertations, has been created by Nehru Library, Ch. Charan Singh Haryana Agricultural University, Hisar with financial support from Indian Council of Agricultural Research, New Delhi under its National Agricultural Innovation Project.

5. Methodology

The data needed for the application of Bibliometric Analysis was collected from the e-version of database prepared from the Doctoral Dissertations submitted to the 45 State/Deemed Agricultural Universities. The data has been presented in the tabulation and graphical form.

6. Analysis and Interpretation of Data

Year-Wise Distribution: Total 167 Doctoral Dissertations were selected for the study. The following table presents the Year-wise distribution.

Table 1: Year-wise distribution of Doctoral Dissertations

S. No.	Year	No. of Doctoral Dissertations	Rank
1.	1994	01	XI
2.	1995	01	XI
3.	1996	00	XII
4.	1997	04	VIII
5.	1998	01	XI
6.	1999	03	IX
7.	2000	09	VII
8.	2001	12	VI
9.	2002	14	V
10.	2003	12	VI
11.	2004	09	VII
12.	2005	21	III
13.	2006	26	I
14.	2007	22	II
15.	2008	15	IV
16.	2009	15	IV
17.	2010	02	X
	Total	**167**	

Distribution of 167 Doctoral Dissertations which were awarded during 1994-2010 has been give in detail in Table 1 and Maximum number of Doctoral Dissertations were awarded in 2006(26) and minimum number of Doctoral Dissertations awarded in 1998(01).

Note: Doctoral Dissertations in 1996 is 0.

Sub-Category-Wise Distribution: Table 2 shows the sub-Category-wise distribution of the Dairy Science Doctoral Dissertations.

Table 2: Sub-Category-wise distribution of Doctoral Dissertations

S. No.	Sub-Category Dissertations	No. of Doctoral	Rank
1.	Animal Products Technology	25	IV
2.	Dairy Technology	39	I
3.	Dairy Microbiology	33	II
4.	Dairy Extension Education	30	III
5.	Dairy Chemistry	19	VI
6.	Dairy Economics	20	V
7.	Dairy Engineering	1	VII
	Total	**167**	

Maximum numbers of Doctoral Dissertations 39 Nos. are submitted on Dairy Technology. The Dairy Microbiology 33 Nos. is second choice of researchers.

Guide-Wise Distribution: Guide-wise distributions of Doctoral Dissertations are shown in Table 4. This Table indicates that overall 85 guides guided 167 Doctoral research scholars. Table 4 indicates that maximum 08 Doctoral Dissertations are guided by Dr. Ram Kumar and 06 Doctoral Dissertations are guided by Dr. D.N.Gandhi and rest of Doctoral Dissertations by several other guides.

Table 3: Guide-wise distribution of Doctoral Dissertations

S. No.	Guide Name Dissertations	No. of Doctoral	Rank
1.	Aggarwal, P.K.	03	V
2.	Annal Villi, R.	03	V
3.	Atreja, S.K.	01	VII
4.	Bandyopadhyay, A.K.	02	VI
5.	Batish, V.K.	03	V
6.	Berwal, J.S.	01	VII
7.	Bhambure, C.V.	01	VII
8.	Bhosale, D.N.	03	V
9.	Biswas, Subhasish	02	VI
10.	Chauhan, A.K.	01	VII
11.	Chauhan, J.P.S.	01	VII
12.	Dabur, R.S.	01	VII
13.	Darshan Lal	02	VI
14.	De, S.	01	VII
15.	Desraj	01	VII
16.	Dhaka, J.P.	04	IV
17.	Dharam Pal	03	V
18.	Fulzeie, R.M.	03	V
19.	Gandhi, D.N.	06	II
20.	Ghatak, P.K.	02	VI
21.	Ghosh, Bikash C.	01	VII
22.	Govindarajulu, M.	01	VII
23.	Goswami, S.L.	01	VII
24.	Goyal, G.K.	03	V
25.	Grover, Sunita	01	VII
26.	Gupta, Jancy	05	III
27.	Gupta, Vijay Kumar	02	VI
28.	Harish Chander	01	VII
29.	Jain, D.K.	04	IV
30.	Jha, Sujeet Kumar	02	VI
31.	Kadian, K.S.	01	VII
32.	Kalra, K.K.	02	VI
33.	Kanawjia, S.K.	03	V
34.	Kapoor, C.M.	04	IV
35.	Khan, B.L.	01	VII
36.	Kulkarni, Satish	01	VII

Contd.

37.	Majumder, S.C.	02	VI
38.	Malik, B.S.	05	III
39.	Malik, R.K.	02	VI
40.	Mann, Bimlesh	01	VII
41.	Mann, R.S.	02	VI
42.	Misra, A.K.	01	VII
43.	Mukundan, M.	01	VII
44.	Narasimhan, R.	02	VI
45.	Palta, P.	01	VII
46.	Panda, P.C.	03	V
47.	Patel, A.A.	02	VI
48.	Patil, G.R.	02	VI
49.	Prasad, D.N.	01	VII
50.	Rai, T.	01	VII
51.	Ram Chand	02	VI
52.	Ram Kumar	08	I
53.	Rao, H.G.Ramachandra	01	VII
54.	Rao, K.J.	01	VII
55.	Rattan Chand	04	IV
56.	Sadasivam, P.	01	VII
57.	Samanta, R.	01	VII
58.	Sandhu, J.S.	01	VII
59.	Sangwan, R.B.	01	VII
60.	Sankhala, Gopal	02	VI
61.	Shah, B.P.	01	VII
62.	Sharma, D.P.	01	VII
63.	Sharma, G.S.	01	VII
64.	Sharma, R.S.	01	VII
65.	Singh, Chandrodai	02	VI
66.	Singh, Kishan	05	III
67.	Singh, Kulwant	01	VII
68.	Singh, R.R.B.	01	VII
69.	Singh, Rajvir	05	III
70.	Singh, Rameshwar	03	V
71.	Singh, Sukhminder	02	VI
72.	Singh, T.	01	VII
73.	Sirohi, Smita	01	VII
74.	Solanky, M.J.	02	VI
75.	Srivastava, D.N.	02	VI
76.	Surendra Nath, B.	01	VII

Contd.

77.	Thompkinson, D.K.	02	VI
78.	Venkateshaiah, B.V.	01	VII
79.	Verma, B.B.	01	VII
80.	Verma, N.K.	01	VII
81.	Vijayalakshmi, S.	02	VI
82.	Wadhwa, B.K.	02	VI
83.	Wankhede, D.B.	01	VII
84.	Yadav, D.N.	01	VII
85.	Yadav, M.P.S.	01	VII
	Total	**167**	

University/Institution-wise Distribution: Table 4 depicts the university/Institution-wise research output in the form of Doctoral Dissertations. Among the 11 Universities/Institution. National Dairy Research Institute, Karnal stands first with 118 Doctoral Dissertations. Chaudhary Charan Singh Haryana Agricultural University, Hisar with 16 Doctoral Dissertations occupies the second place.

Table 5: University/Institution-wise distribution of Doctoral Dissertations

S. No.	University/Institution Name	No. of Doctoral Dissertations	Rank
1.	Anand Agricultural University	06	V
2.	Chaudhary Charan Singh Haryana Agricultural University	16	II
3.	Dr. Balasahed Sawant Konkan Krishi Vidyapeeth	02	VII
4.	Kerala Agricultural University	01	VIII
5.	Mahatama Phule Krishi Vidyapeeth	03	VI
6.	Marathwada Agricultural University	01	VIII
7.	Narendra Dev University of Agriculture and Technology	01	VIII
8.	National Dairy Research Institute, Karnal	118	I
9.	Karnataka Veterinary, Animal and Fisheries Science University, Bidar	02	VII
10.	Tamil Nadu Veterinary and Animal Science University	07	IV
11.	West Bengal University of Animal and Fishery Science	10	III
	Total	**167**	

Keywords-wise Distribution: Table 5 shows the Keywords-wise distribution of the Dairy Science Doctoral Dissertations. Total 99 subject areas have been covered. Maximum numbers of doctoral dissertations 16 Nos. are submitted on Dairy Farming The only Milk subject is second choice of researchers with 13 doctoral dissertations submitted on this subject. 07 doctoral dissertations are found in the Panner.

Table 6: Keywords-wise (Related to Dairy Science Subject) distribution of Doctoral Dissertations

S. No.	Keywords	No. of Doctoral Dissertations	Rank
1.	Dairy Farming	16	I
2.	Milk	13	II
3.	Paneer	07	III
4.	Cheese	06	IV
5.	Milk Products	06	IV
6.	Buffalo Milk	03	V
7.	Ghee	03	V
8.	Dairy Farms	03	V
9.	Dairy Products	03	V
10.	Livestock	03	V
11.	Raw Milk	03	V
12.	Acidophilus Milk	02	VI
13.	Buffaloes	02	VI
14.	Cattle	02	VI
15.	Cows	02	VI
16.	Curd	02	VI
17.	Dairy Husbandry	02	VI
18.	Dairy Industry	02	VI
19.	Dairy Microbiology	02	VI
20.	Entrepreneurship	02	VI
21.	Farmers	02	VI
22.	Fermented Milk	02	VI
23.	Milk Production	02	VI
24.	Sweets	02	VI
25.	Animal Health	01	VII
26.	Animal Husbandry	01	VII
27.	Annatlo	01	VII
28.	Antimycotic Effect	01	VII

Contd.

29.	Antioxidants	01	VII
30.	Bacteriophage	01	VII
31.	Bananas	01	VII
32.	Basundi Making Machine	01	VII
33.	Bifidobacterium	01	VII
34.	Bovine	01	VII
35.	Cardiovascular System	01	VII
36.	Careinogenesis	01	VII
37.	Cereal Byproducts	01	VII
38.	Cheddar Cheese	01	VII
39.	Cheese	01	VII
40.	Chicken	01	VII
41.	Chicken Meat	01	VII
42.	Chicken Patties	01	VII
43.	Coconut Fat	01	VII
44.	Crop Husbandry	01	VII
45.	Cultured Milks	01	VII
46.	Dahi	01	VII
47.	Dairy Cooperatives	01	VII
48.	Desserts	01	VII
49.	Enzymes	01	VII
50.	Farming Systems	01	VII
51.	Food Microbiology	01	VII
52.	Food Pathogens	01	VII
53.	Frozen Dessert	01	VII
54.	Fruit	01	VII
55.	Goats	01	VII
56.	Groundnut	01	VII
57.	Guavas	01	VII
58.	Herbal Sandesh	01	VII
59.	Ice Cream	01	VII
60.	Information Technology	01	VII
61.	Ingredients	01	VII
62.	Institute-village Linkage Programmes	01	VII
63.	Jalbhara	01	VII
64.	Khurehan	01	VII
65.	Kradi	01	VII
66.	Lactobacillus Acidophilus	01	VII
67.	Lactobacillus Casei	01	VII
68.	Lassi	01	VII

Contd.

69.	Lingnocellulosics Wastes	01	VII
70.	Livestock Development Assistants	01	VII
71.	Mango Pulp	01	VII
72.	Market Economy	01	VII
73.	Market Milk	01	VII
74.	Marketing	01	VII
75.	Microbiology	01	VII
76.	Milk Chocolate	01	VII
77.	Milk Fat	01	VII
78.	Milk Market	01	VII
79.	Milk Processing	01	VII
80.	Mist Dahi	01	VII
81.	Mixed Farming	01	VII
82.	Mozzarella Cheese	01	VII
83.	Pathogens	01	VII
84.	Pedas	01	VII
85.	Pizza	01	VII
86.	Poultry Meat	01	VII
87.	Poultry Products	01	VII
88.	Pradeshik Cooperative Dairy Federation(PCDF)	01	VII
89.	Probiotics	01	VII
90.	Processed Cheese	01	VII
91.	Rabit Meat	01	VII
92.	Saccharomyces	01	VII
93.	Sheep	01	VII
94.	Starch	01	VII
95.	Tannins	01	VII
96.	Technology	01	VII
97.	Thermophilic Bacteria	01	VII
98.	Turmeric	01	VII
99.	Whey	01	VII
	Total	**167**	

Conclusion

The present study was undertaken to trace the development of Dairy Science research at doctoral level during 1994-2010 atf different Agricultural universities/institutions (Krishiprabha). It is found that highest number of doctoral dissertations i.e. 26 has been submitted in the years of 2006 and the lowest in 1996. The sub-Category "Dairy Technology" is the first choice of the researchers i.e. 39 and The "Dairy Microbiology" subject is second choice of researchers. Total 33 doctoral dissertations submitted on this sub-Category.

Bibliography

Arunima Kumari. An Introduction to Research Methodology. 2008. Agrotech Publishing Academy; Udaipur. p25.

Buttlern (L). Information Sources in library and information science doctoral research. Library & Information Science Research.21, 2; 1999. P227-245.

Chikate (RV). Citation Analysis of theses in library and information science submitted to University of Pune: A pilot Study. Library Philosophy and Practice; 2008, Dec.

Dixit (Purvendra Kumar). Bibliometric Study of M.D. Dissertations Submitted to Medical Colleges in U.P. during 1996-2005. Jiwaji University. Gwalior. Ph.D. Thesis. 2006.

Directory of Open Access Repositories (2011) (http://opendoar.org/)

dyuthi.cusat.ac.in

etheses.saurashtrauniversity.edu

etd.ncsi.iisc.ernet.in

Ghai (Daljeet). Citation analysis of Ph.D. Dissertations in Library and Information Science submitted to the University of Madhya Pradesh and Punjab (1975-1999). Jiwaji University, Gwalior. Ph.D. Thesis. 2001.

Gooden (AM). Citation Analysis of chemistry Doctoral Dissertations: An Ohio state university case study. Issues in science & technology librarianship. 32; 2001.

Gopinath (MA). Research in Library and Information Science. Library Science with a Slant to Documentation. 15, 3; 1978. p144.

Indian Council of Social Science Research (http://www.icssr.org/)

Kumar (PSG). Doctoral studies in library and information science in India: a study. DESIDOC Bulletin of Information Technology. 18, 1; 1998. p5-9.

Kumar (S) and KUMAR (S). Bibliometric study of the journal of Oilseeds Research since (1993-2001). SRELS journal of Information Management. 42, 3; 2005. p305-334.

Krishi Prabha: Indian Agricultural Doctoral Dissertation Repository (http://202.141.47.8:8080/equestthesis/)

Nederhof (Anton J). Bibliometric monitoring of research performance in the Social Science and the Humanities: a review. Scientometrics. 66, 1; 2006. p81-100.

Pachauri (Nirendra Kumar). A Scientometric Study of PhD Theses submitted in Botany in Universities in U.P during 1998-2007. Jiwaji University, Gwalior. Ph.D. Theses. 2009.

Padhi (P) and GARG (KC). From Librametry to Informetrics and an overview of Indian Contributions. In : DHAWAN (SM),Ed.. Library and Information Studies in Cyber age. 2004. Authors Press; New Delhi.

Patra (Swapan Kumar) and Prakash Chand. Library and Information Science Research in India: A Bibliometric study. Annals of Library and Information studies. 53; 2006, Dec. p219-223.

Patra (Swapan Kumar) and others,. Bibliometric study of Literature on Bibliometrics. DESIDOC Bulletin of Information Technology. 26,1; 2006. p27-32.

Pritchard (A). Statistical Bibliography or Bibliometrics. Journal of Documentation. 25, 4; 1969. p348-349.

Sangam (SL). A Citation analysis of doctoral dissertation in science during 1964-1982. University of Karnataka. Ph.D. Thesis. 1986.

Sharma (Ramnivas). Bibliometric and Citation Analysis of Ph.D. Theses in Library and Information Science 2001 to 2008. Jiwaji University, Gwalior. Ph.D. Thesis. 2012.

Shodhganga http://shodhganga.inflibnet.ac.in/

Ujjappa (Kamappahavarj). Citation analysis of doctoral dissertation in library and information science. . University of Karnataka Ph.D. Thesis. , 1991.

Wikipedia (2011): http://en.wikipedia. org/wiki/Bibliometrics

Vidyanidhi (http://vidyanidhi.org.in)

15

Digital Library: Development of Digital Library

Rishabh Kumar Jain
Research Associate (e-Granth Project)
Nehru Library, CCS Haryana Agricultural University, Hisar
E-mail: rishabh.jain965@gmail.com

Inroduction

In the present I.T. (Information Technology) environment a number of libraries are being converted into digital libraries as the advantages of being a digital library is now well understood by every one. Over the years information has been produced digitally and libraries have become major providers of information in digital format. The information managers should have knowledge of computer, networking, internet and digital resources, etc to manage these resources and provide access to end users.

Need of Digitization

Collection in print format is prone to and deterioration. This type of collection has a short life despite preservation practices affected by numerous factors such as weather, temperature, fire, humidity, insects, water, bugs, etc. Although it is not possible to replicate the original document's spirit as in physical form still the information contained in the form of text and graphics can be preserved in the digital form. The digitization process converts the physical analog data into a virtual digital equivalent of the same that can be displayed on a computer screen or reproduced in physical form again using printing techniques. Thus due to digitization practice the information of a print document could be made survive long after the original is gone.

Digital Library Definitions

The term digital library itself defines the collection of a library. Digital Library occupies or contains the articles/materials in digital/electronic format. There electronic object may include text, images, videos, audio, and multimedia compositions are also included.

William Y Arms (2000) defines that- "An informal definition of a digital library is a managed collection of information, with associated services, where the information is stored in digital formats and accessible over a network. A crucial part of this definition is that the information is managed."

Wikipedia defines as - "A digital library is a library in which collections are stored in digital formats (as opposed to print, microform, or other media) and accessible via computers. The digital content may be stored locally, or accessed remotely via computer networks. A digital library is a type of information retrieval system."

Micheal Lesk (1997) defines digital library as – "Digital Libraries are organized collections of digital formats. The combine the structuring and gathering of information, which libraries and archives have always done, with the digital representation that computer have made possible."

The DELOS Digital Library reference model defines that a digital library as- An organization, which might be virtual, that comprehensively collects, manages and preserves for the long term rich digital contents, and offers to its user communities specialized functionality on that contents of measurable quality and according to codified policies.

Some elements that have been identified as common to these definitions are:

1. The DL is not a single entity.
2. It requires technology to link the resources of many.
3. The linkages between the many digital libraries and information services are transparent to the end users.
4. Universal access to digital libraries and information services is a goal of many digital libraries.
5. Digital library collections are not limited to documents surrogates: they extend to digital artifacts that cannot

the represented or distributed to printed formats." (Jain, Jindal & Babbar, 2006, 23).

Thus, a digital library is nothing but an extension of a conventional library by means of advanced technology. It is a storehouse of distributable electronic resources with the availability of several free digital Library software packages at the recent time, the creation and sharing of information through the digital format. Digital Library is a knowledge centre, learning centre, a node of knowledge in a worldwide information network.

Objectives of Digital Library

To capture, store, organized information in digitized way for its better dissemination using network facilities.

1. To give lifelong learning opportunities to the users.
2. To introduce, provide and retrospective services.
3. To promote economical and efficient release of information.
4. To avoid routing and redundant activities..
5. To provide rational view of all information with any format.
6. To maintain huge digitized databases.
7. To improve the cost effectiveness of library operations.

Advantages of Digital Library

1. Digital libraries provide excellent opportunities for a broad range of patrons to find appropriate research materials all at one place.
2. Digital libraries can be customized according to users need.
3. Information can be consulted, shared by multiple users at the same time, update quickly, and available 24/7.
4. The user is able to use any related searching technique/ term (word, phrase, title, author, and subject) to search the entire collection. Digital libraries can provide very user-friendly interfaces, giving clickable access to its resources.

5. Digital libraries have the potential to store much more information easily because digital information requires very little physical space to contain them and media storage technologies are more affordable than ever before.
6. Digital library make easier to copy digital information without errors, no fear of maintaining one physical object permanently. So rare publications and artifacts may be preserved in better way by providing access to their digital versions.
7. The users of digital libraries need not to go to the library physically, people from all over the world can access to the information as long as an internet connection is available.

Developments in Digital Library Softwares

Well-designed digital library software has the potential to enable non-specialist people to conceive, assemble, build, and disseminate new information collections. This has great social impact because it democratizes the dissemination of information. In particular, it will revolutionize the way in which education is conducted and educational materials are prepared.

Digital Libraries are being created today for diverse communities and in different fields e.g. education, science, culture, development, health, governance and so on. With the availability of several free digital Library software packages at the present time, the creation and sharing of information through the digital library collections has become an attractive and feasible proposition for library and information professionals around the world. Library automation has helped to provide easy access to collections through the use of computerized library catalogue such as On-line Public Access Catalog (OPAC). Digital libraries differ significantly from the traditional libraries because they allow users to gain an on-line access and work with the electronic versions of full text documents and their associated images. Many digital libraries also provide an access to other multi-media content like audio and video on the internet.

There are many open source and commercial digital library softwares available for building digital libraries:

1. DSpace (Digital Space).
2. GSDL (Green Stone Digital library).

3. E-Print.
4. Fedora: An Open Source Digital Repository Management.
5. CD Sware: The CERN Document Server Software.
6. CLOCKSS.
7. LOCKSS (lots of Copies Keep Stuff Safe).
8. ETD-db (Electronic Theses and Dissertation Database).
9. Roads.
10. Libronix Digital Library System.
11. First Search.
12. Dinest.
13. Ages Digital Libraries Software (My Ages).
14. AGES Software.
15. GDL (Ganesha Digital Library).

Some Popular Open Source Digital Library Software

Some important features of the popular open source digital library software are discussed hereunder.

DSpace

DSpace is a suite of software which has the ability to server digital library collections and builds new collections. It provides a new way of organization information and publishing it on the internet or on CD-ROM. DSpace was released by HP-MIT (Massachusetts Institute of Technology) Alliance in 2002 and since its releases are very popular open source digitization software. It is open source software available from http://www.dspace.org under the terms of the GNU General public License.

DSpace installation is very easy. It supports a wide variety of data, including Theses/Dissertations, faculty publications, lectures notes, student's dissertations, learning objects, question papers, project reports, annual reports, gray literature, unpublished documents, maps, 3D digital scan of objects, photographs, film, video, link to open knowledge object, and other form of contents successfully and enables the upload from every terminals with antic user interface.

Features of DSpace

1. DSpace is written in JAVA, based on Postgre SQL database.
2. DSpace holding are made available primarily via a web interface, but it also support the OAI-PHM v2.0, and is capable of exporting METS (Metadata Encoding and Transmission Standard) packages.
3. Controlled Vocabulary support for XMLUI, follow Dublin core metadata standard.
4. Decentralized submission process.
5. Google Analytics support for JSPUI.
6. Import/Export capabilities.
7. Access control over items in repository at collection and individual item levels.
8. Well tested and widely used by library and information centers.
9. Accepts all types of digital contents.

Green Stone Digital Library (GSDL)

Greenstone Digital Library Software (GSDL) promoted by the New Zealand Digital Library Project Research Group at the University of Waikato, and sponsored by the UNESCO and Human Info NGO in Belgium. It is a open source, multilingual software written on C++, JAVA and Perl available from http://www.greenstone.org/ under the terms of the GNU General Public License.

Greenstone software provides a way of building, maintaining, and distributing digital library collections, opening up new possibilities for organizing information and maintaining it available over the internet or on CD-ROM. The aim of the Greenstone software is to empower user, particularly in universities, libraries and other public service institutional to build their own digital libraries. The complete interface available for the Greenstone digital library software in English, French, Spanish, Russian, Dutch, Arabic, German and Kazakh etc.

Features of Greenstone

1. Greenstone builds collection using almost popular and standard digital formats such as TEXT, PDF, RTF, HTML, XML, JPEG, MP3, word, postscript, and many other formats which include audio as well as video.
2. UNICODE based multilingual capabilities and user friendly multimedia interfacing.
3. Use of Dublin Core and other metadata schemes.
4. Supports creation and management of collection by administrator.
5. Z39.50 client available on Linux systems.
6. Increase Portability.
7. Efficiency of Access.
8. Flexibility.
9. Availability.
10. Strengthens - mechanisms and capacity - Information Systems / Services.

E-Print

E-Print is open access repository software. It has been produced by the University of Southampton, School of Electronic and Computer Science with minimum technical experts. The first version of the software was publicly released in 2000 and latest version v3.3.11 was released in January 2013.

E-Print is intended to make a highly configurable web-based archive and is a platform for building repositories of Scientific data, student's theses, lectures notes, project reports, teaching material, images, audio-video data, exhibitions and performances etc that can be stored digitally by making changes in configuration. E-Print works on Linux/Unix Operating System and it need MySQL, Perl modules and Apache web server. The software can be installed by any institutions worldwide with modifying configuration files. By its integrated advanced search, extended metadata and other features, the software can be customized to institutions requirement. We can download/ Install E-Print from (http://www.eprints.org/software/).

Features of E-Print

1. Supports management and access to digital contents.
2. User friendly interface.
3. Support to submission standard formats like word, images, audio, text, postscript, plaintext etc.
4. E-Print also supports by default MS PowerPoint and MS Word format uploading.
5. OAI-PMH data provider.
6. Use Dublin Core metadata scheme.
7. Metadata can be customized for different archives and document types.
8. Software checks for duplicate entries while uploading the digital documents on the basis of "Title".
9. Supports to import metadata of items via DOI (via CrossRef), XML, PubMED ID, PubMED XML format.

Fedora

Fedora (Flexible Extensible Digital Object Repository Architecture) was jointly produced by Cornell University and University of Virginia Library. Fedora first version (Fedora1.0) was publicly released in the year of 2003. It is open source repository software available from http://www.fedora-commons.org for digitations of libraries. Fedora also released a latest version (Fedora3.6.2) in November 2012. The Fedora Repository is extremely flexible and can be used to support any type of digital content such as content management systems, digital collections, scholarly publishing enterprises, e-research, archives, institutional repositories, open access publishing, digital asset management, and digital libraries. Fedora open source software gives institution/ organizational flexible service oriented architecture for managing and delivering their digital contents.

Features of Fedora

- Store all types of content and its metadata in any formats.
- Digital content and its metadata can be managed and maintained.

- OAI-PMH provider service that is designed to take advantage of Fedora's features.
- Access data via Web APIs (REST/SOAP).
- Provide RDF search (SPARQL).
- Drupal module that allows users to view and manage objects stored in Fedora.
- Rebuilder Utility for disaster recovery and data migration.
- Full text search service.
- Web-based Administrator GUI.
- Global Search (full text) Search Service.
- Multiple users driven front-ends.
- JMS messaging service.

Conclusion

With the availability of lots of data in print and digital format it is very much necessary for the libraries to organize these contents with proper systems. Users desire and expect contents in transportable form which can be utilized in various digital environments. In the present time, Digital Library in academic institutions are growing with a hope of power the shared values, research outputs, teaching materials, images etc. presenting themselves as a new paradigms of sharing information.

References

Arms, William Y (2000) "Digital Libraries." Published by MIT Press. PP. 2 https://www.google.co.in/search?tbo=p&tbm=bks&q=isbn:0262511274

EPrints Digital Library Software Evaluation available at http://shodhganga.inflibnet.ac.in/bitstream/10603/3731/16/16_chapter%207.pdf

http://en.wikipedia.org/wiki/Digital_library.

http://www.fedora-commons.org

http://www.delos.info/index.php?option=com_content&task=view&id=345

http://www.slideshare.net/yhen06/advantages-and-disadvantages-of-digital-library-14454641

Jain, P K, S C Jindal, and Parveen Babbar (2006). "Digital libraries in India: Initiatives and problems." International conference on digital libraries 2006: Information management for global access held on 5-8 Dec.2006, New Delhi. Pp 22-31.

Kamila, Kanchan (2011). "Institutional repository building through GSDL: A case study of Burdwan University." Paper presented at International Conference on Digital libraries and Knowledge Organization (ICDK-2011) MDI Gurgaon.

Lesk, Micheal (1997). "Practical digital libraries: Book, bytes and bucks." Published by Morgan kufmann Publisher, Inc. pp.xix. https://www.google.co.in/search?tbo=p&tbm=bks&q=isbn:1558604596

Naganna, N, Mallinath kumbar, and Rajive Kumar Pateria (2012). "Open source software for building digital librart: An evaluative study." Libraries in digital era. New Delhi, Arihant Prakashan Pvt. Ltd. 2012.

Rajput, P.S., V.K. Chaudhary, and J.N. Gautam (2011). "Digital library for all: Creation framework and obstacles." Paper presented at International Conference on Digital libraries and Knowledge Organization (ICDK-2011) MDI Gurgaon.

Seify, Leili and Khaiser Nikam (2011). "Developemnt of cultural heritage digitization and access in Indira Gandhi National Centre for the Arts: A case study." Paper presented at International Conference on Digital libraries and Knowledge Organization (ICDK-2011) MDI Gurgaon.

Singh, Bindeshwari Pratap, Rishabh Kumar Jain, Veenu, and B.R. Yadav (2012). "Free open source software (FOSS) and their use in the library and information management." Paper presented at National Conference of Agricultural Libraries and user community (NCALUC-2012). ANGRAU, Hyderabad.

Trivedi, Mayank(2010). "Digital Libraries: Functionality, Usability, and Accessibility" Library Philosophy and Practice. http://unllib.unl.edu/LPP/trivedi-diglib.pdf.

Vaidya, Bina (2011). "Digital library development preservation and management of digital information: The state of digitization and preservation activities in Nepal." Paper presented at International Conference on Digital Libraries and Knowledge Organization (ICDK-2011) MDI Gurgaon.

❑❑❑

16

Library Consortia

Saurabh Nagariya
Librarian
Vandana Global Ltd.
Raipur, Chhattisgarh
E-mail: saurabhmlib@gmail.com/saurabhnagariya@yahoo.com
and
Barsha Gupta
Trainee
Central Library
Bundelkhand University, Jhansi U.P.
E-mail: 123varshagupta@gmail.com

Introduction

The total area of education is continuously changing where imperative information is exploring constantly. There is highest need of information and knowledge for best and efficient education and the library plays a vital role in it. The users demand various aspects of information and enhanced quality of information service. Therefore present day's library has gone from traditional environment to e-environment. We can use e-journals, e-books; CD & DVD etc .Library consortia play a most important role of academic libraries.

Definition

A consortium is an association of a group of organizations or group of academic libraries, which come together for achieving the common objective .The basic aim to formulate consortia is for resources sharing and save the budget for development of organizations. A library consortium can be local, regional, state, national and inter institutional level.

Need

1. Education Area Continuously changing.
2. Users demanding broader varieties of information services.
3. Information Explosion.
4. Limited Budget.

Advantages of Consortia

1. Electronic resources at substantially lower cost.
2. Optimum utilization of funds.
3. Facilities to build up digital libraries
4. Helpful to provide better library services like CAS and SDI
5. Cost Sharing for Technical and training support
6. Electronic Journals demand neither library space nor shelling costs nor can they be stolen from the library
7. The consortium have been offered better terms of licenses for use, archival access and Preservation of subscribed electronic resources, which would not have been possible for any single institution; and available 24/7.

Disadvantages of Consortia

1. Require training of staff in handling electronic documents etc.
2. Consortia require high initial investments in licensees and information and communication technology.
3. Copyright problems.
4. Unreliable telecommunication links and insufficient bandwidth.
5. Lack of archiving and back files availability.
6. Internet Access necessary.
7. Users are not accepting e-journals at par with the printed Journals.

Consortia in India

1. INDEST (Indian National Digital Library in Engineering Sciences and Technology) (http://paniit.iitd.ac.in/indest/).

   The Ministry of Human Resource Development (MHRD) has set-up the Indian National Digital Library in Engineering Sciences and Technology (INDEST) Consortium on the recommendation made by the Expert Group appointed by the ministry under the chairmanship of Prof. N. Balakrishnan. The Ministry provides funds required for subscription to electronic resources for (58) institutions including IISc, IITs, NITs, IIMs and a few other centrally-funded Government institutions through the consortium headquarters set-up at the IIT Delhi. The INDEST- Total Members (1370).

2. FORSA (Forum for Resource Sharing in Astronomy and Astrophysics) (http://legacy.icolc.net/FORSA.html).

   The Forum for Resource Sharing in Astronomy & Astrophysics (FORSA) came into existence in the year 1982, for sharing the resources available in astronomy libraries in the country. In 2004, this group has extended its membership to Physics and Maths libraries in the country who have common interests to carry forward the aim of FORSA and its activities. Currently FORSA has twelve members and it works towards the goals and services which the founder members have started.

3. ICICI Knowledge Park (Industrial Credit and Investment Corporation of India) (http://ikplibrary.wordpress.com/about/).

   ICICI Knowledge Park is the first wet lab Research Park in India. Structured as a not-for-profit company, the mission is to set up a world-class centre for business driven research. This is achieved by developing an innovation hub around a research park so that the region becomes globally competitive. The Park is spread over an aesthetically landscaped 200 acre campus in Genome Valley life science cluster near Hyderabad. While the current focus of IKP is in Life Sciences, innovation in any knowledge-based sector that requires wet labs is encouraged.

The Project was made possible by ICICI Bank providing the initial equity, management support and soft funding and the State Government of Andhra Pradesh giving 200 acres of land free of cost for establishing the Park.

4. CSIR Library Consortia (Council for Scientific and Industrial Research) (http://www.csir.res.in/External/Utilities/Frames/aboutcsir/main_page.asp?a=topframe.htm&b=leftcon.htm&c=/external/heads/aboutcsir/about_us.htm).

   The Council of Scientific & Industrial Research (CSIR) —the premier industrial R&D organization in India was constituted in 1942 by a resolution of the then Central Legislative Assembly. It is an autonomous body registered under the Registration of Societies Act of 1860.CSIR aims to provide industrial competitiveness, social welfare, strong S&T base for strategic sectors and advancement of fundamental knowledge.

5. HELINET (Health Sciences Library & Information Network) (http://www.rguhs.ac.in/HELINETHOSTCO NSO RTIUM/homehelinethost.htm).

   HELINET stands for Health Science Library and Information Network is first of its kind in the country. The consortium was started with a vision to improve the quality of education and research in the Health Science institutions of the state through enhanced access to high quality medical information. HELINET's goal is to deliver information to user's desk-top, with round-the-clock access.

   The major benefit of this consortium was expanded access to core international e-journals. Before the launch of the consortium, access to foreign medical journals by each college was limited to around 100. HELINET has made it possible for each college to access and share the contents in more than 600 journals, in effect increasing the access provision by 6-times.

6. INFLIBNET (Information & Library Network Centre).

7. UGC- InfoNet (University Grants Commission).

8. UGC-DAE Consortium for Scientific Research.

   DAE Library Consortia (Department of Atomic Energy).

9. IIM's Library Consortia (The Indian Institute of Management).
10. ISRO Library Consortium.
11. DeLCON -DBT e-Library Consortium.

Conclusion

Library consortia are really helping the students, faculties and the researcher to provide the information and save their time. They are providing physical and electronic delivery of materials.

References

Ramesh Yernagula, & P. K. Kelkar : Library Consortia: benefits and models of E-journals Consortia (http://www.isical.ac.in/~serial/consortia/CBSOR-11.pdf)

Sadanand Y. Bansode- Library Consortia in India: Issue & prospects – TRIM V3 (2) July- Dec 2007 – Page 138-152.

17

Cloud Computing: Issues and Concern with the Libraries

Seema Parmar
Assistant Librarian
Nehru Library, CCS Haryana Agricultural University
Hissar, Haryana
and
Rajive Pateria
Assistant Librarian
Nehru Library, CCS Haryana Agricultural University
Hissar, Haryana
and
Bhanu Partap
Assistant Librarian
Nehru Library, CCS Haryana Agricultural University
Hissar, Haryana

Introduction

Information Technology (I.T.) with its multi advantageous services has influenced the working of every sector whether it is education, industries, livelihood, agriculture, and other sectors *viz* government, business, health, employment, environment and security etc. Consequently, taking the benefit of I.T., most of the organizations have automated their systems to perform their routine activities in a better way as well as to offer more improved services.

The Internet has made it possible to communicate and share the services and resources of one organization with others irrespective of time and place which has brought the different organizations at a single forum within the network.

Internet with its advantageous services is now no more a miracle for the present generation, instead it has become the necessity of everyone's life. Next Generation is considering Internet as a toy to play for their required information. This plaything has been accompanied with a new module of services on desktop, named as 'Cloud Computing' or 'Location-Independent-Computing'.

Concept of Cloud Computing

The 'cloud' is considered as a label for online computing resources rather than the entire Internet. The term 'cloud computing' also distinguishes the kinds of things we have been doing online for a couple of decades from a totally new age of online software and processing power.

Cloud computing is a subscription-based service where we can get networked storage facilities and various computer applications on as pay- as use basis. In Cloud Computing IT resources and applications are rented and shared among multiple customers much as storage space or particular applications. These services are delivered over an Internet connection the "cloud" which replaces the company data space or server providing the same service on as pay as use basis. Thus, Cloud Computing is simply that IT service where various clients are accessing data through a networked cloud. "There are many synonyms for cloud computing such as, 'on-demand computing', 'software as service ', 'information utilities', 'the internet as a platform', and others. Cloud computing refers to use of web for computing needs which could include using software applications, storing data, accessing computing power, or using a platform to build applications". (Bansode and Pujar, 2012).

Definitions

There are many definitions for cloud computing:

- Gartner defines cloud computing as "a style of computing in which massively scalable IT-related capabilities are provided 'as a service' using Internet technologies to multiple external customers".
- Forrester defines cloud computing "as a pool of abstracted, highly scalable, and managed compute infrastructure capable of hosting end-customer applications and billed by consumption".

- Scale defines cloud computing is 'simply the sharing and use of applications and resources of a network environment to get work done without concern about ownership and management of the network's resources and applications".

National Institute of Standards and Technology, defines cloud computing as "a model for enabling convenient, on-demand network access to a shared pool of configurable computing resources (e.g. networks, servers, storage, applications, and services) that can be rapidly provisioned and released with minimal management effort or service provider interaction (Pandya, 2012). All these all definitions encompass the key 5 cloud characteristics:

1. On Demand Service
2. Broad Network Access
3. Resource Pooling
4. Scalable & Elastic Services
5. Metered Services (Pay-Per-Use).

The clouds makes it possible for you to access your information from anywhere at any time. While a traditional computer setup requires you to be in the same location as your data storage device, the cloud takes away that step. The cloud removes the need for you to be in the same physical location as the hardware that stores your data. Your cloud provider can both own and house the hardware and software necessary to run your home or business applications (Huth & Cubela, 2011).

Some of the companies such as Amazon cloud, Salesforce.com, IBM Smart Cloud, Microsoft, Rock space, Fortress ITX, Areti Internet, Joynet, Teremark, Layered Technologies, Google, Akamai etc. are providing Cloud Computing services:

Types of Cloud Computing (Cloud Services)

There are mainly three categories of cloud service:

1. Software-as-a-Service (SaaS).
2. Platform-as-a-Service (Paas).
3. Infrastructure-as-a-Service (IaaS).

1. Software-as-a-Service

In this type of service software in the form of service is delivered to the user/customer . For this the user need not to install and run the application on his/her own system to access any program but he can access any program from any online device like home PC, work PC, netbook, tablet or smartphon under cloud. The maintenance responsibility is of the host company in such type of service. Most SaaS applications are also collaborative. For example, two or more people can work on the same application at the same time, which makes remote working easier. Because Saas applications are delivered over the Internet, they are continually updated. SaaS applications therefore do not have version numbers. Instead new functionality is constantly added incrementally.

Examples: Google Docs, Google Checkout, Hotmail, Gmail, Yahoo mail, Skype, Google Apps, Zoho, Acrobat.com, SlideRocket, etc. are some of the examples of this type of Cloud Computing.

Applicaton in libraries: OpenURL resolver, journal listing service, instructional guides, reserves statistics, and IM/chat service. Their major limitations are threat to data security and oppose open source movement.

2. Plateform-as-a-Service

PaaS is a hosting environment and a software application development platform that allow a user to develop, debug, deploy, and control personally created or acquired applications using service provider application development tools and infrastructure such as: database, middleware, programming languages, OS, network, server or storage (Barr and Schofield, 2008). In this type of service PaaS vendors facilitate the customer everything necessary to quickly create, test and deliver other novel online applications. These applications may be made available to one organization on fee basis or publicly on a free basis.

Some technical programming knowledge is required to use most PaaS offerings. PaaS does speed up the process by automating some coding tasks. All current PaaS offerings require programmers to work in their own specified programming languages and to use only the supplied tools to create new applications. However, once this knowledge is acquired pretty much anybody-be they a computer science student working in their bedroom or a large corporation-can create new web-based applications and deliver them rapidly at minimal cost.

One of the major advantages of many PaaS offerings is that new applications do not have to be migrated between systems. This is because applications are created from scratch on the same platform from which they will be delivered to their final users. It is therefore exceedingly unlikely that a new application that has been properly tested will not work perfectly the moment it goes live on the web.

PaaS is not a panacea. One of the biggest potential drawbacks of developing new applications using PaaS is vendor lock-in. There are currently a relatively small number of PaaS vendors available, and all of them have their own standards and programming tools. Anybody who uses PaaS to develop applications therefore inevitably becomes reliant on their chosen vendor. This makes the choice of vendor critical, and is likely to drive most users to of large organizations like Google and Microsoft.

Examples: Google App Engine, Force.com, Microsoft Windows Azure, Zoho Creator, Google Maps, ADP Payroll Processing, Google Sites, Moonfruit, Webs.com, IBM's Smart Business Cloud Solutions, Oracle Platform, etc. are some of the examples of this type of Cloud Computing.

Application in libraries: Integrated library system, archives management software, initial website application,etc.

3. Infrastructure-as-a-Service

It is also known as HaaS (Hardware-as-a-Service) which includes both storage services and computing power. In this service consumer is provided the capability of processing, storage, networks, and other fundamental computing resources where the consumer can deploy and run arbitrary software, which can include operating system and applications. The consumer does not manage OS, storage, deployed applications, and possibly limited control of select networking components (e.g., host firewalls).

Thus, infrastructure as a service (IaaS) is where a vendor offers computer hardware in the cloud on which their customers can store data and develop and run whatever applications they please. IaaS allows companies to move their existing programs and data into the cloud and to close down their own local services and data centres.

In brief it can be said that IaaS vendors basically rent out the servers to their customers on which their customers store their data and run applications. Many of the servers the vendors supply are virtual rather than real. What this means is that while cloud data centers contain rack upon rack of server blades, these physical servers are subdivided by a software process called 'virtualization'. After the Internet itself, virtualization is the most fundamental technology that allows cloud computing to occur. Using virtualization, any physical server can be split into any number of virtual servers, each of which can then be used entirely independently by a different user.

Examples: Amazon.com (Elastic Compute Cloud [EC2] and Simple Storage), IBM, etc. are some of the examples of this type of Cloud Computing.

Application in libraries: Hosting IR discovery layer.

Sanchati and Kul Karni (2011) have suggested some other services in libraries which are as follows:

Unified Search Service : Although majority of libraries are using OPAC (Online Public Access Catalog) but a uniform access platform is not available to share the OPACs. However, with the adoption of cloud computing, the integrated library resources support distributed uniform access interface, promote usage of library resources, answers users' questions by using high-quality navigation.

Real-time Access Services : Due to innumerable advantages of electronic resources, users prefer to access electronic journals and electronic databases. However, by introducing cloud computing, libraries can establish a shared public cloud jointly which can have infinite storage capacity and computing power bringing obvious benefits to libraries. It can help to reduce the substantial cost involved on purchase of electronic databases. Moreover, users can visit the shared resources by any terminal equipment, such as PC, mobile phone or PDA using internet access.

Knowledge Service : In the context of knowledge economy, knowledge resources are directly affecting the productivity and national development. So the mode of dissemination of information and knowledge has become the most challenging task for librarians today. However, at this juncture, cloud computing and establishment of shared public cloud can help a great deal to save on manpower and resources. Moreover, with cloud computing, librarians won't have to maintain their own equipments or deal with users personally which will provide more time and energy to librarians to offer their users the needed information and knowledge-based services.

All-people Service : With this model, libraries can provide services to all the people with the help of cloud computing. Anyone who can legally identity the network authentication has the right to visit the joint resources of libraries on the internet.

Deployment Models: A cloud deployment model represents specific type of cloud environment and it is classified based on ownership and size. According to Saxena and Azimuddin Khan (2012) there are four common deployment models:

Public Cloud: In this type a cloud service provider make the cloud infrastructure available to public but on subscription basis. The cloud service provider is the owner of this infrastructure and manages & maintains it. This is economical service for a consumer to develop and deploy a service in the cloud. Google App Engine, Microsoft window Azure, IBM Smart Cloud etc are included in this type of model.

Private Cloud: In this type of model the infrastructure is established, maintained and controlled for a specific institution or organization. This is operated in house or by a third party or by both. It is more secure. Amazon VPC, VMware Cloud Infrastructure Suite, and Microsoft ECI data center are the examples of private clouds.

Community Cloud:It is just like the public clouds but it is accessible to a specicial community of consumers who have common interests and needs. It is also operated in -house or by a third party. Google Apps for Govt. and Microsoft Govt.Community Cloud are the examples.

Hybrid Cloud: It is combination of two deployment models but they may support the requirement to retain some data in an organization and it requires providing services in the cloud. Window Azure, VMware vCloud are the examples.

Cloud Computing and Library Services

Libraries from the very beginning were satisfying the user needs with their own inhouse resources. During the end of the 20th century information technology had changed the whole scenario of disseminating the services of the libraries irrespective of place and time. The internet and consortia played on important role in providing 24x7 hours information services to the user in a collaborative manner through resources sharing. Recently the libraries have been moving towards other recent technologies for better sharing of resources without spending much time, human energy and funds. Cloud computing is one of these technology which is emerging as a major technology in the libraries around the world. It offers much improved services then strengthen the sharing of resources of all kind among libraries through the web or cloud. "With these development heterogonous resources are accessible to any one, anywhere because of the application of domain "independent software". (Singh and Veralakshmi, 2012).

According to Fox (quoted in Bansode and Pujar, 2012) "one of the key pressures that pushes libraries to cloud solutions and proves to be an impediment to the migration is the availability of IT support services. He also observes that goals and policies of organisation might also force libraries in making use of cloud computing services". These factors make SaaS and PaaS approaches appealing for libraries. However, according to Kroski (quoted in Bansode and Pujar, 2012) "Libraries are experimenting with all types of cloud computing services including that of infrastructure services, i.e., IaaS". Libraries are using cloud computing in number of areas starting from library automation, digital libraries, website hosting, federated search, etc. In the last two decades of 20th century, computerization of libraries' all traditional activities like cataloging, the public catalog, acquisition, and serials check-in etc. meant for digitization of library.

Advantages of Cloud Computing for Libraries

- Many a libraries are using some library software, maintaining website or portal, institutional repositories and they are managing their servers having huge data their self but maintenance of these servers has always been a major problem to the LIS professionals as these require a heavy cost as well as IT skilled staff or hired experts. So libraries are facing deferent type of problems in management of these types of hardware and software especially due to the problem of data security. In such cases the libraries can adopt the concept of cloud computing keeping in mind the various advantageous things like data integrity, updates, maintenance, backup, disaster management etc.

- After adopting this technology the operational cost of electronic resources will be reduced and access will be nsured through virtualized environment.
- The cost of infrastructure, maintenance and hired I.T. experts within or outside the organisation will be reduced.
- It is boon to green IT companies as the virtual servers facilitates high bandwith, large storing capacity, disaster management and more data security.
- It is a cost effective or more economical technology as it is based on as use-as pay concept.
- This technology makes libraries enable to take joint decisions on collection development, preservation, digitization, and online shared services in real time.

In addition to the above this technology will prove effective for routine activities of libraries. According to Goldner (2010), following are the other personas that a library can avail the benefits from cloud:

- For having suitable and preferred automation software using SaaS from cloud.
- Digitization and storage using IaaS from cloud.
- Providing the reference services using the cloud tools as Google Chat, Skype, and Mailing service.
- Advertising the library new acquisitions and services using the multimedia resources of cloud.
- Acquisition Librarians managing diverse collections.
- Cataloging librarians seeking to describe an ever increasing body of information and information sources the library is managing.
- Serials librarians working to maintain control and access to collections spidered across the web.
- Electronic resource librarians managing burgeoning collections, and ever-changing list of vendors using the combined expertise and resources.

Cloud Computing Initiatives for Libraries

There are a number of organizations and business houses, involved in the business of integrated library software, etc. A few major initiatives pertinent to libraries are:

OCLC's Webscale

OCLC can be said as an example which is making use of cloud computing for libraries. Since last many years OCLC has been providing tools for cataloguing over internet and allow member institution for copy cataloguing thus it is acting as a cloud computing vendor.

Ex-Libris Cloud

It is a popular USA's library software vendor, which at first developed a number of current products and they were implemented at local level as solutions. At a later stage, they were modified for a hosted environment. "Alma"-the library system, was conceived as a cloud-based service which was transformed the traditional library resources management. It has not only saved the total cost of implementing software but provided effective services to users.

Duraspace's DuraCloud

To enable the different organisations and libraries to share scholarly literature with using DSpace and Fedora Commons, Duraspace provides open source repository solutions. "DuraCloud" service of Duraspace offers digital preservation support services in the cloud, which proved useful for libraries. Using this service libraries may move their content in cloud and stock up it with different service providers thus avoid the risk of data loss.

OSS Labs

OSS labs from India is using Amazon's elastic cloud computing platform owing to the various capabilities of Amazon such as high durability of data, scalability, flexibility and strong information security based on ISO 27000 standards,. With using Amazon's cloud services, it provides the Koha and DSpace hosting to the libraries alongwith the free software maintenance and update services.

Security of Cloud Computing

As data owners store their data on external servers, there have been increasing demands and concerns for data confidentiality, authentication and access control. The Data Owner (DO) places the data on the Cloud Service Provider (CSP) which user wants to access. As the CSP is un-trusted, DO places encrypted data on CSP. Upon receiving a data access request from the user, DO sends required keys and a certificate to the user. User then presents the certificate to CSP and gets the encrypted data upon successful verification by CSP.

According to Kim and Korea (2009) the foremost part of selecting cloud providers are:

Choosing a cloud provider

a) Each cloud service provider serves a specific function, giving users more or less control over their cloud depending on the type of requirement. When we choose a provider, we need to compare our needs with the cloud services available. Depending on our personal or public need the cloud service model will vary.

b) The foremost important thing we must look into is the security measures that our cloud provider already has in place. The cloud service provider must have standard for ensuring the data security.

c) Cloud Computing service provider must adopt the most sophisticated and up-to-date tools and procedures, and strive to provide better security and privacy.

Availability of Data

It is impossible to provide 100% availability, unless high availability architecture is adopted and both the platform and applications are fully tested. Data provider should seek service level agreements (SLAs) that will motivate the cloud service provider to ensure desired levels of availability. The data provider must select viable vendors, and even then have a contingency plan. It is one serious availability concern with cloud computing. This is when the cloud computing vendor goes out of business, or becomes unable to deliver the service as the users may have initially been led to expect.

Compliance

Data provider must maintain business legal documents and assure their integrity in order to comply with various laws, rules and regulations.

Support

Both data provider and end users require support for problem resolution. Today's free SaaS cloud users are left pretty much than their own. Data provider need to pay for support. Cloud computing service provider must hire and train adequate staff to provide better support. In fact, cloud services should be designed for easier usability. All the concerns need to be careful about this issue. Vendor lock-in is a concern that the users always have but in practice they live with. Interoperability and industry-wide standards have alleviated this concern in the case of other technologies. This does not seem to have received much press as a major concern yet, probably because the market is in its infancy and not many users have faced the problems yet.

Pros to End User

1. The third party provider owns and manages all the computing resources (servers, software, storage, and networking) and electricity needed for the services. The users only need to "plug into" the cloud.
2. The users do not need to make a large upfront investment on computing resources; the space needed to house them; electricity needed to run the computing resources; and the cost of maintaining staff for administering the system, network, and database.
3. The users can increase or decrease the level of use of the computing resources and services flexibly and easily.
4. The users pay most likely much less for the services, because they pay only for the computing resources and services they use, and the subscription-based or pay per-use charges are likely much lower than the cost of maintaining on-premises computing resources.
5. The users can in practice access the cloud for services anytime from anywhere.

6. Hides the technological complexity from the user and enables enhanced flexibility.
7. Multi-tenancy is an important characteristic in cloud systems, where the location of code and / or Data is principally unknown and the same resource may be assigned to multiple users.
8. User can acquire and operate necessary resources in almost no time versus much time needed to plan, buy and install their own resources.
9. Cloud computing put all these complexities on provider sides enabling clients to easily operate hardware and software appliances.

Cons

Cloud computing is still in its early years. Organizations usually prefer to adopt proven methodologies that come with success stories and best practices from previous adopters. Some of the risks of adopting cloud computing include:

1. Risk or data loss.
2. Failure in compliance.
3. Constant connectivity required.
4. Dependency.
5. Quality problems with cloud service provider.
6. Time and budget Constraints.
7. Cloud computing lacks the standards needed for loose coupling between providers and clients.
8. Lack of transparency in terms of continuity and reliability.
9. Lack of Legislation.

Thus seeing the above advantages and disadvantages of cloud computing model, we need to focus more on the issues while selecting the cloud provider. All these are equally applicable for individual, institution, community of organizations and to libraries. Libraries must take care of the disadvantages, so that those issues do not interrupt in retrieving most precise piece of information for the user. Libraries instead can even develop their own clouds, depending on the collaboration of the supportive institutions, using the interfaces and DB2 support provided by the Cloud Service Providers. A library can have its own long-term Information Repositories.

Conclusion

Cloud Computing is one of the effective technological buzz of the time. It has considerable impact even on libraries as compared with the IT industry, Technological Firms, & Informational World Market. Libraries would have a visible change in future, in terms of housekeeping operations, services provided, and generated. Libraries have a huge scope with the implication of cloud computing to improvise their services and relevance with the information society and to come in the workflow of the information seekers. Cloud Computing is the biggest solution for the libraries lacking with fund and budget. It serves as the perfect tool for maximum output with minimum expenditure.

References

Abidi, Faiz and Abidi, Hasan Jamal (2012). Cloud Libraries: A novel application of Cloud Computing. International Journal of Cloud Computing and Services Science)IJ-CLOSER), 1 (3), pp.79-83. http://iaesjournal.com/online/index.php/IJ-CLOSER

Ahmed, Mohammed Imtiaz and others (2012). Cloud computing explorations in Chhattisgarh (India). (Paper presented in SAARC conference for library and information professionals, December 01-02, 2012, Greater Noida). New Delhi: Zenith Publications, pp. 645-655.

Bansode, S.Y. and Pujar, S.M.(2012). Cloud Computing and Libraries. DESIDOC Journal of Library & Information Technology, 32(6), pp. 506-512

Barnatt, Christopher (2010). A brief guide to Cloud Computing: an essential guide to the next computing revolution. London: Constable & Robinson.

Barr, J (2010). Host your web site on the cloud: Amazon web services made easy. Seattle:SitePoint.

Goldner, M. (2011). Winds of change: libraries and cloud computing, product and technological essence, Vol. 5 (12), pp. 1-13.

Kim, Won and Korea, Suwon (2009). Cloud Computing: status and prognosis, Journal of Object Technology, Vol. 8(1), pp. 65-72. http://www.jot.fm/issues/issue_2009_01/column4/

Mehta, Poonam and Shete, Chandrakant (2012). Cloud Computing: An avenue to launch libraries on Web. (Paper presented in SAARC Conference for Library Professionals, December 01-02, 2012, Greater Noida). Trends and development in library and information science, New Delhi: Zenith Publications, pp. 631-643.

Pandya, Miteshkumar (2012). Cloud Computing for Libraries: A SWOT analysis, INFLIBNET 8th Convention, PLANNER-2012, pp.387-394.

Sanchati, Rupesh & Kulkarni, Gaurav. Cloud computing in digital and university libraries. Global J.Comp. Sci. Technol., 2011, 11(12), 37-42.

Saxena, Karunesh and Azimuddin Khan. (2012). Cloud: The new vistas of computing for higher education and research. University News. 50(16), pp.17-21.

Scale, Mark-Shane E. Cloud computing and collaboration. Library Hi Tech News, 2009, 26(9), 10-13.

Singh, Shashi Prabha and Veralakshmi, R.S.R. (2012). Cloud Computing: A Promising Economic Model for Library and Information Centers. DESIDOC Journal of Library & Information Technology, 32(6), pp. 526-532.

18

Information Literacy Competency For Higher Education and the Role of Librarians

Stanley Madan Kumar
University Librarian (Retd)
No.80, "Sri Ranga", 2A Main
10th Cross, Laxmaiah Block
Ganganagar, Bangalore 560 024
E-mail: sunnystanmk@gmail.com
and
Subramani, M.K
Assistant Librarian, Forestry College
Ponnampet 571 216
Kodagu Dist. Karnataka
E-mail: subramanifcp@gmail.com

Introduction

Increasing quantum of information being generated and distributed in electronic form and management of these resources has become a real challenge to the library professionals. How to integrate and handle this information increasing at phenomenal speed and how quickly and effectively it can be accessed and provided is the real concern. This has given rise to the concept of 'poly-media library'. This concept has brought to the front the importance of Information Literacy (IL) for academic pursuits as well as for life-long learning.

What is Information Literacy?

Generally, Information Literacy (IL) is defined as the ability to identify when there is a need for information, to be able to identify, locate, evaluate and effectively use that information for dealing with the issue/problem at hand. IL is very important for life-long learning and is common to all learning environments.

Unesco (2009) describes IL as the ability to recognize information needs and use ICT features and applications to access, retrieve, store, manage, integrate, evaluate, create and communicate information effectively.

Standards for Information Literacy

Recognizing the importance of IL, The Association of College and Research Libraries (ACRL) and the International Federation of Library Associations (IFLA) and several national and professional bodies have evolved standards for assessing IL competency of students in higher education.

ACRL Standards are mentioned hereunder.

Standard I

The information literate student determines the nature and extent of the information needed.

Standard II

The information literate student accesses needed information effectively and efficiently.

Standard III

The information literate student evaluates information and its sources critically and incorporates selected information into his/her knowledge base and value system.

Standard IV

The information literate student individually or as a member of a group, uses information effectively to accomplish a specific purpose.

Standard V

The information literate student understands many of the economic, legal and social issues surrounding the use of information and accesses and uses information ethically and legally.

IL and Higher Education

Cultivating innovative abilities of students is a crucial requirement of higher education in the present era of knowledge-based economy. It is also a linchpin to promote competence-oriented education.

Sheer abundance of information will not help students in their pursuit for excellence. They need a complimentary cluster of abilities essential for effective use of information. Some of these competencies are:

1. Acquiring required information effectively and efficiently.
2. Incorporating selected information into one's knowledge base.
3. Using information effectively and efficiently.
3. Possessing good information ethics including IPR, copyright, plagiarism issues.

With the advent of Information Age the necessary skills of IL has aroused widespread concern about proper utilization of information, especially in the universities and centers of higher learning. Using the computers, net working and multimedia technology, integration of information technology and academic courses are being explored/experimented.

Traditional Teaching Mode

Traditional teaching model centering around teacher, classroom and book learning is gradually being replaced by independent learning and collaboration. Conditions are being created to test new teaching model, digitization of related subject fields, hypertext, databases, visualization, teaching multimedia, networking, learning-based modes etc. Network learning has openness, controllability, flexibility as against the closeness of space-time limitations of traditional class room teaching.

Outdated curriculum, rigid teaching methods, less practice and scientific teacher training are some of the main reasons for the deficient higher education of the Third Word. The present day IL education in India is in the embryonic form.

IL and Librarians

The core mission of higher education is developing life long learners possessing intellectual abilities of reasoning and critical thinking beyond formal class room settings. The basic skills needed for IL education are related with the library. Collaboration between librarian, teachers and administrators will ensure success of IL education.

Librarians who are also the IL course teachers need to master new information methodology and view points rapidly and accurately, keep track of latest developments in related disciplines as well. The application of ICT in libraries has provided immense opportunities for digital resources to be distributed the way the users prefer.

Goals of IL Training

Information is changing so fast that students will not succeed unless they are well versed with IL. The goals of IL skills training are as under.

1. To make students aware of the rich store of information available outside the class room.
2. To help students acquire the basic skills needed to locate the desired information.
3. To encourage team-based interaction in a project outside the lab environment.
4. To give students practice and confidence in making oral presentations.
5. To allow students delve deeper into a subject of their interest.

Pedagogue for IL

Migrating to e-learning environment calls for a change in the attitude of teachers and learners. Teachers need to upgrade their skills of tutoring via networks. Learners must be infused with enthusiasm to be info-literates.

Historically, the IL educations was initiated by academic librarians. The following pedagogical approaches were generally followed (Ali et al 2009).

a. Stand-alone Courses

Compulsory orientation course for the freshers. Optional credit or non-credit courses for others who take up research project as part of their PG programmes. This course may be an independent course or part of Research Methodology course.

b. Computer-assisted Tutorials

These are used as a package of training to develop information skills in distance educations programmes. They include interactive web-based tutorials, virtual tours, OPAC tutorials. These packages encourage self-learning principles for individuals and user-groups.

c. Course-integrated Instruction

This mode has become very popular among the academicians. It uses problem-based learning approach.

d. Point-of-need Instruction

Library has to play a prominent role because the skills needed for IL education are related to library. Librarian has to interact with the students about various types of resources they would use. His goals are three-fold.

1. To make students aware of the variety of print and digital resources that are available.
2. To develop an awareness of specific databases and other resources which would help them to locate appropriate information.
3. To give some basic practice in locating books, journal articles and also internet resources.

Point-of-need instruction is required for successful IL outcomes of the learners.

e. Simulation

The most effective way to learn a software application is to watch demonstrations and practice. Simulation provides an environment to perform demonstrations and for the students to practice. Handouts are provided that give step-by-step instructions for using each resource.

The input from the student is checked for correctness. If correct, the response of the software is printed on the simulated screen. In addition, some reinforcement message is also given. If not correct, the error message is printed on the screen and more detailed feed back about the error is also provided.

Pre-Text and Post-Text Analysis

A pre-text analysis helps the librarian in formulating the IL Course Outline to fit the specific needs of the students.

A post-text analysis helps in evaluating the change (if any) in the students' perception of the usefulness of IL course in their academic pursuits and on the job as well as knowledge of availability and breadth of knowledge.

Internet ramification of information sources of knowledge, varieties of a-v materials, digital publication, databases and network information sources have become important ways to access information.

Since 1990s , the multimedia and network technology have become popular teaching modes as they provide user-friendly and visually interactive learning environment. This has resulted in bringing the book information under crises and stress.

Assessment Methods for IL

Communication and information research skills are, however, more difficult to integrate into the prevailing curriculum which is already very demanding because of extensive inter-disciplinary and multi disciplinary subjects.

Therefore, the assessment method should match the purpose of assessment, taking into account the issues of reliability, validity and feasibility. Types of assessment include multiple-choice tests, essay assignments, direct observation of information search activities of students, group projects. Each of these modes has its own strengths and weaknesses.

Conclusion

Today's educated workforce need skills beyond what is traditionally taught in colleges and universities. Lifelong skills have become extremely important. Present generation students must be able to identify problems, decide what information they need to solve the problem, locate the needed information, analyze it, synthesize it and communicate the solution to others.

Because of the ever-increasing complexity of information, individuals are faced with diverse, abundant information options, raising questions about its reliability, authenticity and validity.

A well designed IL programme is important to increase learner's ability to conduct quality researches in their academic pursuits and future career. IL is one of the digital age literacy for higher education. IL makes the learners fully recognize that the most important things in the society is not the knowledge per se but the ability to acquire knowledge.

References

Ali (R), Abu-Hassan (N) and Daud (MYM), 2009. Information literacy of engineering students: A case study. Intl. Conf. on Engineering Education (ICEED), Kuala Lumpur, Malaysia, 2009.

Association of College and Research Libraries, 2004. Information Literacy Competency Standards for Higher Education. Jan. 2004 http://www.ala.org/ala/mgrps/divs/acrl/standards.pdf

Feldmann (L) and Feldmann (J), 2000. Developing information literacy skills in freshmen Engineering Technology students. 30th ASEE/IEEE Frontiers in Education Conf. (Kansas city) 18-21 Oct. 2000.

Li (Xiaolo) and Wang (Xu), 2009. Information literacy education for improving innovative ability of post-graduate in China. First Intl. Workshop on Education Technology and Computer Science, 2009.

Stanley (Madan Kumar), 2010. The changing reference culture: An agenda for digital reference service. ICSSR-OUAT National Seminar on Dynamics of e-Resources and Usage Trends in digital era (Bhubaneswar) p 254-262.

UNESCO, 2009 Towards Information Literacy indicator. http://www.ifla.org/files/information-literacy/publications/towards-information-literacy 2008-en.pdf.

19

Social Media and Academic Libraries: Trends and Challenges

Stanley Madan Kumar
University Librarian (Retd)
University of Agricultural Sciences
Dharwad-580 005
E-mail: sunnystanmk@gmail.com
and
Devaraj
University Librarian I/c
University of Agricultural Sciences
GKVK, Bangalore-560 065
E-mail : devaraj1805@gmail.com

Introduction

Studies have indicated that four significant forces viz. IT, Mobile, Cloud and Social Media would create unique work environment in the coming years. Social media presents both opportunities and challenges. It has reached a stage where a single tweet can make or mar an organization. It has emerged as a force to reckon with.

Social media surpasses all geographical limitations and enables to create cost-effective network strategies. Facebook, Twitter, Google, LinkedIn, Orkut are some of the major social networking sites.

Synchronous and Asynchronous Tools

Wikipedia defines social media as "primarily Internet-based tools for sharing and discussing information among human beings".

Internet-based communication tools are grouped under two categories viz. Synchronous and Asynchronous.

Synchronous tools are one-way communication processes. Users can only read the contents. Web1.0 belongs to this class.

Asynchronous tools allow a person to communicate at his convenience. Web2.0 belongs to this class. Here users are both consumers and producers. This group of tools -

1. allow people to communicate, collaborate and build virtual community.
2. can be shared, reused and allow syndication.
3. Users can easily take benefit of others' knowledge.

Growth of Social Media

With the break-through achieved in digital technology and ICT, social software applications have diversified from chat and instant messaging to multiple applications, changing the mode of inter-personal communication and interaction with information.

Social networking sites spread information faster than any other media. Researchers can have accesses to sources that were earlier remained unknown or had restricted accessibility.

Impact on Libraries

Social media tools are being increasingly used in academic libraries to promote library services and highlight their resources, and market the same to current and prospective users. Recent studies are concentrating on the perceived benefits of social media in libraries. More emphasis is laid on promoting the use of their services rather than the users' reaction and their expectations.

Librarians generally regard social media tools as a way to connect the patrons-- especially the student community-- with the library resources. Though social media is primarily used to communicate information to the current and prospective users the rate of activity, way of content creation and modes of delivery vary from individual to individual and institution to institution. Sharing and collaboration make the research process more transparent and the results accessible to wider and larger community.

Social media provide libraries with a human face beyond their walls; provide them ways to communicate, collaborate, educate and market their services. Technology can make libraries more dynamic and relevant to people who think that they can get all their information from the web.

The most important aspect of social media is its viral effect. The looming mobile phone market, especially smart phones, has already accentuated it.

Changing Academic Scenario

Internet-based continuing education programs (Distance Education, Online Education) have almost doubled in the last decade and have ushered in radical changes in the traditional education system.

Libraries have recognized the popularity of social networking among youngsters, especially college and university student community. for communication and interaction. Open Education resources, sharing knowledge via free online educational offerings and down-loadable text books is catching on. This trend has shaken traditional higher education from its brick and mortar moorings.

Social Software

In todays' knowledge society, apart from technical skills and access to information technologies, it is increasingly important for people to have diversified and supportive social connections. The digital boom has brought about changes in information field which is instantaneous, swift, consistent and interfaced.

Use of social media tools - also known as Social Softwares - has increased at a phenomenal speed. Applications have diversified from simple chat and instant messaging to multiple apps changing the way people communicate and interact.

(a) Blogs

One of the simplest tools of content management. Comprises of dated entries in reverse chronological order with most recent postings appearing first. Blog is described as a cross between a diary, a website and an online community. Information can be posted by the individual or collected from other websites or can also be contributed by other users.

(b) Instant messaging

Also called Micro-blogging. Popular mode of communication among Internet users. Very useful for quick, short messages. Allows users to log-in from different user ID, simultaneously. Posts can be written or received with a variety of digital devises like cell phones. A great way to stay in touch with people of one's choice.

(c) You tube

A consumer media for people to watch and share original videos, worldwide. Library events, diaries etc., can be spread and shared.

(d) Book marking

Practice of saving addresses of websites to be remembered and visited at a later date. They are tagged with keywords. Tags can be designated as private or public.

(e) Podcasting

An audio or video file broken into parts and broadcasted over Internet. Users can also contribute to a podcast and keep updating the contents. It is a voice recording on a computer or saved on and MP3 digital audio-player and listened at a later date/time.

(f) Wikis

Open-ended collaborative group sites; allows registered users to freely create and edit web page contents using any web server. Wikis support hyperlinks and has simple text syntax for creating new pages and cross links. Users can find out any information about anything, such as basic facts, product information etc. As more people add knowledge to the database, the more useful it becomes.

(g) Mashup

A web application that collects information from one or more sources and presents it in a new or unique format. Mashup is a hybrid of blogs, wikis, content aggregators, instant messaging and social networking. Lib2.0 is a mashup. Users can edit OPAC data and metadata. Users' tags can be saved, borrowed and lent.

(h) RSS

The acronym is described variously as Rich Site Summary, RDF Site Summary, Really Simple Syndication. This tool is comparable to SDI service of yester years.

This tool is used to read contents from multiple web sites. Users are allowed to syndicate content from several sites into a single web page or into an RSS Aggregator. They no longer have to hunt for materials on their topics of interest. Users can learn about changing web contents and information without actually visiting each web site. By subscribing to RSS, users can keep themselves updated on news items, new services as soon as they appear on Internet.

(i) Tagging

Allows users to add and change data (content) as well as metadata. Users can create subject headings in the form of words, phrases, codes, strings of characters etc., This feature of user-participation is more democratic, dynamic and collaborative, and also helps in lateral searching as in the tags serve as thesaurus.

(j) Streaming

An important Web 2.0 enhancement, a sequential delivery of multimedia content over the network. Generally, the content is supplied on request and includes short films, music and similar such materials.

Impact on Library Services

Traditional libraries are facing many challenges from the socio-economic and technological advances being achieved. The concept of "ownership of library resources" is replaced by the concept of "accessibility to library resources".

A quarter of century ago computers were viewed as a luxury which many could not afford. The main sources of information were newspapers, radio and to some extent TV. Geographical location of the university, the nature and size of library collection had an impact on the adoption and use of the social media.

In the conventional network, devices like phones, fax machines, computers, documents are linked. In social network individuals and organizations are linked which cross traditional boundaries. As social networking facilities are freely available on Internet, librarians and information service providers are taking full advantage to close the gap between the library and information users.

Libraries have to take advantage of latest ICT advances in order to make their services, effective, popular and user' friendly. Networks are being used to communicate with potential library users as well as extending the services to other libraries. One of the Lib 2.0 application is Social Networking.

Social media apps are highly valued for their ability to connect libraries with users who may be unaware of their existence. Librarians can create services which are very much suitable and accommodative to the changing information needs of user community.

Onus on Academia

Librarians and teachers have realized that social media is a great way to connect with student community. Teachers create chat room forums and groups, extend class room discussions, post assignment tests, provide homework outside of class rooms. Teacher-Parent communication is also encouraged regarding academic and extramural progress of their wards. On their part, students use social media to reach professionals, funding agencies and prospective employers for internship, scholarship and job opportunities.

A Word of Caution

Social media is not without its drawbacks. Misuse of personal details, infringement of privacy, threat of predators, identity theft, data theft, viruses are some of the hindrances. Such cases raise crucial questions about the safety of social networking sites and apps.

Pathological Internet-use Disorders

Excessive use of social media can lead to psychological problems like stress, depression, feelings of loneliness, anxiety, ADHD, inability to have in-person conversations, schizophrenia and other psycho-disorders. Users become addicted to virtual friends. Real world is greatly impeded by increasing use of social media.

These hindrances make one to reflect that it is much better to live in 'real world' with real people rather than in a 'virtual world'.

Conclusion

ICT is providing library professionals with both opportunities and challenges. The challenges facing the library profession has never been more demanding than they are in today's digital age.

Studies have also indicated that libraries take for granted the actual techno-level understanding of the users and give more emphasis on library's social media apps, instead of understanding the impact these services have on the users and the latter's response. We should remember that convenience is what governs the choice of selecting the point of assistance.

We need to question ourselves "Why the end users prefer going to Google instead of library? Have we failed to come up to the expectations of the end users?"

References

Belden (D), 2008. Harnessing social networks to connect with audiences. Internet Reference Service Quarterly 63(1):99-111

Collins (Gary) and Quan-Haase (Anabel), 2012. Social media and academic libraries :Current trends and future challenges. ASIST,2012, Oct 26-31

Haythornthwaite(C),2005.Social networks and Internet connectivity effects. Information, Communication & Society 8:125-147

http://en.wikipedia.org/wikis/use of social network_websites_in investigation

http://socialnetworking librarian.com/2010/12/21/social media and library trends

Kishore (Avineni) and Reddy (C Krishna), 2012.Collection in the backdrop of social media. A study of Dravidian University Library. Proceedings of the International Conference on Collection Development in the Digital Environment (Chennai) (2012): 315-320

Mathews (B), 2008.Twitter and the library. Thoughts on the syndicated lifestyle. Journal of Web Librarianship 2:589-593

Padmanabhan (Sumikhi) & Thilagavathi (N),2011. Role of social networking sites. National Seminar on ELITE-2011 (Chennai) (9-10 Dec): 92-101

Sadeh (T),2007. Time for a change; New approaches for a new generation of library users. New Library World 108: 307-316

Venkateswarulu (Y Ch),2011. Social networking technologies: An observation. National Seminar on ELITE-2011 (Chennai) (9-10 Dec): 20-26

20

Role of E-Books as Important Electronic Resources in Digital Environment

Subarna K. Das
Associate Professor
Dept. of Library and Information Science
Jadavpur University, Kolkata-700032
E-mail:skd_ju2002@yahoo.co.in

Introduction

Electronic resources for libraries includes online databases , electronic(e-) journals , electronic(e-) books ,full text articles and web sites, where online journals have firmly established themselves as essential resources for libraries and information centers and their users, as appointed books in most of disciplines. Electronic books (e-books) have not found the same favour. The potential of e-books to support learning activity has been acknowledged, and new services have emerged in recent years, but uptake has been slow.

E-Books

According to Cox and Mohammed, (quoted by Lee 2002), an "eBook is a term used to describe a text analogous to a book that is in digital form to be displayed on a computer". Lee (2002) also included the definitions of an e-book from the Hi-Tech Dictionary and The New Concise Oxford English Dictionary respectively as "a book that has been converted to digital form and could be read on a computer, usually through network services or CD-ROM. E-books could expand over print media by adding several specific features such as hypertext links, search and cross-reference functions and multimedia" and "an electronic version of a printed book which can be read on a Personal Computer or hand held device designed specifically for this purposes" According to Wikipedia (2005), the free encyclopedia, an "ebook is an electronic (or digital) version of a book. The term is used ambiguously to refer to either an individual work in a digital format, or a hardware device used to read books in digital format. Some users deprecate the second meaning in favour of the more precise 'ebook device'".

History

The inventor of the first e-book is not widely agreed upon. The first e-book may be the Index Thomisticus , prepared by Roberto Busa beginning in the late 1940s. In 1930, he wrote an entire book on this invention and titled it "The Readies" playing off the idea of the "talkie". In 1949 a teacher from Galicia, Spain - Angela Ruiz - patents the first electronic book. Her intention was to decrease the number of books that her pupils carried to the school.Alternatively, some historians consider electronic books to have started in the early 1960s, with the NLS project headed by Doug Engelbart at Stanford Research Institute (SRI), and the Hypertext Editing System and FRESS projects headed by Andries van Dam at Brown University. Van Dam have coined the term "electronic book", and it was established enough to use in an article title by 1985. In 1971 the operators of the Xerox Sigma V mainframe at the University of Illinois gave Hart extensive computer-time. Seeking a worthy use of this resource, he created his first electronic document by typing the United States Declaration of Independence into a computer. Project Gutenberg was launched afterwards to create electronic copies of more texts - especially books.In 1992, Sony launched the Data Discman, an electronic book reader that could read e-books that were stored on CDs. One of the electronic publications that could be played on the Data Discman was called The Library of the Future . In the 1990s, the general availability of the Internet made transferring electronic files much easier, including e-books.

Technologies Available for Reading E-books

There are two types of technologies available for using e-books:

- Online or Internet-based.
- Offline or specific e-book reader based.

In the online version the user can read the text through an Internet browser and this opens up possibilities of linking to other resources, cross-text searching, utilization of dictionaries and so on. There are several organizations which each offer access to tens of thousands of e-books from a range of different publishers. Examples include:

- Netlibrary (http://www.netlibrary.com).
- Ebrary (http://www.ebrary.com).
- Questia (http://www.questia.com).

In the offline version users will read e-books through special e-book reader software, which can be downloaded, from the Internet. Much of this software is format specific, such as for *example :* Adobe reader in PDF format http://www.adobe.com/products/ebookreader)

Advantages and Disadvantages of E-books

E-books are becoming popular because they have several advantages when compared to printed books. E-books provide multimedia information, full-text searching, reference linking, flexibility in searching and browsing, selection of different types of fonts, portability, and interoperability on a variety of devices. For users who are frequent travelers, or who have to carry out research in remote places e-books offer a substitute for print books and provide easier portability. For teachers and students, e - books are a very good classroom teaching tool. E-books which are available online can be accessed 24/7 from a 'local' desktop, are able to be accessed remotely and more than one person can to access the same e-book at a time. For publishers, e-books offer economies in publishing costs and involve no storage, shipping and handling charges. For librarians, e-books do not go out of print, are easy to download, can be customized to suit individual needs (especially by those who may be physically handicapped), allow many people to access the same book at the same time, are free from problems of being misplaced, and do not suffer from wear and tear or theft. In spite of these advantages, e-books are still not very popular. Elements that are considered important to study regarding academic use of e-books are:

- Content.
- Software and Hardware Standards and Protocols.
- Digital Rights Management.
- Access.
- Archiving.
- The Market and Pricing.

Content

Inspite of big vendors and reputed web publishers initiatives to built-up packages of e-books collections , the corpus of academic level e-books available is still not up to the mark and have failed to represent many disciplines. Thus collection building is hampered by publishers' conservatism in providing rights to titles for e-books distribution and vendors' cost to reformat content from proprietary versions. Scholars and researchers need to rely on authenticity and integrity of the content of e-book. E-book content should match any print version and include all its elements: text, graphs, and illustrations. It is anticipated that academics will increasingly incorporate information that can only be presented as non-print media (e.g., visualizations, interactive content, etc.). Content needs to be separated from access and manipulation features, and needs to be transferable, in a non-proprietary format, into a variety of software and hardware readers, both to offer readers a choice of additional features, and to make it possible for libraries to loan e-book content.

Software and Hardware Standards and Protocols

Non-commercial monographic electronic texts for scholarly exchange have been available on the Internet since the early years of UNIX file exchange, file transfer (FTP), gopher and, finally, hypertext transfer (HTTP) protocols.At this point, although publishers are creating books electronically, more often than not text is created in a proprietary form that requires reformatting or scanning of the print version for adaptation to an individual vendor's system. Of the current formats, large vendors are using HTML, XML or PDF as default. To serve a large and varied academic clientele and to build a strong scholarly collection for long-term access, electronic books must be provided in a standards-based format that includes:

- Non-proprietary software and hardware for interoperability of files
- Identifiers
- Metadata.

A pragmatic factor in using e-books is the ease of reading and using them, yet e-book hardware devices are still not quite practical or cost effective enough to penetrate very deeply into the market. A variety of devices are being developed to replicate some of the virtues of printed monographs, including portability and network-independence, so that e-books themselves will function on a variety of platforms. The two basic kinds of e-book readers on the market today are the full-sized reader and the palm-sized reader. Currently, all readers use proprietary file formats.Given the range of users in an academic environment, it will be important that e-books are not hardware or software dependent. Libraries will undoubtedly be providing technical support for multiple online and portable reading devices.

Digital Rights Management

One of the most critical elements in the development of electronic publishing that will impact libraries involves digital rights management systems (DRMS). Still being developed, DRMS are either hardware or software (or both) that enforce control over intellectual property, such as limit by user, time, fee, and/or extent of content. Due to publishers' concerns about rights, e-book vendors are normally able to offer only limited usage rights for printing, downloading and copying. Normally, interlibrary loan is not allowed, and classroom use is not always allowed. The degree of control e-book publishers choose to exercise over the access, sharing and loaning of intellectual property will make e-books either more or less compatible with the free flow of information needed in the scholarly setting. To support open research, libraries will need "ownership" or "first sale" rights that allow perpetual access and fair use, such as classroom use and the ability to loan the textual content (without value-added features) to other libraries. It will not be feasible to create a print copy of entire monographs for interlibrary loan, as is done for journal articles. Without lendability, e-books become supplementary to any print version required for archiving and interlibrary loan. When the market evolves to a point where a print version is not also available, libraries will need to have the capability of "loaning" and archiving e-books.

Access

Issues of access include user awareness and the ability to accommodate simultaneous users. Vendors working with libraries normally offer a one-copy-one-user model, following a traditional print monograph purchase model. The number of simultaneous users for e-book titles will become an issue, particularly in consortia arrangements. Depending on the type of information being purchased, a single user may not be using the entire book text, but only querying a portion of it. A single chapter in an edited work may be what is needed, rather than the entire volume.

Archiving

Currently, e-book vendor purchase models allow some flexibility, such as a premium price for perpetual access (and potential archiving) versus more modest pricing for annual access to a revolving group of titles. The ability to manipulate an e-book collection easily to eliminate older editions is attractive where currency matters. In other disciplines where long-term research is essential, assurance of perpetual access will be vital.

The Market and Pricing

Few reputed vendors like netLibrary offer e-books to libraries--particularly with academic content. Publishers have been conservative in moving into the e-book market, and direct publisher offerings are only recently beginning to appear.

Pricing options include:

- One-time purchase of a title with a premium for perpetual access
- Purchase of a title with annual access fee premium
- Annual subscription fees access with ownership
- Annual subscription fee access without ownership.

For libraries, pricing for e-books should include two separate and distinct elements:

- An initial one-time purchase price, less than the equivalent print version
- A separate minimal ongoing fee for access and archiving costs.

The demand for simultaneous access to individual e-book titles should not require libraries to purchase multiple copies of e-books, and pricing models should be developed that permit some level of simultaneous access.

General Experiences of Libraries with E-books

It has been observed that acquisition of e-books has little or no impact on their purchase of titles in print. Some suggested that they felt the role of e-books was not to replace print but to serve as a duplicate copy. Some comments that the e-books are not the panacea for book storage or archiving.The most common method may be used for publicity of e-books is to use a link or announcement on the library's web site. Other ways included writing articles for faculty or campus newsletters; creating flyers; sending targeted emails; and including e-books in bibliographic instruction. Libraries felt that promotion and education of users is still a factor in evaluating use.Most of the academic institutions in our country had no formal user feedback mechanisms. This is very essential for developing balanced collection of e-books in any academic institute.Factors that might discourage use of e-books is the cost, both of the e-books themselves and the equipment needed to access them. The majority of the users still find that the e-books are hard to read and browse, and that they are used to reading printed books and do not want to change the habit. User education, publicity, raising awareness about the software/hardware used for e-books, increasing the bandwidth and making available ebook reader devices along with e-books through libraries can increase.

Conclusion

E-books are not as popular as other types of e-publications, such as e-journals and e-newspapers. The possible reasons for this could be because the technology for creating/accessing e-books (both hardware and software) is not yet matured, users' perspectives about e-books need to be changed and the awareness of e-books needs to be raised. It is not clear that academic libraries can replace print with e-books as a long-term collection goal. There are still concerns about adequate rights to information to support the academic mission of open scholarly communication.

References

Hane, P.J. "Getting into deep content". NewsLink, 55, May 2004. http://www.infotaday.com[accessed [9th Feb.2013]

http://www.safaribooksonline.com (visited on 20/4/13)

http://safari.oreilly.com (Visited on 12/4/13)

http://www.netlibrary.com(Visited on 14/4/13)

http://www.ebrary.com(Visited on 18/4/13)

http://www.wikipaedia.com (Visited on 16/4/13)

Irish Universities Safari Electronic Books User Survey, http://wwwlibrary.nuigalkay.ie/survey/e-books.html. [Accessed 8 Jan 2013].

Sue, Polanka (2011). No shelf required : e-books in libraries , New Delhi : Ess Ess

21

Open Source Software for Modern Libraries: A Comparative Study of ABCD, Koha and Newgenlib

Surendra Kumar Pal
IISER Library
Indian Institute of Science Education and Research Thiruvananthapuram-695016.
E-mail: surendrapal@iisertvm.ac.in/ surendrapal2015@gmail.com/ hotmail.com/yahoo.com
and
Bharat Praveen Sonker
Central Library
Shri Ramswaroop Memorial College of Enginnering and Management
Lucknow- 227105
E-mail: bharatpraveensonker@gmail.com

Introduction

Library automation in the first giant step towards the use of ICT based products & services in libraries. It brings great revolution and saves tremendous time of users and library staff for collecting and disseminating information. Library automation refers to use of computers, associated peripheral media such as software for automation, magnetic tapes, disks, optical media etc. Library automation makes the provision to provide the 'right information to right reader at the right time in a right form in a right personal way' it is the basic aim of libraries. There are some open source software available e.g. Evergreen, CDS Invenio, Koha, NewGenLib, PMB, PhpMyLibrary, OpenBiblio as well as many commercial software: SOUL, Alice for windows, Netlib, LibSys etc.

Objective of Study

1. To Know more about Open Source Software for Libraries.
2. To Understand the functionality and technology used in ABCD, Koha and Newgenlib.
3. To explore the special features of these softwares.
4. To get Clear-cut idea which software is more better for Automated Libraries.

Types of Software: Although in the cyber age freeware, open source, and shareware are commonly used as synonyms actually there is difference between these terminologies and their use. Their definitions and differences between them are stated as follows:

1. **Proprietary (Commercial) Software:** User has to purchase proprietary software for its use and in course of time he becomes totally dependent on the commercial developer and has to pay high cost for its purchase, maintenance, and improvement. User is unable to modify software for his own needs, makes him feel helpless at the mercy of external software.
2. **Shareware Software:** Shareware can be downloaded free of cost to try as a sample, but for the ultimate use, user is supposed to pay for it. It is developed and released by someone who keeps full control of the intellectual property. The user does not have access to the source code and cannot modify it. There is also no collaboration or community around shareware.
3. **Freeware Software:** Freeware is the software which can be downloaded, used and copied without restrictions. No access to the source code, no community, no development, and no improvement can be possible.
4. **Free/Open Source Software (FOSS):** The FOSS or free/libre/open-source software (FLOSS) is software that is both free software and open source. It is liberally licensed to grant users the right to use, copy, study, change, and improve its design through the availability of its source code rather than its cost. This approach has gained both momentum and acceptance as the potential benefits have been increasingly recognised by both individuals and

corporations as free software. This terminology came from the ideological movement against proprietary from FSF (Free Software Foundation) in 1985 and open source from OSI (Open Source Initiative) in 1998.

Open Source Software in Library: Open source software is typically created and maintained by developers crossing institutional and national boundaries, collaborating by using internet based communications and development tools. Both libraries and open source have same philosophy i.e., 'community first'.Blake Carver's modification of Ranganthan Law is: (i) Software is for use, (ii) Every computer its user, (iii) Every reader his source code, (iv) Save the time of the user, and (v) A system is a growing organism.

Reasons for Choosing Open Source Software: Price of the library software are very high, most of the libraries are not in a position to buy high priced commercial software due to severe budget constraints. V. Vimal Kumar [5] has mentioned various aspects regarding this like no restriction of use, free of costs; community involvement in development and maintenance of software; competence of software compared with other commercial software; and the legal aspects. The obvious reason for the organizations like libraries to choose open source software for automation purposes is the cost of software, which is free. There is no restriction but everyone can use, study, modify and distribute the open source software, regardless of a person's status, wealth, social background etc. It is also the open source software is interoperable, customizable according to the needs and fulfills the standards. The most judicious reason in favour of it is the legal aspect of the use of open source software. The licenses are copyright protected and committed to user's freedom of use, modify and redistribute the programme.

Benifits of Open Source Software in Libraries: Following benefits from open source software make it ideal to use in the libraries:

1. Code of software is open to modify, improve, and redistribute.
2. No dependence on vendor or producer.
3. It is more reliable, Easy to Customization.
4. Perform better as our needs.

5. More secured, Community Support.
6. Use without restriction & on reduced cost.

Thus the philosophy, flexibility, freedom, cost and continuity of OSS makes this software as an ideal choice for libraries.

Integrated Library Management System: An integrated library system (ILS), also known as a library management system (LMS), is an enterprise resource planning system for a library, used to track items owned, orders made, bills paid, and patrons who have borrowed. An ILS usually comprises a relational database, software to interact with that database, and two graphical user interfaces (one for patrons, one for staff). Most ILSes separate software functions into discrete programs called modules, each of them integrated with a unified interface. Examples of modules might include:

1. Acquisitions (ordering, receiving, and invoicing materials).
2. Cataloging (classifying and indexing materials).
3. Circulation (lending materials to patrons and receiving them back).
4. Serials (tracking magazine and newspaper holdings).
5. OPAC (public interface for users).
6. Administrations (Report Generation, Policy Changing).

Each patron and item has a unique ID in the database that allows the ILS to track its activity. Larger libraries use an ILS to order and acquire, receive and invoice, catalog, circulate, track and shelve materials. Smaller libraries, such as those in private or non-profit organizations often forgo the expense and maintenance required to run an ILS, and instead use a library computer system. The present study discusses some of the widely used open source library management software in terms of their features and capabilities. The information furnished in Table 1 and 2 is taken directly from the software websites and related weblinks.

Special Features of Selected ILMS: Koha is the first open-source Integrated Library System (ILS) in use worldwide. Koha was created in 1999 by Katipo Communications for the Horowhenua Library Trust in New Zealand. The first installation went live in January of 2000. ABCD, in Egnlish, is "Automation of liBraries and Centres of Documentation". The name itself already expresses the ambition of the software suite to provide not only automation functions for traditional libraries but also other information providers such as documentation centers. It is developed by BIREME (WHO, Brazil) in collaboration with the Flemish Interuniversity Council, Belgium, using UNESCO?s ISIS database technology. NewGenLib is an integrated library management system developed by Verus Solutions Pvt Ltd. Domain expertise is provided by Kesavan Institute of Information and Knowledge Management in Hyderabad, India. NewGenLib version 1.0 was released in March 2005. On 9 January 2008, NewGenLib was declared Open Source Software under GNU GPL Licence by Verus Solutions. Currently NewGenLib 3.0.3 U2 is the latest version running. It is estimated that 2,500 libraries across 58 countries are using NewGenLib as their primary integrated library management system.

Table 1 : Showing General Information about ABCD, Koha and Newgenlib

ILMS	Developer	Licence	Site	Download Website
Koha	Katipo Communication for Horowhenua Library Trust	GNU-GPL	http://koha-community.org/	May 05, 2013
ABCD	BIREME (WHO, Brazil)	ABCD	http://fmv.jku.at/abcd/# download	abcd-0.3.tar.gz
Newgenlib	Verus Solutions, Hyderabad, India	GNU-GPL	http://www.verussolutions .biz	NewGenLib 3.0.3 U2

Table 2 : Showing Special Features of Koha, ABCD, Newgenlib

ILMS	Written in Language	Requirements	Plateform	Usefull For
Koha	Perl	Apache web server, MySql database, Perl, KohaW32 install	Window, Linux, Unix	Small and Big Libraries
ABCD	Java	ISIS database	Window	Small to Big Libraries
Newgenlib	Perl	J2SE kit, PostgreSQL, JBoss Application Server, Java Runtime Environment, Newgenlib files, backup in plain SQL, newgenlib.ear	Window, Linux	Small and Big Libraries

Table 3 : Showing Technical Features of Koha ABCD and Newgenlib

ILMS	Standard	Functional Modules	Digital Library Support	Technical Suport
Koha	Z39.50, SRU, and SIP2, MARC, AGRIS, OAI- PMH	OPAC, Full Catalogue, Circulation, Serials, Acquisition, Patron Management, Branch Management, Reservations.	No	Strong Wide Community Support & Commercial Support also
ABCD	Z39.50,MARC CEPAL and AGRIS, OAI-PMH	Administration, Cataloguing, Acquisition, Loan, OPAC, ABCD site, Serial Control	Yes	Poor Community Support
Newgenlib	MARC-21, MARC-XML, AGRIS,z39.50 SRU/W, OAI-PMH	Acquisitions, Cataloguing Serials management Circulation,Administration, MIS Reports, End of Day Process	Yes/ RFID Support	Community Support & Commercial Support

Table 4 : Showing Details about Modules Support

Modules	ABCD	Koha	Newgenlib
Catalouging	YES	YES	YES
Circulation	YES	YES	YES
Acquisition	YES	YES	YES
Serials Management	YES	YES	YES
Patron Mgt	YES	YES	YES
Report	YES	YES	YES
Institutional Repository	Partially	NO	YES

Table 5 : Showing Circulation Features

	ABCD	Koha	Newgenlib
Supported metadata standards	ABCD is independient of formats. The same mechanisms, interface and forms can be used to create and maintain any structure, whether bibliographic or not	MARC 21 and UNIMARC	All Metadata Standard
Managing of various types of material (books, serials, DVDs, audio and video tapes etc.)	Yes	Yes	Yes
Cataloging via Z39.50	Yes	Yes	Yes

Table 6 : Showing Report Statistics

Pre-defined reports	Yes (Only for CEPAL and MARC21 Format)	Yes	Yes
Custom Report	No	Yes	Yes

Findings and Analysis of the Study

1. Koha is widely used and developed during last 10 years, has better support and greater community; ABCD is still a young software and its community will grow in time, Even Newgenlib is also just equal to Koha while it is also developed very soon in India
2. ABCD has also offline local version of software which is easy to set-up and use (good for small libraries without system administrators and/or servers/internet connection).
3. Koha has wider range of additional functionalities and Web 2.0 features, while the other having less Functionalities.
4. ABCD is more flexible when it comes to metadata standards -it supports all standards and non-standards, while Koha supports only UNIMARC and MARC21. But Newgenlib is supporting all formats of Standards.
5. These three softwares support multi-branch mode.
6. These three ABCD, Koha ans Newgenlib satisfy all the basic functional requirements of a Integrated library management system.
7. Koha has more and better developed additional functionalities and enhanced contents than ABCD at this moment, as well as 10-years of developement and a great community and support behind it, so it is a better solution for libraries implementing web based ILMS.
8. ABCD is on the other hand a better solution for local use (offline) at small libraries without system administrator and/or servers/internet connection, as well as for libraries using other bibliographic standards (or non-standards) than UNIMARC or MARC21. While this facilities is not in others.

Conclusions

In this study it is clear that these three software would be applicable in Indian libraries as far as its different features are concerned. But Koha is somewhat more strong in all modules with advance feature compare to ABCD and Newgenlib. Somehow Newgenlib is also more better because it provides all Cataloguing Standard and also Institutional Repository while this facilities is not availabilities in Koha but In ABCD it is accessible in offline mode while for another Internet Connection is needed. In this study I found that Koha is more prominent software than Newgenlib and ABCD, but in coming days, this Indian Open sources will dominate the Koha. Because NewgenLib has same features compared to Koha and commercial software under study and also having Feature to Institutional Repository like Dspace Greenstone. In a developing country like India, where library budget is a major constraint, the first Indian origin open source software is incredibly useful. In the new paradigm of information society, software like NewGenLib open source software is a basic requirement as a primary resource.

References

"ABCD". Last Modified May 05, 2013, http://fmv.jku.at/abcd/ (accessed on 3 April 2012).

Anuradha, K.T, "Koha: An Overview", Presented in NCSI-IDRC Workshop on Integrated Library Automation Packages: Basics of KOHA and NewGenLib. Accessed on May 05, 2013. URL: http://dharmaganja.ncsi.iisc.ernet.in/workshopnew/index.html

Dhamdhere, Sangeeta Namdev. ABCD, an open source software for modern libraries. Chinese Librarianship: an International Electronic Journal, 32(2011). Accessed on May 05, 2012. URL: http://www.iclc.us/cliej/cl32dhamdhere.pdf

De Smet, Egbert. The ISIS-software family: From Free and Open? to "Free and Open Source Software?. Innovation: Journal of Appropriate Librarianship and Information Work, 36(2008). Acessed on May 05, 2013. URl : http://www.innovation.ukzn.ac.za/InnovationPdfs/No36Egbert%20de%20Smet.pdf.

De Smet, Egbert. (2010). Some ISIS- software history and technical background on the new FOSS integrated library system ABCD. Liber Quarterly: The Journal of European Research Libraries, 19(3/4), 324-335.

Francis, A.T. Software Problems in Library Automation in India, In ed by Mahapatra et al. Ahmedabad: INFLIBNET/UGC, (1998). p. 60 -64.

Koha. Lat Modified May 05, 2013, http://koha-community.org.

Kumar, V. Free/open source integrated library management systems: Comparative analysis of Koha, PhpMyLibrary, and OpenBiblio. Paper presented at the National Library Week Celebration, University of Calicut (2005). Accessed on May 5, 2013, URL: http://eprints.rclis.org/8074/

Kumar, Vimal and Abraham, Thomas Eight. Eight things you should know about Open Source Integrated Library Systems. In UGC Sponsored National Conference on Open Source Software in Libraries, Cochin University of Science and Technology, (2009) 24-25 November. Accessed on May 05, 2013

NewGenLib. Last Modified May 05, 2013, http://www.verussolutions.biz/

Sherikar, Amrut & Jange, Suresh. Open source software development: Historical and current perspectives for academic librarianship. Accessed on May 05 2013 URL: http://ir.inflibnet.acin/dxml/bitstream/handle/1944/1219/196-201.pdf

Sonker, Sharad Kumar. Implementation of Koha: an open source library Management software. Accessed on May 05, 2013. URL http://ncsi et.ncsi.iisc.ernet.in/gsdl/ collect/tracol/index/assoc/ HASH01cc.dir/doc.doc.

The open source initiative. Last Modified May05, 2013 http://www.opensource.com.

22

Implementing RFID Technology for Enhanced Library Services

Tarvinder Singh Handa
Senior Library & Information Assistant
IIT, Ropar- 140 001
and
Arvind Mittal
Senior Librarian
Sukham Memorial Central Library, Bhai Gurdas Group of Institute, Sangrur- 147301

1. Introduction

Radio Frequency Identification popularly known as RFID is a term used for a radio-enabled device that communicates with or interrogates a tag or smart label, which is embedded with a single microchip processor and an antenna. "This is an automatic identification method that relies on storing and remotely retrieving data using devices such as RFID tags or transponders (Mamdampur and Rajgoli, 2011)". This technology is similar in concept to a cell phone (Singh and Midha, 2008) which refers to the subset of automatic identification that uses radio waves to automatically identify bulk or individual items (Chavan, 2012).While the origin of RFID lie more than 50 years in the past, passive RFID technology is actually only in its infancy (Sarma, 2008).

The origin of the term lies in the invention of "tags" that reflect back or re-transmit a radio frequency signal. The two components of RFID are tags and readers. The tag or label is equipped with a single microchip processor, an antenna and an ID code that can be embedded in almost in any object. RFID readers are radio-enabled devices that communicate with or interrogate RFID tags or labels wirelessly and obtain the ID code on the tags from a distance of several inches. The RFID readers can be fixed or made portable just like barcode scanners. RFID can also be referred as a high-tech version of bar-code technology.

2. The RFID- Defined

RFID is an acronym for Radio Frequency Identification, which is a wireless communication technology that is used to identify tagged objects (Daniel et al., 2007). Briefly, the RF in RFID stands for "radio frequency" the ID means "identifier" (Coyle, 2003). This is a wireless system that works in conjunction with an organization's information technology infrastructure such as inventory management and efficiency in supply chain management (Nisha *et al.*, 2006).

Thus, RFID is a system that facilitates the tracking of objects, primarily for inventory tracking, via a three part technology comprised of a reader, a transceiver with decoder and a transponder known as tag.

3. Libraries and RFID Technology

Until recently, majority of libraries used barcode technology to keep record of lending, borrowing and shelving status of their items. But barcode technology has its own limitations as it is slow to read and more prone to sabotaging which can further lead to massive loss to a library and its valuable stock. This is where RFID technology can come to the aid of library managers and users.

This technology improves the speed and accuracy of most circulation and shelving functions and frees library staff to provide direct service to customers. It also helps protect your collection and ensure that your community gets the more value out of the library.

4. RFID Technology: An Overview

The RFID system combines radio frequency and microchip technologies to create a smart system that can be used to identify, secure and inventory items. This technology, though new to libraries, has been in use in other sectors for more than twenty years (Handa, 2010). In libraries, RFID is used to automate circulation and collection management. RFID technology was developed in 1980s, primarily for use in the industry sector (Dawes, 2004).

4.1 Components of RFID

The RFID system consists of following components as its infrastructural elements:

4.1.1 Tag

Also known as transponder, the tag consists of an antenna and silicon chip encapsulated in glass of plastic (Chavan, 2012). This is flexible, paper thin smart label, approximately 2x2 inches in size that is applied directly to items in library. Within the tag, there is a microchip and an antenna. This assembly is generally covered with a protective overlay. The back of the assembly has an adhesive so the assembly can be permanently installed in an item as shown in the figure below:

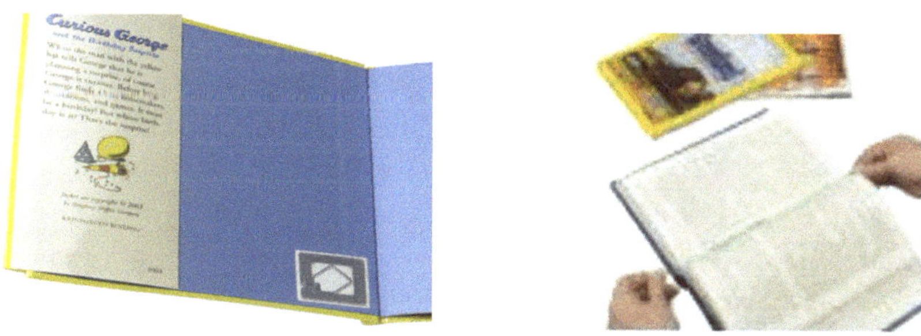

Fig. 1 : The fixing of a tag/tattle tape

The tags contain a very small amount of information. For example, many tags contain only a barcode number and security bit (128 bits) but some tags contain as much as 1024 bits (Chavan, 2012). Tags also vary in size ranging from a grain of rice to two inch square, depending on their application.

4.1.2 Reader

The reader or receiver is composed of a radio frequency module, a control unit and an antenna to interrogate electronic tags via radio frequency (RF) communication. The reader serves as a link between RFID tags and the server. The reader can send information in two directions. It can read information from a tag and send it to the server (Read Mode), or on the other hand, it can send information from the server and send it to an RFID tag (Write Mode).

When a tag is passed through exit readers, the information stored on the chip in the tag is interpreted by the reader and sent to the server, which in turn, communicates with the integrated library system when the RFID system is interfaced with it.

The RFID exit gate sensors (readers) at the exit point are basically of two types. One type reader reads the information on tag going by and communicates it to a server. The server, after checking the circulation database turns on an alarm if the material is not properly checked-out. The other type relies on a "theft" byte in the tag that is turned on or off to indicate that the item is properly checked-out or not.

4.1.3 Antenna

The antenna produces radio-signals to activate the tag and read/write data to it. Antenna is the channel between the tag and the reader, which controls the system's data acquisition and communication.

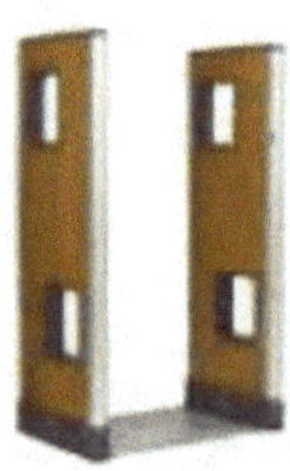

Fig. 2 : 3MTM EM sensor gate

Fig. 3 : 3MTM RF sensor gate

The electromagnetic field produced by an antenna can be constantly present when multiple tags are expected continually. Antenna can be built into a doorframe to receive tag data from person's belongings passing through the door (Nisha et al., 2006).

4.1.4 Server

The server is the heart of the comprehensive RFID system. It is the communication gateway among the various components. It receives the information from one or more of the reader and exchanges information with the circulation database. The server typically includes a transition database sit ha reports can be produced (Sujatha, 2007). Its software includes the SIP/SIP2 (Session Initiation Protocol), APIS (Application Programming Interface) and NCIP or SLNP necessary to interface it with integrated library software. The server typically includes transaction database so that reports can be produced (Chavan, 2012).

4.2 Working of RFID in libraries

The read/write device in a passive RFID system transfers the energy which is necessary for communication with the tag/ transponder and receives data from it. The tag in-turn returns a unique identification code (ID) to the reader. On the basis of ID code, detailed information regarding and item can be obtained.

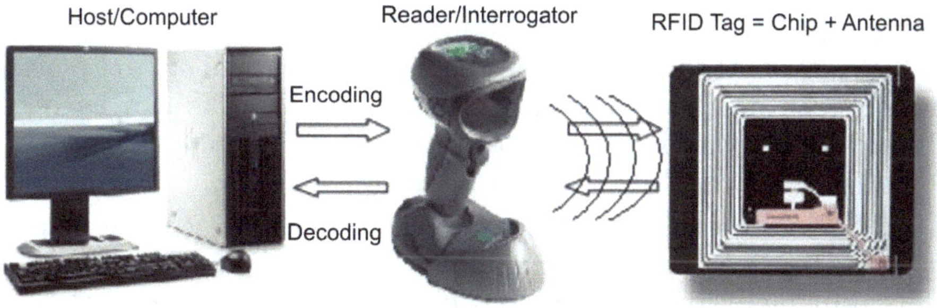

Fig. 4 : Functioning of RFID System

In order to check a book out, there is no need to open it as RFID tags can be read through the item in which they are placed. The interrogator or reader at security gates controls the communications with the tags.

5. Areas of RFID Application in Libraries

RFID technology can be successfully implemented in certain housekeeping operations of a library. Some of them are described as under:

5.1 Circulation

The amount of time required to perform a basic circulation transaction is greatly reduced with RFID application. The library staff do not need to scan barcodes one by one (Namdpur and Rajgoli, 2011). Moreover, a fully tagged collection allows the user to perform the self-check option. The RFID tags installed in library material contain a theft bit and are programmed with item information, allowing for greater security of same. Multiple items can be read simultaneously and in any orientation. As the item is checked-in the theft bit is turned on, and then off at checkout. This simplifies and increases the speed and efficiency of circulation operation.

5.2 Self Check-out/ Check-in

By far the most popular use of RFID to date has been for providing self-service facilities, enabling library users to borrow their own items and process multiple loans simultaneously (Fortune, 2010). The Self-out system is user friendly, highly intuitive and reduces queuing times. The station is basically a computer with a normally touch screen, a built-in RFID reader and special software for personal identification and material identification. At this station, the books to be checked out are placed on the desk and both user card and stack of books can be read simultaneously that is, recording the user' identification, the borrowed items and deactivating the antitheft.

The borrowed books can be placed on desk station one by one without any intervention by staff. The items to be returned are instantaneously updated in the integrated library software and the anti-theft device is again activated.

Fig. 5 : The Self check in/out kiosk

5.3 Inventory control

RFID is a highly advantageous technology for a wide variety of inventory tracking situations (Coyle, 2005). Libraries with bigger collections face a daunting challenge in keeping track of their resources. They hold thousands or even millions of individual items, each one unique in nature, each vitally important for the potential user who wants it for his/her own needs. With RFID, those items are where they are supposed to be, where customers and librarian can find them.

With the aid of portable hand-held reader/scanner, a library staff member may examine a particular stack section as if items are either missing or out of place (Daves, 2004). In situation where search for a particular item is required the information is first entered into the portable scanner of the base station. When mismatch item is found on the shelves a beep sound alerts the library staff.

Fig. 6 : Inventory Control Process

5.4 Security and reliability

The library security system through RFID can be ensured through Electronic Article Surveillance (EAS) gate, which is the anti-theft part of RFID library management system using RFID tags embedded in the various library items.

When an unauthorized item passes through security gates, the alarm will sound and lights will flash. The EAS anti-theft gate has the option to trigger a camera to record the situation when a patron passes through with an unchecked item.

6. The Future Perspective

There has always been a desire for efficient collection management, organization; description and dissemination of knowledge since the first libraries came into existence. Technology is seen as a key in approaching these ends. The use of RFID in library housekeeping operations has seen a tremendous change in terms of improving service efficiency and reduced time frame.

Once the RFID is in place in libraries, a great shift can be expected in the near future. RFID technology is still relatively new to libraries, but there is a wealth of experience with the product in the retail and industrial sectors (Dawes, 2004). This technology promises to offer solutions for today's libraries and has solid growth potential for the future (Ward, 2003). Fortune (2010) further comments that as the technology develops and existing issues of interoperability are overcome, RFID will begin to transform the way in which library services are delivered and both public and academic libraries are expected to host a broad range of service channels to meet the needs of all their users.

For libraries, the RFID solutions are intuitive, easy to use and attractive because they are grounded to decades of research and subjected to rigorous testing. Thus the RFID technology holds the onus of providing the managers in libraries an opportunity to deliver a better learning environment by connecting their patrons to the whole world of information.

7. Conclusion

In the twenty first century, the libraries of all nature are bound to deliver hassle free services to their respective clientele. The RFID technology promises to provide the technological basis for ubiquitous identification, data exchange, and time, location and environment sensing. Although this technology has found a wide acceptance in libraries of developed countries, its application in libraries of developing countries is relatively limited. This may be due to the high cost of implementation and some technical hurdles faced in some cases. It is hoped that as the technology matures even more and competition grows in the manufacturing industry, better tags and equipment is likely to become more economical and affordable. It is therefore envisioned that RFID technology will soon be pervasive in libraries of all kinds to help the staff work with ease and provide robust service platform for their clients.

References

Chavan, S.P. (2012). Use of RFID technology in libraries. Online International Interdisciplinary Research Journal, 2(4), pp. 235-341.

Coyle, K. (2005). Management of RFID in libraries. The Journal of Academic Librarianship, 31(5), pp.486-489.

Daniel, H., Puglia, A. and Puglia, M (2007). RFID: a guide to radio frequency identification, New York: John Wiley & Sons, Inc., p.1.

Dawes, T.A. (2004). Is RFID right for your library? Journal of Access Services, 2(4), pp.7-13.

Fortune, M. (2010). Guidelines for the use of RFID in libraries. Online: http://www.mickfortune.com/Store/MLA_RFID_Guide.pdf

Handa, T.S. (2010). Radio frequency identification (RFID) application in libraries. In: Amudhaveli, A. and Singh, J., Ed. Challenges and Changes in Librarianship: Papers in honour of Prof. Sewa Singh, 2 Vols. 2010. B.R. Publications: Delhi, pp.829-837.

Mamdapur, G.M.N. and Rajgoli, I.U. (2011). Implementing radio frequency identification technology in libraries: advantages and disadvantages. International Journal of Library and Information Science, 3(3), pp.46-57.

Nisha, F., Bakshi, S. and Ali, N. (2006). RFID system: a boon for libraries. In 4th International Convention caliber-2006, Ahmedabad: Inflibnet, pp.554-555.

Sarma, S. (2008). RFID technology and its applications. In Miles, S.B.; Sarma, S.E.and Williams, J.R. Eds. RFID Technology and Applications, Cambridge University Press: Cambridge, pp.16-32.

Singh, G. and Midha, M. (2008). RFID: A new technology in library management systems. Journal of Interlibrary Loan, Document Delivery & Electronic Reserve, 18(04), pp. 439-447.

Sujatha, G. (2007). Radio frequency identification (RFID) in library management. Pearl, 1(22-24) Online: http://www.wikipedia.com

Ward, D. (2003). Radio frequency identification systems for libraries and archives: an introduction. Library & Archival Security, 18(2), pp.7-21.

23

Use of Electronic Resources by the Faculty Members of Indira Gandhi Krishi Vishwavidyalaya, Raipur (C.G.)

Uaday Kumar Watti
Asstt. Librarian
Indira Gandhi Krishi Vishwavidyalaya, Raipur (C.G.)
E-mail : ukwatti2007@rediffmail.com
and
Brajesh Tiwari
Associate Professor
Deptt. of Library and Information science
Guru Ghasidas Vishwavidyalaya, Bilaspur(C.G.)
E-mail: brajeshtiwari65@gmail.com

1. Introduction

Today we are living in the Era of Information. Over last decade, electronic resources have become increasingly substantial components of academic library collection. This is due to the continuous development of Information Technology and its impact on library collection development policies due to changing demand of users for the pin pointed and exhaustive information within a short time. With the growing popularity of e-resources, the traditional libraries are gradually migrating from print documents to e- resources where providing access to information is considered more important than owning it. This is further augmented by the advent of Internet. Which has opened up windows of opportunity to different Information sources.

Meanwhile, the publishing industry has witnessed as evolutionary change. Most of the publishers are bringing out their products on magnetic and optical storage media which are more effective than the print versions of the same. With most of the information available on electronic formats, users expect that their needs and requirements be met by the library with the best and more effective resources. The librarian will have to meet this challenges environment by acquiring new skills and providing new services. They must become proficient in electronic collections management and further commitment to render services to different categories of users. Electronic formats are cheaper to obtain, store and retrieve.

The Nehru Library of Indira Gandhi Krishi Vishwavidyalaya, Raipur was established in 1987. This library is automated through LIBSYS software in 2004. It is recognized by the ICAR as the regional library of central India. This library has e-resources such as -

1. CD Rom Database (Agricultural Sciences) from 1970 to till date,
2. Online Journal of Consortia for e-resources in Agriculture (CeRA),
3. E-thesis of full text database (Krishiprabha),
4. E-reports of various projects and Annual reports of various organizations,
5. Internet facilities and,
6. OPAC services (Online public access catalogue).

So for no survey has been undertaken to investigate the usefulness of above e-resources to users. So this study has been conducted to reveal the usability of these subscribed e-resources.

Objective

1. Utility of E-resources by the Faculty members,
2. Awareness about different types of e-resources,
3. Purpose of use of e-resources,
4. The Frequency of use of e-resources,
5. To know the extent of the use of electronic resources,

6. To get the valuable suggestions for the improvement of the library e-resources services.

Review of Literature

1. Gurdev Singh et al. (2010) studied the "use of e-resources in college libraries of Delhi" and found that majority of students i.e. (97.56%) and teachers i.e. (100%) are aware about the e-resources. It was also found that the exchanging of the information through email by the teachers is (68.29%), sometime the use of e-resources by the teachers is (51.21%) and students is (60.97%) and frequently use of e-resources by the teachers is (41.46%) and students is (19.51%).
2. Sanjeev Kumar et al. (2010) studied the use of e-resources at Punjab Agricultural University library. He found that 94% respondents used Internet as the source of information. Most of the respondents used On-line journal, On-line database and CD-Rom databases for study, research and teaching.
3. Sunil Kumar Satpathy and Biswanath Rout (2010) in their study "use of e-resources by the faculty members with special reference to CVRCE Bhubaneswar" have discussed the advantages and usefulness of e-resources over print resources.
4. Sewa Singh and Navneet Kaur (2010) had conducted the study on "use pattern of e-resources by Social Scientists of Guru Nanak Dev University, Amritsar". It was found that most of the respondents (83.57%) are familiar with e-resources.
5. E. Kanniyappan *et al.* (2010) studied the use and impact of e-resources in an academic and research environment and found that most of the respondents (52.66%) use only e-journal and 32% of the respondents use both e-journal and print journals.
6. Lalitha K. Sami and Rabia Iffat (2009) studied "use of electronic information services in research libraries" and found that the technical staff (64.47%) accepts the wide range of available e-resources for improvement of their research work.

7. Dineshan Koovakkai et al. (2006) studied "Electronic information use among the Faculty". It was observed that the most of the teachers prefer Google and Yahoo search engine for the e-journals for their research and education though the availability of e-resources is not high. So, he suggested to use and aware the e-resources as much as possible.
8. Baljinder Kaur et al. (2006) studied "use of e-resources of TIET Library Patiala". It is found that all the users have knowledge of using computers, email, internet etc, but maximum of users (72.7%) use printed materials. It is due to unawareness about various e-resources. It was suggested that the library should provide education/ awareness program to the users for using the online services daily.

2. Scope and Limitations

The study confined to the use and usage of electronic resources by the Faculty members (Teacher and Scientist) of Central Library, Indira Gandhi Krishi Vishwavidyalaya, Raipur (CG). This study of e-resources includes On-line journals, Off-line databases, e-books, e-reports, Internet services and OPAC services etc.

3. Methodology

For the proposed study a structured questionnaire was prepared and distributed to the users of library. The collected data (questionnaire) was tabulated and then analyzed with the application of Statistical Tools.

4. Data Analysis and Discussion

The survey involved 50 faculty members. The study is presented by the various Tables based on the various parameters.

Table -1 clearly shows that the respondents gradually increase to the age group of 46-50 and decreases thereof. In the age group of 46-50, the percentage of respondents is maximum i.e. 28% and in the age group of 31-35 and above 56, the percentage of respondents is minimum i.e. 6%.

Table 1 : Classification of respondent according to age group

Age Group	Faculty Member	% of Respondents (Faculty Members)
31-35	03	6%
36-40	11	22%
41-45	08	16%
46-50	14	28%
51-55	11	22%
56 to above	03	6%
Total	50	100%

Table 2 : Visiting the Library

Table -2 shows that very less number of faculty members visit the library daily i.e. 12%. However, 18% visited in 2-3 days in a week, 48% visited once in a week and 22% visited occasionally. It clearly indicates that more number visit the library once in a week.

Frequency of Visit	Faculty members	% of Respondents (Faculty Members)
Daily	06	12%
2-3 days in a week	09	18%
Once in a week	24	48%
Occasionally	11	22%
Total	50	100%

Table-3 reveals the purposes of use of e-resources in which out of 50 faculty members, 24 members (48%) use all the e-resources of library, whereas 13 (26%) use e-resources for teaching and research, 9 (18%) use for writing paper, 3 (6%) use occasionally.

Table 3 : Purpose of using E-resources

Purpose	Faculty members	%
Writing paper	09	18%
For Teaching	13	26%
To Improve knowledge	06	12%
For doing Research Work	13	26%
Seminar/ Workshop preparing	03	6%
All of the above	24	48%

Table-4 reveals that out of 50 faculty members, 2 members (4%) use on-line journals daily, 16 (32%) use once in a week, 9 (18%) use once in a month,16 (32%) use occasionally and 7 (14%) never use the on-line journal.

Table 4 : Frequency of use of On-line Journals

Frequency of use	Faculty member	%
Daily	02	4%
Once in a week	16	32%
Once in a month	09	18%
Occasionally	16	32%
Never	07	14%

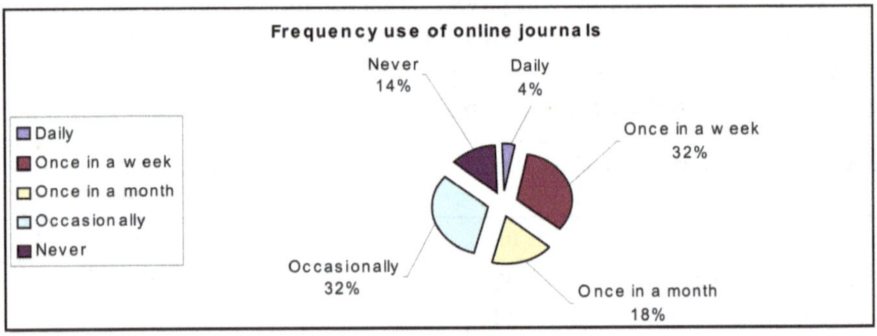

Table-5 reveals that out of 50 faculty members, 1 member (2%) use the off-line CD-Rom Database daily,11 (22%) use once in a week, 9 (18%) use once in a month,17 (34%) use occasionally and 12 (24%) never use the off-line CD-Rom Database.

Table 5 : Frequency of use of Offline CD-Rom Database

Frequency of use	Faculty member	%
Daily	01	2%
Once in a week	11	22%
Once in a month	09	18%
Occasionally	17	34%
Never	12	24%

Table-6 reveals that out of 50 faculty members, 9 members (18%) use the e-thesis (Krishiprabha database) once in a week, 9 (18%) use once in a month,13 (26%) use occasionally and 19 (38%) never use the e-thesis (Krishiprabha).

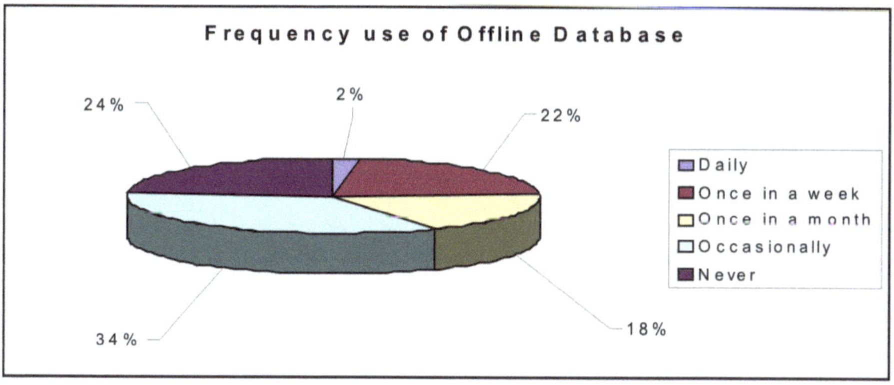

Table 6 : Frequency of use of e-thesis (Krishiprabha Database)

Frequency of use	Faculty member	%
Daily	-	-
Once a week	09	18%
Once in a month	09	18%
Occasionally	13	26%
Never	19	38%

Table-7 reveals that out of 50 faculty members, 6 members (12%) use the OPAC (Online public access catalogue) once in a week, 2 (4%) use once in a month,15 (30%) use occasionally and 27 (54%) never use the OPAC (Online public access catalogue).

Table 7 : Frequency of use of OPAC (Online public access catalogue)

Frequency of use	Faculty member	%
Daily	-	-
Once a week	06	12%
Once in a month	02	4%
Occasionally	15	30%
Never	27	54%

Table-8 reveals that out of 50 faculty members, 1 member (2%) uses the e-book daily, 13 (26%) use the e-book once in a week, 7 (14%) use once in a month, 15 (30%) use occasionally and 14 (28%) never use the e-book.

Table 8 : Frequency of use of e-Books

Frequency of use	Faculty member	%
Daily	01	2%
Once a week	13	26%
Once in a month	07	14%
Occasionally	15	30%
Never	14	28%

Table-9 reveals that out of 50 faculty members,1 member (2%) uses the e-report daily,9 (18%) use once in a week, 4 (8%) use once in a month,18 (36%) use occasionally and 18 (36%) never use the e-report.

Table 9 : Frequency of use of e-report

Frequency of use	Faculty member	%
Daily	01	2%
Once a week	09	18%
Once in a month	04	8%
Occasionally	18	36%
Never	18	36%

Table-10 reveals that out of 50 faculty members, 35 members (70%) use the internet daily,11 (22%) use once in a week, 1 (2%) uses once in a month, 3 (6%) use occasionally.

Table 10 : Frequency of use of Internet

Frequency of use	Faculty member	%
Daily	35	70%
Once a week	11	22%
Once in a month	01	2%
Occasionally	03	6%

Table-11 reveals that out of 50 faculty members, 9 members (18%) need the training program once in a month for e-access, 21 (42%) need once in a year, 8 (16%) need thrice in a year, 8 (16%) need occasionally and 4 (8%) does not need e-access.

Table 11 : Need of Training

Frequency	Faculty member	%
Monthly	09	18%
Once in a year	21	42%
Thrice in a year	08	16%
Occasionally	08	16%
Never	04	8%

5. Suggestions

The following points based on the finding of the study are put forward to familiarizes the use of e-resources among the users:

1. There are very less time to visit the library for the faculty members due to extra (research and education) load on them. This is due to shortage of staff in the respective departments. Therefore, there should be sufficient number of staff in the departments.
2. The library visit of the faculty members should be made compulsory at least once in a week.
3. There should be networking facility between Library and different departments.
4. Internet facilities should be provided to all the departments.
5. The information related to e-resources should be circulated to all the departments.
6. Sufficient number of computer terminals should be installed in the Library for accessing of e-resources.
7. Training programmes related to e-access should be conducted time to time.

6. Conclusion

The development of ICT has changed the seeking and dissemination pattern of information in the library. The e-resources are the easiest and fastest way to manage and retrieve the information. The study reveals that the users are not showing interest to access the e-resources daily. So, necessary steps (i.e. subscribing more e-journals, motivation to use e-resources, training programs to access e-resources etc.) should be taken to make the e-resource more popular among users.

References

Arun Kumar. 2009. Use and usage of electronic resources in business schools in India. FIIB. ICAL 2009. University of Delhi: 573-578.

Kanniyappan, E., Nithyanandam, K. and Ravichandran, P. 2010. Use and impact of e-resources in an Academic and Research environment. Indian Journal of Information, Library and Society. 23(1-2): 26-40.

Kaur, Amritpal and Randhawa, Sarwan Singh. 2010. Use of electronic databases in University Libraries of British Columbia: a study. SRELS Journal of Information Management. 47(6): 641-652.

Koovakkai, Dineshan and Hanna Noor, K.V. 2006. Electronic Information use among the faculty. Library Hearld. 44(4): 313-320.

Lohar, Manjunath and Kumbar, Mallinath. 2008. Use of CD-Rom and Internet resources by the students in JNN college of Engineering Shimoga: a study. SRELS journal of Information Management. 45(2): 235-241.

Lohar, M.S. and Roopashree, T.N. 2006. Use of electronic resources by faculty members in B.I.E.T. Davanagere: a study. SRELS journal of Information Management. 43(1): 101-112.

Patil, D.B. and Parameshwar, S. 2009. Use of electronic resources by the faculty members and research scholars in Gulbarga University Gulbarga: a study. SRELS journal of Information Management. 46(1): 61-72.

Sami, Lalitha K. and Iffat, Rabia. 2006. Electronic resources and public libraries. SRELS journal of Information Management. 43(2): 171-176.

Sanjeev Kumar and Sharma, Yogita. 2010. Use of e-resources at Punjab Agricultural University Library: a study. IASLIC Bulletin. 55(4): 238-243.

Satpathy, Sunil Kumar and Rout, Biswanath. 2010. Use of e-resources by the faculty members with special reference to CVRCE, Bhubaneswar. Desidoc Journal. 30(4): 11-16.

Singh, Gurdev and Arora, Taruna. 2010. Use of e-resources in college libraries of Delhi. Library Herald. 48(4): 363-375.

Singh, Sewa and Kaur, Navneet. 2010. Use pattern of e-resources by social scientist: study of Guru Nanak Dev University, Amritsar. Indian Journal of Information, Library and Society. 23(1 & 2): 16-25.

24

Use of E-journals in A Engineering College Library with Special Reference to Gates Institute of Technololgy (GIT) Gooty, A.P: A Study

Y.Ch.Venkateswarlu
Librarian
Gates Institute of Technology
Gooty, Anantapur
Andhra Pradesh

1. Introduction

Electronic journals are an important source for scientific technical research and development. This resource is widely used by research and development workers and other users of the libraries to carry out qualitative research, education and gain knowledge. In recent years there has been a surge in the number of electronic journals available to libraries for their users to access. More titles are made available by publishers and subscription agents. There is a common view amongst Liberians that libraries are forsaking traditional print resources in favor of electronic resources. With the application of information technology, particularly internet, there has been a shift from traditional print journal to electronic journals. This type of use survey is essential to improve the existing library services, to plan new services, rationalize the use of the limited financial resources in an economic way, evaluate the performance of the library and enhance the user satisfaction.

Gates Institute of Technology is a private engineering college in Gooty, Anantapur (Andhra Pradesh) established in the year 2001sponspored by Gujjal Raghunatha Reddy Trust Gooty,A.P. This college has 6 Under-Graduates and 4 Post-Graduate Departments in engineering, management, and computer science. Gates Engineering College Library has 30,000 volumes subscribing to 135 national and international print journals. Apart from that all the departments have the facility to access to online e-journals through IEEE, JGATE, Springer, MgHill, ASTM Digital Library, ASME and EBSCO publication. The library is also a member of DELNET through which the users can access the bibliographical data bases of books, journals, thesis etc. of other member libraries.

2. Statement of the Problem

The problem of the present study is "use of E-journals in an engineering college library with special reference to Gates Institute of Technology (GATES) Gooty, A.P.

3. Objectives of the Study

The following are the specific objective of the study:

- To examine the extent of awareness about the e-journals services among the engineering students.
- To know the location from where engineering students access e-journals.
- To find out the purpose of using e-journals.
- To examine the problems while using e-journals.
- To know the level of satisfaction with the available e-journals.
- To examine the need for conducting user awareness programmes in using e-journals.

4. Hypotheses

- Most of the engineering students are aware of electronic journals.
- Most of the engineering students are not satisfied with availability of electronic journals related to their subject field.

- Most of the engineering students are not facing problems while accessing the electronic journals.
- Most of the engineering students realize the need of user awareness programme.

5. Methodology

To conduct this survey, questionnaire tool was used. The present study is conducted using a sample of 100 final year engineering students of civil, electronics, electrical and mechanical branches. Copies of questionnaire were distributed to 100 engineering students in the month of November 2012. However, 80 of them responded and the same used for analysis.

6. Data Analysis

The data collected from the engineering students is analyzed and presented in the following Tables.

6.1 Awareness of E-journals

Table 1 shows the distribution of engineering students according to their responses with regard to awareness of available e-journals.

Table 1 : Awareness of E-journals

Awareness	No. of students	Percentage
Yes	73	91.25
No	7	8.75
Total	**80**	**100.00**

It is evident from Table1 that 91.25 percent of the engineering students are aware of available electronic journals in the library and only 8.75 percent of them have replied negatively in this regard.

6.2 Source of information about E-Journals

The distribution of engineering students according to the sources from which they came to know the availability of electronic journals is shown in Table 2.

Table 2 : Source of information about electronic journals.

Sources	No. of Students	Percentage
Library Staff	55	68.75
Friends/Faculty	21	26.25
Others	4	5.00
Total	**80**	**100.00**

It is evident from Table 2 that 68.75 percent of the engineering students came to know about the availability of electronic journals from the library staff 26.25 percent of them from friends and faculty, and a few 5% of them from other sources.

6.3 Place for accessibility of E-journals

Table 3 : Place for accessibility of electronic journals

Sources	No. of Students	Percentage
Central Library	72	90.00
Main computer centre	28	35.00
Departmental Computer centre	56	70.00

(Multiple answers were permitted)

It is evident from Table-3 that 90% of the engineering students are accessing the electronic journals from the central library, 70% of them from departmental computer centers, and 35% of them from main compute center. It is concluded that the majority of the students are accessing the e-journals from central library and computer centre in their own department.

6.4 Purpose of using E-journals

A question has been put to the engineering students to indicate the purpose for which they are using the electronic journals. Their responses are analyzed and shown in Table-4.

Table 4 : Purpose of using electronic journals

Purpose	No. of Students	Percentage
To update the knowledge(general)	31	38.75
For research (project work)	61	76.25
For Study (exams)	26	32.50
To write papers (articles)	42	52.50

(Multiple answers were permitted)

It can be seen from Table 4 that 76.25% of the engineering students are using electronic journals for their research work. It is also evident that 52.50% of them are using e-journals for writing articles, 38.75% of them are using to update their general knowledge. Only 32.5% of them are accessing e-journals for their studies.

6.5 Problems in using e-journals

A question has been put to the engineering students to indicate the level of problems they faced while using the electronic journals. The responses given by them are shown in Table-5.

Table 5 : Problems in using electronic journals

Level of problems	No. of Students	Percentage
Major problem	49	61.25
Minor problem	22	27.50
No problem at all	9	11.25
Total	**80**	**100.00**

It is evident from Table 5 that majority of the students (61.25%) are facing major problems in using electronic journals, and also 27.5% of them are facing minor problems and only 11.25% of them are facing no problems. This clearly indicates that library needs to organize training programmes at regular intervals in order to reduce the problems of the students. The library staff also needs to assist the students till they get familiarity in using the electronic journals. This will motivate the students to use the facility electronic journals are shown in Table-6.

Table 6 : Types of problems in using electronic journals

Types of problems	No. of Students	Percentage
Internet connectivity	11	13.75
Limited access terminals	57	71.25
Slow speed	49	61.25
Lack of training	19	23.75
Other problems (power cuts, Ups down etc.)	33	41.25

(Multiple answers were permitted)

It is evident form Table -6 that majority of the engineering students faced problems of limited access terminals 71.25% followed by slow speed 61.25% about 41% pointed out other problems like power cuts and non functioning of UPS. Lack of training in the use e-resources has also been stated as one of the problems by 23.27% of the students.

Value of Information Access through E-journals

The distribution of engineering students according to their assessment of value of information accessed through electronic journals is shown in Table-7.

Table 7 : Value of information access through E-journals

Information accessed	No. of students	Percentage
Most helpful	38	47.50
Helpful	42	52.50
Least helpful	-	-
Total	**80**	**100.00**

It is evident form Table that 52.5% of the engineering students found the information accessed through electronic journals as Helpful for their research and 47% of them considered the information content of electronic journals as "Most helpful".

6.6 Skills regarding the use of E-journals

The distribution of engineering students according to their skills for accessing the electronic journals is shown in Table-8.

Table 8 : Skills regarding the use of E-journals

Skills	No. of Students	Percentage
Expert	17	21.25
Moderate	57	71.25
beginners	6	7.50
Total	**80**	**100.00**

It is evident form Table-8 that 71.25% of engineering students consider their level of personal skills as "Moderate" for accessing the electronic journals. About 21.25% of them identified themselves as "experts" whereas only 7.5% of them considered themselves as 'Beginners' in terms of use of e-journals.

6.7 Level of satisfaction with E-journals

A question has been put to the engineering students to indicate the level of satisfaction with the availability of e-journals subscribed by the library. the responses given by them are shown in Table-9.

Table 9 : Level of satisfaction with E-journals

Level of satisfaction	No. of Students	Percentage
Satisfied	45	56.25
Neither satisfied not dissatisfied	21	26.25
Dissatisfied	14	17.50
Total	**80**	**100.00**

It is evident from Table-9 that more than half of the engineering students 56.25% are satisfied with the availability of electronic journals in Gates Institute of Technology library 26.25% of them are neither satisfied nor dissatisfied, and 17.5%of them are dissatisfied. So there is a need to improve the satisfaction levels of engineering students by improving the quality and quantity of electronic journals subscribed.

6.8 Need for user training programmes

A question has been put to the engineering students to indicate whether they need any awareness programme in using the electronic journals. The responses given by them are shown in Table-10

Table 10 : Need for user training

Need of user training	No. of Students	Percentage
Yes	59	73.75
No	21	26.25
Total	**80**	**100.00**

It is evident from Table 10 that majority of engineering students73.7% felt that providing the awareness programme in the use of electronic journals is essential however 26.25% of them have not shown any interest in this regard.

7. Findings

- Most of the engineering students (91.25%) are aware of the availability of electronic journals in library.
- Majority of engineering students are able to know about the availability of electronic journals in library from library staff (68.75%).
- Most of the engineering students (90%) are accessing electronic journals from central library and departmental lab/computer centers (70%).
- Most of them (76.25%) are accessing the electronic journals in support of their research work.
- Majority of them (61.25%) are facing major problems in accessing electronic journals. The specific problems faced by them are limited access terminals and slow speed.
- Most of the engineering students (52.2%) felt that electronic journals are helpful in their research work.
- Majority of the engineering students (71.25%) consider themselves as having moderate skills in the use of electronic journals.
- More than half of the engineering students (56.2%) are satisfied with the available electronic journals in library.
- Though most of them are getting assistance from the library staff in the use of the electronic journals, majority of them have expressed the desire and need to have user training programme in the use of electronic journals.

Suggestions

- A considerable percentage of engineering students are dissatisfied with the electronic journals available in central library for their needs. Hence, number of journals available though consortia should be increased to access more journals in their respective fields.
- Internet bandwidth need to be increased as most of the students complained about the problem of slow downloading of online information.

- To provide more access to electronic journals efficiently and effectively, the number of computers with internet connectivity has to be increased in the central library as well as departmental labs in the campus.
- The college authorities and departments should organize regular workshops and seminars to encourage the usage of electronic journals.
- User's studies should conducted to know about electronic information needs of users as well as problems they are facing while searching information through consortia.
- Keeping in view the demand and need expressed by the students, the library has to organize user training programmes in the use of electronic journals periodically for the new comers.

References

Fosmire. M and Young, E. Free scholarly electronic journals, what access do college and university libraries provide. 61, 2000, 500-508.

Halliday (leah) and Oppenheim (Charles) Developments in digital journals. Journals of Documentation 57, 2001, 260-283.

Raza, M. and Eqbal, M. Management of E-journals in digital environment. Library Herald. 41,2003,275-286.

Ramaih, CK. Use of chemistry periodical literature in a university library, ILA Bulletin, 24, 2988, 14-36.

Woodward, H et al. An electronic journal user survey. Journal of Digital Information, 3, 1998, 9-18.

25

Digital Preservation in the Context of Institutional Repositories in Academic Libraries of India

Sunil Kumar Satpathy
Deputy Librarian
National Institute of Technology
G.E./Road, Raipur (C.G)-492010, India
E-mail: drsksatpathy@gmail.com

---

1. Introduction

Over the years, the library and information environment has seen remarkable changes in its collection, organization and services due to impact of Information Communication Technology (ICT). One of the most significant benefits which libraries have acquired with the help of ICT during past two decades is the Institutional Repositories (IR). IR has changed the image and importance of academic libraries in preserving the institutional knowledge to a great extend. "With the rapid development of Information Communication Technology (ICT), many new services have been introduced in libraries to satisfy the need of users in a better way. Institutional Repository is a type of information service which involves collection, organization, preservation and dissemination of digital scholarly materials such as theses, dissertations, technical reports, journal articles and teaching materials. It is created and maintained by an individual library/organization or a group of libraries/organizations with an aim to preserve the institutional knowledge .Thus basically it is an online locus for collecting, preserving and disseminating the intellectual output of an academic or research institution in digital form, created and maintained by the institution itself (Satpathy, 2012).The creation of Institutional Repositories in libraries, mostly academic libraries of India are in a good flow and a good numbers of IRs are now seen in India also.

Some issues related to digital preservation in Institutional Repositories are yet to be sorted out properly and unanimously accepted by all institutions. The paper tries to discuss some issues related to the digital preservation in IRs for the benefit of libraries.

2. Concepts and Definition

2.1. Institutional repositories

Clifford Lynch defines Institutional Repositories as "a set of services that a university offers to the members of its community for the management and dissemination of digital materials created by the institution and its community members. It is most essentially an organizational commitment to the stewardship of these digital materials, including long-term preservation where appropriate, as well as organization and access or distribution" (Lynch, 2003)

Hockx-Yu opines that "while some repositories focus on particular subject domains, an institutional repository stores and makes accessible the educational, research and associated assets of an institution. Although most of the currently established institutional repositories are 'e-prints' repositories providing open access to the research outputs of a university or research institution, the content does not need to be limited to e-prints but could potentially include research data, learning material, image collections and many other different types of content."(Hockx-Yu,2006)

The main objectives of an institutional repository are to provide access to institutional research output and other institutional digital assets, including unpublished or grey literature .It also facilitates its organization, preservation and dissemination. The basic contents of IR are preprints, post prints, author post prints, publisher PDFs, technical reports, working papers, theses and dissertations, books and chapters of books, research databases, conference proceedings, text audio-video recordings, teaching materials, digital research, materials, unpublished work, datasets, research papers, working papers etc. Thus, Institutional Repository is a digital archive of the intellectual products of faculty members, research staff and students of an institution to enhance the use of information by users conveniently.

2.2. Digital preservation

Digital Preservation is the process of ensuring sustainable access to digital scholarly and heritage materials over the time."In the long term, both the physical and digital materials suffer some degradation. The equivalent process of degradation for digital materials is typically caused by format obsolescence - due to changes in hardware, software etc in comparison with degradation of physical materials and can be ameliorated by specialized technical processes such as format migration. Hence a good digital preservation strategy needs to be formulated.

As defined by Jones and Beagrie (2002), digital preservation refers to the series of managed activities necessary to ensure continued access to digital materials for as long as necessary. The ease with which digital information can be created, combined with the huge increase in computer power and network bandwidth, has led to the proliferation of a vast amount of 'born-digital' data, especially in science and engineering, where petabytes (10 " 15 bytes) of data are being generated by scientific instruments on a daily basis. This data deluge has forced many to address the issue of long term preservation and creation so as to ensure that data generated today can survive the changes of technology and can be accessed in the future. The challenge for digital preservation is not just the volume of data. The hardware and software used to store and access digital information are constantly upgraded and superseded. Technology obsolescence is generally regarded as the greatest technical threat to ensuring continued access to digital material. The speed of changes in technology means that the timeframe during which preservation action must be taken is very much shorter than for paper, often measured in just a few years. Similarly Jantz & Giailo opines that " digital preservation encompasses activities which are neccssary for long term maintenance of a byte stream including metadata) sufficient to reproduce a suitable facsimile of the original document; and for tho continued accessibility of the document contents through time and changing technology"(Jantz & Giailo,2005).

Digital preservation includes a wide range of activities starting from storage to transformation, depending on the nature of the resources and the source. Also the range of preservation services could be equally wide. Since such services are not yet widely practised or available, a useful starting point is to consider by the libraries for long-term preservation of digital materials for the target contents of digital Library or Institutional repositories.

3. Need for Digital Preservation

The volume of digital materials in Institutional repositories is not a problem for digital preservation rather technology obsolesce is regarded as the greatest technical thereat to ensure continued access to digital materials. The hardware and software used to store and access digital information are constantly upgraded and superseded. Further speed of access is another factor. Hence there is every need to take proper action for the preservation of digital materials because the timeframe during which preservation action require to be taken due to speed changes of technology is very short in comparison to print materials. Owing to their relatively short existence, few institutional repositories so far have encountered problems with long-term access or experienced an unmanageably large volume of content. (Hockx-Yu,2006)

4. Digital Preservation in Institutional Repositories: Issues and Challenges

In order to understand the process necessary to achieve the long-term digital preservation of objects placed within a repository, it is useful to break down what is understood as effective preservation. Wheatley (2004) summarized its key functional goals as follows:

- data is maintained in the repository without being damaged, lost or maliciously altered;
- data can be found, extracted and served to a user;
- data can be interpreted and understood by the user; and
- the above can be achieved in the long term.

Digital preservation is a complex process and involves many unsolved organizational, managerial and technical issues that make it a challenging task for libraries that are managing institutional repositories. Till date digital preservation has not been embedded as an integral part of the library function. Also there is neither much experience nor commonly agreed practice as to how digital preservation can be best performed. Digital preservation requires new work rows, new skills and close co-operation among different professions ranging from traditional preservation management skills to computing science.

Digital preservation in Institutional Repositories includes a lot of technical issues and challenges related to practical implementations of preservation standards and technical knowledge There is a need for more automation and tools such as identifier services, registries for file format, registries for representation information, automatic metadata generation and extraction, and for automatic ?le format recognition and validation.

Some of the prime issues and challenges related to digital preservation in Institutional Repositories can be summarized as follows.

a) Hardware/Software failure: The hardware components are expected to suffer transient recoverable failure like power loss and catastrophic irrecoverable failures like burnt-out power supplies. Similarly all software components are expected to suffer from bugs that pose a risk to stored data.

b) Communication errors: Communication of information will either succeed or fail within a specified time period or will deliver the content unaltered that systems cannot assume.

c) Failure of network services: The external network services including domain name and persistent URLs suffer both from transient and irrecoverable failures. For instance domain name will vanish or to be reassigned or cancelled and a persistent URL may fail to resolve if the resolver services fails to preserve its data.

d) Technology Obsolesce: All hardware, software and media components are expected to degrade or obsolete with time causing serious irrecoverable errors. This problem is acute particularly for removable media.

e) Direct & Indirect attack: It involves modification of the stream of information communication or creates a false stream. The direct attacks can be of different types such as modification of messages, masquerade (one entity pretends to be a different entity), replay (passive capture of a data unit and its retransmission), denial of service (it prevents the normal management of communication facilities) etc. The Indirect attacks are in the nature of transmission of data. Some important types of indirect attacks in information communication are release of message content and traffic analysis. These types of attack are very difficult to detect because they do not involve any alteration of the data.

f) Financial Constraints: There are ongoing costs for power, cooling, bandwidth, system administration, domain registration, and so on in digital preservation. Hence budgets for digital preservation must be expected to vary over time. So the digital preservation system are more vulnerable to interruption in the name of financial constraints

g) Policy of the parent institutions: Lack of clear cut policies in creation and maintenance of Institutional Repositories by the parent organization poses another problem.

5. Suggestions for Developing a Digital Preservation Strategy

Preservation is an important aspect in the context of Institutional Repository. It is an indicator of the seriousness with which an institution holds its Institutional Repositories. Hence without an underlying strategy for digital preservation, the institutional repository and its contents lack sustainability. Some basic logical steps in framing strategic plan for digital preservation in IRs can be discussed as below.

5.1. Formulation of policies on institutional repositories and Digital preservation

The basic and first step in developing a strategic digital preservation plan is to frame policies on Institutional Repositories and digital preservation by the parent institutions. Such policy framework is meant to provide the required mandate, decisions, financial support and commitment from the authorities for the digital preservation of contents available in the Institutional repositories.

5.2. Selection for digital preservation

The amount and types of digital collections in IR grows with the time .Hence it is highly essential to select materials for digital preservation keeping in view the demands of users and reference value in future. Selecting materials for digital preservation needs to depend on following criteria:

- Materials which are both valuable and endangered.
- Contents of the materials.
- Availability of techniques, procedures and standards for the selected materials.
- Copy right of the materials.
- Demands of the users.
- Long term use of the materials.

5.3. The role format in digital preservation

The long-term preservation of digital objects is simply not possible without a detail understanding of the internal details of the formats in which the digital objects are encoded... Formats need to be understood in the general sense so that generic tools and services can be created.

"The concept of representation format permeates all technical aspects of digital repository architecture and is, therefore, the foundation of many, if not all, digital preservation activities. While analog content is generally directly usable by a human agent despite the passage of time (consider, for example, the ongoing accessibility and utility of 500 year-old incunabula), digital content is always dependent upon technical mediation for effective access. A digital object is merely an opaque string of bits without the intermediation of some technical system that is capable of transforming those bits into an appropriate representation interpretable by the human perceptual and cognitive facilities. This intermediation requires a detailed understanding of the particular means used to encode an object's intellectual content into a digital form; in other words, its format. The data neccssary for the proper interpretation of digital formats is known as representation information as defined by the OAIS Reference Model ,ISO, 2003. (Abrams, 2004).

Two categories of representation information are necessary for effective digital preservation:

(1) Representation information about the formats used to encode digital objects.

(2) Representation information about individual encoded digital objects, more familiarly referred to as object

technical metadata or significant properties (Hedstrom and Lee, 2002).

5.4. Selection of metadata

Selection of metadata for creation of IR and digital preservation is an important aspect..."As the archival storage disallows to update, metadata of corresponding file cannot be updated. Therefore separate components of the metadata are kept in different locations, according to their function. Administrative metadata should be entered into a separate database, as it will need to be updated. This will also be archived as data sets at frequent intervals. Copies of bibliographic metadata will be managed via the library OPAC (Semple, 2004).

Research shows that preservation metadata forms a crucial element of digital preservation. It is commonly agreed that preservation metadata is the key to successful digital preservation. Information recorded about a digital object, both at time of creation, and during its life cycle, is crucial to the long-term readability of the file. Compiling a preservation metadata schema however is more difficult. One of the best way to overcome metadata problem is to digital preservation from the outset is to involve the authors in contributing preservation metadata during the creation and ingest process and to embed digital preservation into the repositories workflow, which will ease the later preservation tasks.

5.5. Continuous management and maintenance

Digital preservation work is not a one time job, rather is a continuous job on the part of the libraries who maintains IRs. The digital archive requires continuous regular maintenance to keep it secured, which includes regular processes to check the fixity of files i.e. to find out if the content is corrupted and needs repairing, to ensure replications etc.

5.6. Collaborative efforts by the libraries

Although creation and maintenance of IRs in India is mostly done by the individual libraries, collaborative efforts by similar types of libraries in the line of library networks, consortia etc may prove to be effective in terms of collection, finance, resources and services. At least the collaborative efforts in finding solution in metadata selection, role format, registry services, software and hardware selection, access mechanisms, framing digital preservation strategies etc can be made to provide better services through IRs and to ensure log term digital preservation.

6. Conclusion

In the context of Institutional repositories, digital preservation is most important aspects on the part of libraries. There is seen continuous debate that to what extend libraries, which maintain institutional repository, are responsible for digital preservation. Some are in the opinion that digital preservation is the responsibility of the publishers and the legal deposit libraries, while others are in the opinion that long term preservation is an important functions of Institutional libraries However the disagreement on digital preservation by libraries does not weaken the case for libraries playing a role in digital preservation. Even those who regard the institution as having only a short-term responsibility for preservation of institutional research outputs do not deny that there is a preservation role for libraries.

Further, the broad view of institutional repositories as a means to manage and preserve the institutional knowledge base and research outputs effectively expands its contents beyond e-prints to include research data e-learning materials and other forms of institutional intellectual outputs, which are generally not published or preserved elsewhere. The users of academic libraries which include faculty members, researchers, students and staff will require ongoing availability and confidence in the future accessibility of the content within the repositories, which the libraries have to be ensured. It needs to be ensured that content within the repositories remains accessible and retains its authenticity, reliability and integrity for as long as it is needed.

Also it is the responsibilities of the libraries to perform the duties of digital preservation to preserve human knowledge with full confidence and sincerity, for which libraries are recognized since time immemorial. All stakeholders-librarians, publishers, administrators, policy makers and funding bodies should get together to initiate and develop a strategy for preserving digital materials of IRs.

Digital preservation is not a unique problem that institutional repositories face alone. Also it is fact that with the development of technology and the numbers and types of digital collections, the pressure on libraries as information providers will continues to intensify over time. The library authorities and LIS professionals need to accept the challenges positively and find solutions for long term digital preservation. The libraries having IRs also need to wok collectively in finding best solutions of it.

References

Abrams,S.L.(2004).The role format in digital preservation. The Journal of Information and Knowledge Management Systems, 34(2), 49-55.DOI 10.1108/03055720410530997

Hedstrom, M. and Lee, C.A. (2002). Significant properties of digital objects: definitions, applications, implication(pp. 218-27), Proceedings of the DLM-Forum 2002, @ccess and Preservation of Electronic Information: Best Practices and Solutions, Barcelona, 6-8 May. http:// europa.eu.int/historical_archives/dlm_forum/doc/dlm-proceed2002.pdf

Hockx-Yu,H.(2006)..Digital preservation in the context of institutional repositories. Program: electronic library and information systems,40(3),232-243..DOI 10.1108/00330330610681312

Jantz, R & Giarlo, M.J. (2005).Digital preservation:Architecture and technology for trusted digital repositories. D-Lib, 11(6). http://www.dlib.org/dlib/june05/jantz/06jantz.html

Jones, M. and Beagrie, N. (2002), Preservation Management of Digital Materials: A Handbook,Digital Preservation Coalition, York. www.dpconline.org/graphics/intro/definitions.html

Lynch,C.A.(2003). Institutional Repositories: Essential Infrastructure for Scholarship in the Digital Age. ARL: A Bimonthly Report on Research Library Issues and Actions from ARL, CNI, and SPARC. 226 . http://www.arl.org/resources/pubs/br/br226/br226ir.shtml.

Satpathy,S.K.(2012). Institutional Repository (IR): need and future trends in Indian libraries. In Veerujaneyulu, K,Mahapatra, R.K. & Vaisakhi,P.(Eds.). Library services in knowledge age.New India Publishing Agencies: New Delhi.

Seadle, M.(2004). .Selection for digital preservation. Library Hi Tech, 22(2),119-121. DOI 10.1108/07378830410543494

Semple, N.(2004). Developing a digital preservation strategy at Edinburgh University Library. The Journal of Information and Knowledge Management Systems ,34(1),33-37. DOI 10.1108/03055720410530979

Wheatley, P. (2004), Institutional Repositories in the Context of Digital Preservation, DPC Technology Watch Series Report 04-02, Digital Preservation Coalition, York. www.dpconline.org/docs/DPCTWf4word.pdf

26

Electronic Resource Management: Opportunities and Challenges

Kamal Lochan Jena
Librarian
College of Engineering & Technology
Bhubaneswar - 751003
E-mail - kljena@rediffmail.com

Introduction

Due to the advent of new technologies now-a-days e-resources became more popular and essential. The information technology has made it possible the availability and accessibility of e-resources. The e-resources are made available both online and offline. Further some are free and some are paid. The free e-resources can be accessed anywhere and anytime on the discretion of the user. But for the paid e-resources to get comprehensive access by using best possible tools and techniques is the library. Multiple resources in the present electronic environment can be seamlessly integrated with a single login gateway which makes is user friendly. Further the explosive growth in network connectivity and rapid advances in computing power systems have altered the speed of communications. Recent advances in the information world have transformed the role of libraries in disseminating information to users. Increase in the number of users and their different needs have made modern libraries apply new communication technology. As a result of this there is a worldwide need and trend to collect, organize, manage, protect and distribute information in digital form.

The management of digital resources has never been an easy process. The rapid expansion of digital resources compounded with changing formats and sales models in the short life of Web-based delivery systems has particularly made the management process more complex. Further, from the very beginning, details relating to purchasing, licenses, access, and usage have been kept in ad hoc systems built by in-house teams or by the individual librarian needing to organize her workflow. It is hard to recall the days when digital resources played only a minor role in library management discussions1. Among all academic e-resources, the e-journal has made the greatest revolution in capturing and dissemination of emerging academic knowledge. Realizing this, some popular and front runner academic publishers had started their publishing in electronic form during 1970s and 1980s. Today e-resources are available in abundance, individually or through packages from different publishers.

Most of the academicians today have become Internet dependent. It is the contribution of information and communication technology and impact of Internet that information processing, storing, searching, dissemination and uses have become expeditious, easy and user-friendly. Today, digital technology is available at our doorstep, capable of effectively creating and capturing information in various formats, making these available to others2. Now-a-days e-resources are available and accessible beyond time and space restrictions which restrict the users to visit the library physically.

Impact of Information Technology on Users and Library

The impact of communication technology on user behavior and attitude has been tremendous. Communication pattern in local research environment significantly influenced e-resources use3. The use of e-resources depends upon the infrastructure and facilities available in comparison to the printed materials, because uses of printed materials need no technology. But with the increase of internet facility the use of e-resources has been increased. Now there is a sea change in the users' behavior and attitude in information searching and use. The users want information just now or never. For this, the libraries are forced to change from physical to virtual environment and adopt the latest Information Communication Technology (ICT) for the effective use of information. Since the printed materials and e-resources have their own importance and merits one cannot replace the other and the libraries have to continue to provide both the services effectively.

Publication of e-books is increasing but their acquisition represents only a small proportion of acquisition of the academic libraries4. But the acquisition of e-resources by the libraries is increasing steadily and exponentially. If the demands and attitudes of the users' will be taken into account the libraries will be forced to acquire more e-resources then earlier to meet the approach of the users. The users' information seeking behavior can be summarized as

- Least reliance on physical structure of libraries;
- More dependence on online world;
- Convenience and instant availability and accessibility of information;
- Impatient behavior to search the information from the print media;
- Easy availability of desktop computers, laptop, palmtops, tablets and even on mobile phones;
- Get satisfaction on the information whatever available easily.

Advances in technology create dramatic changes within libraries. The complex issues surrounding this new electronic and end-user environment have major ramifications and require expert knowledge. Innovation and development of Information and Communication Technologies (ICTs) and different library software and its application in the field of Library and Information Science (LIS) create changes in entire library management system. Electronic services librarians and electronic resources librarians are two specialized titles that have recently emerged within the field of librarianship to fill this niche. Electronic technologies and collection development are two of the top concerns in library and information science today. In a recent analysis of the literature, four major trends in library and information science were identified such as increases in end-user access to computer-based information resources; library use of networks and telecommunications; dependency on CD-ROM-based information sources; and emphasis on collection management activities. This is the age of ICT and everything is available electronically or automatically so academics and publishers believe that there is no role of librarians in this age. But the Librarian plays a vital role in this age also. Library and Information Science professionals face complex challenges by recent trends in ICT. The role of LIS professionals has become more dynamic and challenging. The technology to provide digital access to library reserve collections has been available for some time. Access to information and knowledge will therefore assume a different dimension altogether. The ICT and digital revolution have made dramatic changes in the offing for libraries such as:

- Changes in the form of the library;
- Changes in the relationship between an institution's library and its information technology division;
- Changes in the way collections are acquired, organized, stored and delivered; and
- Changes in the outlook of library buildings and facilities.

It can be summed up that the first and foremost impact of e-resources on libraries is about collection development followed by pricing, maintenance, archiving and management.

Collection Development

The first and foremost responsibility of libraries is the collection of materials irrespective of their forms and types. From the inception of the library the collection of libraries were printed materials, but with the changing of time the forms of materials became changed and now with the revolution of ICT the digital collection become essential for libraries. The assessment of quality is much easier in the printed form than the today's digital form which is more complex. It is because for long times the librarians are dealing with the selection of printed form in a pre-established standardized procedure and practice. But the case of e-resources is not so easy due to the abundance availability and the absence of standard procedure. In the printed form the librarian or the library has the control over the procedure, whereas in e-resources much control is lying with the vendor or supplier. Based on the agreement the vendor or the publisher supplies the e-resources through internet and if any dispute arises the publisher may discontinue the supply and embarrassing situation may arise leading to legal dispute. Further while procuring the e-resources some of the points may be considered like

- Content;
- Conditions of access;

- Updatability;
- Convenience of cataloguing;
- Longevity;
- Convenience of use;
- Technical characteristics and quality of service;
- Factors of value added; and
- Structure of price formation.

It is important to decide regarding the subscription of print version or e-resources. Sometimes the same source is available in both the versions. Further consideration may be made whether individual journal will be subscribed or from the sources available under consortium. The main drawback of e-resources is that the access to the resources is denied after the expiry of the subscription unless perpetual access is agreed upon. Today accessibility is given to the user not the ownership which has its own problem. There are different terms and conditions of accessing, downloading and printing of information. You may not be allowed to download whole issue of the journal, may not send the article through e-mail, may not store articles for future use, etc. The costs of e-resources are not fixed as of printed resources which vary depending upon various variables like number of concurrent users, level of access, nature of the institution, different renewal policies, etc. There are five important elements of collection development: Budgeting, type of material, selection, acquisition and evaluation 6 to be taken into account by all libraries. The whole process of e-resources is comparatively more challenging.

The acquisition of e-books is also made problem due to unpopular pricing model. The packages of e-books are costly as compared to the print version. Further the reading of e-books is not as convenient as printed books. However, printed books and e-books are complementary to each other having their own advantages and disadvantages. At this juncture the library has to keep balance between the print version and the e-resources depending upon the resources available, the demand from the users and the trend towards the use of e-resources.

Libraries shall have to continue their dual collection development policies in hybrid environment in which printed and electronic resources are to be integrated to meet diverse needs of communities they are expected to serve. Libraries shall have to change and adapt to the new environment keeping the future needs of users in view. It is important to consider the range of purchase, pricing models available and determine which one meets the needs of the library in terms of access and archival and value for money 7. Every library today has to add e-resources along with printed material which requires knowledge of pricing policies and models of different.

Publishers as well as scope, coverage and usefulness of data resource so that right choice in selection of resources is made 8.

E-resources and Consortia Purchase

Today is the day of cooperation and collaboration. The ICT has made it possible and easy to make collaboration and internet facility is an addition to it. Further the rising cost of printed materials as well as e-resources has forced to do collaboration among similar institutions and the concept of consortium is the outcome of this. In the consortium the libraries are able to access more information in least price. The concept of library cooperation and sharing of resources is as old as the library itself. No single library is self sufficient to acquire all the documents / information even the richest library in the world. Hence, pooling of resources and sharing of documents / information is the only solution to meet the needs of the users. But the e-resources have changed the scenario of library. Now the acquisition policy have been changed, individual purchase of resources is decreasing and the sharing is increasing. The physical barrier of library is becoming lesser and lesser making the libraries into hybrid libraries or virtual libraries. E-resources purchased through consortia provide wider accessibility with minimum cost. So most of the libraries are eager to join in different consortia. In the consortia thousands of journals and books are available to access and the price is negotiated. Sometimes all the journals and books available in the package may not be useful to all, but one has to accept it.

In the consortium, libraries have to accept the predefined package. The price may be affordable but in terms of use this may not be cost effective. This is because the prices are fixed by the publishers looking to the collective needs of the member libraries baring the needs of the individual libraries. Normally the pricing is fixed with the negotiation of the top bosses of the supplier and the consortia authority.

Cost of E-Resources

Like the printed materials the e-resources have not fixed price. The printed books or journals have fixed rates which can be verified and the librarians are not facing any such problem during the procurement. But in case of e-resources there is no standard pricing model yet. Different publishers have different pricing which goes on changing from time to time. Further the price for the same resource varies for different consortia or groups. Many times the bundle price is much less than the individual pricing which varies from vendor to vendor.

There are different subscription rates depending upon various factors like number of users, availing of inter-library loan, duration of subscription, level of use, on standalone system, on Local Area Network, with IP address or on Proxy server etc. Ables9 described the early stage of pricing which included 'connect time, flat fee per search, computer resources, subscription or flat fee-pricing per year, differential by time of day, 'free with print version.' 'Free with print version was to promote the use of e-resources in the beginning.

Many times the vendors made the pricing depending upon the standard of the institution e.g. the pricing for the journals subscribed by the Indian Institute of Technology (IITs) are much higher than the journals subscribed by the general universities. The same is the case for higher research institutions. The vendors are keeping watch on the funding of the institution. Depending upon the funding to the institution, the higher the cost of subscription is made. Sometime also the charge is made depending upon the usage of the resources. While deciding the price of the e-resources different publishers have different terms and conditions. Always the publishers want to protect their own interest which may not be suitable for the library and the librarian has to negotiate for this.

In the bundle of e-resources the price may not be suitable for the library because many times the publishers made the bundle of such journals which are not relevant for the library and the library is forced to subscribe it in order to subscribe the required e-resource / journal. Many times the librarian has to make negotiation for it also. Sometimes the publishers offered the bundle price for all their publications. But it is not easy to assess the usage of the full package and right decision may not be taken to purchase the whole package for the requirement of of selective titles. But one thing is that the bundle pricing gives access to a wide range of collection, but the usage cannot be ascertained in advance. In case of journals the pricing is also done on the basis of access to the back volume journals made available.

Management of E-Resources

In traditional libraries there is physical availability of documents, whereas in modern libraries where the e-services are available the e-resources are not visible physically. The information or documents are available when one search or browse the resources through the computer. Library subscribe different packages of different publishers and the information are scattered which may not be convenient to the users for searching. But the users want to access the information in one single stroke of key because the user has no time or patience to search different websites, databases or platforms.

For an effective search of appropriate literature the present library softwares have not adequate provision. In order to satisfy the user needs effectively Electronic Resource Management (ERM) is required. ERM services are a way of thinking about Library Management to help libraries optimize the access, usage, data, and workflows of electronic library collections in the physical and digital Library. Electronic resources, particularly electronic journals and e-books, can be viewed as an integral part of library collections. Recent studies have shown that not only are libraries acquiring significant amounts of digital content, but also that this content is both replacing and eclipsing traditional media. For this some libraries have developed their own local system and some have procured the commercial ERM software. But it is difficult to satisfy all types of needs of the users because the users have multiple approaches to access the e-resources. Some of the users' approaches are:

- Users search information on a particular topic from all available resources;
- The search may be on a particular resource;
- The search may be confined to a specific period;
- Integrated federated search may be made both from printed as well as e-resources;

- Articles may be selected for download and printing purpose;
- Users may require the resources to be grouped under different subject categories;
- Users' may require to download the particular issue of journal published on a specific topic;
- Users' may require the bibliography on a particular topic from the available resources;
- In addition to these libraries require the usage statistics for the justification of subscription of e-e, compliance to the terms and conditions of publisher / vendor etc.

Archival of Resources

Online resources are remotely located and remain under the ownership of the publishers or vendors. The libraries get access to these under the subscription mode with certain terms and conditions made agreement between the library and the publisher. Since after the expiry of subscription the library will not be able to access the resources unless mutual agreement is made. Under such case it is advisable to opt for archiving. But this is also not trouble free. If the library decides to do the outright purchase of the resource it will be quite expensive and unaffordable for most of the libraries. If the library wants to make its own archive then it is also a cumbersome and sometime agreement has to be made with the publisher since most of the times publishers are not allowing to download all the resources at a time. Further agreement may be made with the publisher to access the back issues with certain terms and conditions.

Conclusion

E-resources is the emerging source of information for all types of users. But is creates challenges in every levels of selection, acquisition, preservation, maintenance and management. In spite of the challenges e-resources becomes popular due to its many advantages and above all easy to search and use. The e-resources are able to keep the researchers up to date and save their search times and they are able to get their literature huge in amount within their finger strokes in the minimum possible time. Many software developers and service providers are doing their research to make possible the compilation of information as per requirement of the user. Technology has been behind the evolution and development of e-resources, and the same technology may be able to provide better solutions and more opportunities to have complete bibliographical control over world literature which is impossible in case of printed resources. More cooperation and interaction are required among library professionals, publishers, vendors/aggregators, users and software engineers to discuss common issues to arrive at common goal of mutual interests to promote more production, use of these resources with their improved, maintenance and management to the maximum benefit of the users.

References

Ables, E G (1996). Pricing of electronic resources: Interviews with three Vendors. Journal of the American Society for Information Science, 47(3) 235.

Carpenter, Todd . Standards Column - Electronic Resources Challenges and Opportunities. Against the Grain / December 2007-January 2008. P. 79. (http://www.against-the-grain.com).

Chandel, A S and Saikia, Mukesh (2012). Challenges and Opportunities of e-resources. Annals of Library and Information Studies. 59, Sept, p. 148-154.

Dawson, R. (2000). Knowledge capabilities as the focus of organizational development and strategy. Journal of Knowledge Management. 4 (4), 1-9.

Kaplan, L (1975). Library cooperation in United States, Encyclopedia of Library & Information Science, edited by Allen Kent, et al. (Dekker: New York) p 260.

Lutsik, Y N (2009). Creating the electronic collection of a University: Criteria for selecting online access resources. Scientific and Technical Information Processing. 36 (2), p 93.

Newman M, (2010). Librarian eBook survey, Highwire. (Palo Alto CA: Stanford University).

Nicholas, D and Huntington P (2006). Electronic journals: are they really used? Interlending & Document Supply, 34(2), 48.

Ramesh Babu, B (2012). Electronic Resource Management for Academic Excellence. In Innovative Practices in Management of Agricultural Libraries in the ICT Environment. Ed by Mahapatra, Rabindra K, et al. National Conference of Agricultural Libraries & User Community NCALUC - 2012, 5th - 7th Dec, 2012. Electronic Resource Management for Academic Excellence

Torma S and Vakkari P (2004). Discipline, availability of electronic resources and use of Finnish National Electronic Library-Fin Elib, Information Research, 10 (1).

Wilkinson, Francis C and Lewis Linda K (2003). The complete guide to acquisitions management. (Libraries Unlimited: London) 156.

27

Marketing and Promotion of Library & Information Products and Services in Digital Era

Chandresh A. Shah
Library Assistant,
Junagadh Agriculture University, Junagadh
E-mail : Cashah1963@yahoo.com
and
Rabindra K. Mahapatra
Chief Librarian
Orissa University of Agriculture & Technology,
Bhubaneswar- 751003
E-mail : rkmahapatra60@gmail.com

Introduction

Marketing and promotion are important for any organization that provides services to consumers. Marketing and promotion allow an organization to inform, remind, or persuade the consumers by sharing information about goods or services, community involvement, or societal impact. Simply stated, these efforts encompass anything libraries do to let the community know who they are, what they do, and what they offer. The goal of marketing is to keep the product in the minds of the customer: in the case of libraries it is to keep the customer aware of the library, to provide them with knowledge about the library's physical features, resources, services, programs, and events, and to let them know about the benefits libraries offer. Marketing and promotion benefit the library by increasing usage, educating users, and increasing or at least maintaining a positive perception of the library.

Libraries often attempt to create, develop, or maintain a recognizable brand for the consumer. This requires approaching the situation from the users' viewpoint by getting into their space. Many libraries have found Web 2.0 platforms to be effective as most of today's consumers utilize some form of social media. Libraries can communicate to consumers through pod casts, blogs, social book marking, social networking, videos, photos, wikis, and mobile apps.

What is Marketing in Libraries?

In recent years, marketing has been gaining importance in libraries throughout the world. Self-support policies, increasing competitiveness in the marketplace, rising customer expectations, and widening access to information are some of the main reasons for this trend. To survive in such an environment, library and information centers must identify their users' needs and integrate this information into the everyday workings of the library.

The first requirement for successful marketing in library and information services is a clear appreciation for what marketing is and what it can do. Although marketing is not new to library and information services, there are many opinions about what role it plays. Some people equate it with the pursuit of sales rather than customer satisfaction. Others view it as the production of brochures and other low-level marketing communications.

The term "marketing" is established in our vocabulary, although it has been less than three decades since marketing was first applied to the field of library and information services. The premise of marketing is simple and appealing: The customer is at the center of every library activity. This idea is not new—library science thinkers and philosophers were advocating such a philosophy as far back as 1880.

Definition of Marketing

Marketing is a process which carries goods from producers to ultimate consumers. Marketing, in its broader sense, is the social instrument through which the material goods and culture of a society are transmitted to its members. Marketing, in its library sense, refers to the instrument through which information (both raw and processed) are transmitted to its members.

Kotler has rightly defined: "Marketing is the analysis, planning, implementation and control of carefully formulated programs designed to bring about voluntary exchanges of values with target markets for the purpose of achieving organizational objectives. It reties heavily on designing the organization's offering in terms of target markets needs and desires, and on using effective pricing, communication, and distribution to inform, motivate, and service the markets."

In the words of Stanton, "marketing is a total system of interacting business activities to plan, price, promote and distribute want satisfying products and services, and present to potential customers."

Dragon neatly defined the concept of marketing and outlined its major aspects as "follows." Marketing is a systematic approach to planning and achieving desired exchange relations with other groups. Marketing is concerned with developing, maintaining, and/ or regulating exchange relations involving products, services, organizations, persons, places or causes."

Zachert and Williamss considered that' 'marketing is planning that focuses on products,; place or mode of delivery, adjustment of cost/price to the market, and promotion to ! Specifically targeted segments of the special librarian' s market."

The above definitions call for various activities in marketing. They are:

1. Market research and customers' analysis
2. Development of products and services
3. Pricing
4. Distribution
5. Promotion
6. Evaluation of products and services.

All the above mentioned activities of marketing as applied to other industrial sectors are equally applicable in the area of information products and services. Whether it is for profit or non-profit sector, methods remain the same while the policy varies.

Need for Marketing and Library Information Services

- Customer's requirements

- Visibility
- Valuable community resources
- Maintaining relevance
- Scarcity of resources
- Survival
- Beneficial to library images
- Rising expectations.

Market Research

Market research involves the "systematic gathering, recording and analyzing of data" relating to the demand for a service or product (Katz 1988). The parent organization needs to be analyzed in terms of funding sources, the contribution the library makes to the mission of the parent organization, resources available and the needs of the users. There are two basic functions of market research:

(i) To reduce the uncertainty of the decision-making process of marketing.

(ii) To monitor and control the performance of marketing activities.

The information gathered through market research will provide the basis for making marketing decisions.

Functions of Marketing Promotion

The functions of the Library Promotion Division are :

1. Marketing programmes
   - Develop marketing plans for new and existing library resources and services.
   - Manage promotional programmes to enhance the image of the Library and encourage its use.
2. Creating awareness
   - Develop publicity and promotional programmes to create awareness of library services and resources and to sustain users' interest over time.

- Coordinate and manage library exhibition events.
- Host professional visitors of the Library.

3. User relations
   - Establish and manage feedback channels.
   - Coordinate networking with student organizations, faculties and external professional bodies.
   - Coordinate outreach programmes to NTU alumni and friends of the Library.
4. Publicity materials
   - Develop a range of library publicity materials and marketing collaterals.
   - Manage the production of bulletins to update users on the library resources and services.
5. Market research
   - Identify specific research areas of user-library interaction and relations.
   - Conduct and review users' feedback and satisfaction surveys.

The Medium of Promotion

Promotional activities can take many forms and the promotional media will depend on the nature of the target audience and on promotional objectives.

- **Behavioral Skills**

Your manner whether in person or on the telephone, will affect user's rating of the library. You need to be professional and use quality procedures but you also need to smile and establish a personal relationship with as many of your users as possible. If you react positively to complaints, people will be encouraged to tell you about other things they would like change. Instead of defending your position think about their suggestions. Make yourself highly visible, visit the staff room, memorize names, and learn research interests of staff. Make a point of visiting staff rather than waiting for them to visit you. Establish the key players and the people who can and want to help.

- **E-Mail**

Where a large proportion of the users are on e-mail it is an easy way of reaching them, quickly and cheaply. It can be targeted more precisely than most other methods and so is effective at reaching specific audiences. I have found that staff responds quicker to e-mails than any other medium. By maintaining up-to-date address lists different user groups can be targeted with different versions of the advertising 'message'.

- **The Internet**

The Internet has the power to improve the library's image and to allow the library to offer enhanced services. Although it takes time to set up and maintain services on the Internet, it can reap rewards in terms of user satisfaction and recognition. A Library Web home page serves as a promotional tool advertising in-house library services and electronic information resources on the web. The pages should include an e-mail link to the library making the librarian easy to contact.

- **Newsletters and Leaflets**

Newsletters and leaflets are both a means of delivering information. A newsletter can be used to list interesting new web sites, new journals and online services, and perhaps more general science news of interest. It does not have to be long but should be produced on a regular basis. Leaflets and guides can be handed out, and displayed on notice boards. The library notice board should be in a prominent place.

- **The library Website**

Since the library website is the face of the library, the webpage should be designed in such a way that the required information is easy to locate. The page should not only shoe the traditional information buy should also up coming events, new arrival, subscription offers, talks and new services. The website should have the facilities to accept feedback and should have contact details of the library staff.

Marketing and Library and Information Services (MLIS)

MLIS requires a critical analysis of the marketing mix (the 7 Ps of Marketing - product, place, price, promotion, Participants, Physical Evidence and Process) to identify the nature, features, benefits, and value of the products to the customer. The development of an effective marketing strategy requires the specification of the marketing mix. These concepts are utilized in the for-profit sector, but a good library-marketing plan will also profit (in the most altruistic sense, of course!) by examining products offered and assessing the value of the products to the users. Market research helps to determine what library users are looking for in the way of product features such as variety, quality, and design, and what benefits such as good performance, quality, reliability and durability users demand in services, systems, programs, and resources.

The following table shows the 7P's of Marketing in MLIS.

7 Ps	Definition
Product	Products or services of the general reference and information service department. This is, of course, the information, reference, and ancillary services that add value such as personal assistance, referral services, online database searches, document delivery, and interlibrary loan.
Price	Pricing of use of the library is usually that of the time and effort the user spends traveling to the library, as well as the time and effort spent searching for and examining materials and cost of a foregone alternative activity.
Place	Place of service, based upon knowledge of the market of a library, is essential in order to identify users and their discrete information needs and wants. Also, this location element has effect upon how the library can best access their product offerings. To expand the service area, the library may have branches, bookmobiles, or electronic access, FAX, and telephone calls, etc.
Promotion	Promotion includes utilizing persuasive information about general information services, and communicating this information to target market segments that are potential users. Five kinds of promotion include: publicity, public relations, personal representatives, advertising, and sales promotion.
Participants	All human actors who play a part in reference and information services delivery, namely the library's personnel.
Physical Evidence	The environment in which the reference and information services are delivered that facilitates the performance and communication of the service.
Process	The procedures, mechanisms and flow of activities by which the reference and information services are acquired.

Role of Librarian in Marketing

'Benson identifies eight roles for librarians in a global network environments they are;

1. As intermediaries
2. As information evaluators
3. As information organizers
4. As planners and policy makers
5. As internet access Providers
6. As Publishers
7. As navigators
8. As educators

Service is a customer-oriented result. This result is produced when an organization performs activities that are oriented towards meeting customer needs and expectations. The products and services, the libraries can offer vary from print to electronic information. In electronic environment the services include; websites as products; monitoring of internets and internet for web browsing and e-mail service through pass word protected information.

Conclusion

As librarians we should be actively marketing and promoting our library services. The basic aim of marketing is to know and understand our users in order that the library is able to satisfy those needs in an effective way. A marketing plan is an essential tool which will enable us to focus our efforts. The market plan should assess where you are now (market research), where you are going (objectives) and how you are going to get there (strategies).

References

Dragon, A. C.: "Marketing the library". Wilson library bulletin, 53(7), 1979, pp.498-502.

Kotler, Philip: Marketing for non-profit organizations. Ed.2. New Delhi: Prentice-Hall of India, 1985.

Katz, B. and William 1988, How to market professional services, Prentice Hall.

Stanton, W. J. : Fundamentals of marketing. New York: McGraw-Hill, 1981.

28

ICT among State Agricultural University and ICAR Institutes Libraries in India: An Overview of E-Granth

Jadhav U.S.
Assistant Librarian
Karnataka Veterinary, Animal and Fishery Sciences University
Nandinagar, Bidar-585401

Introduction

E-publishing and information accessing have become easy and convenient mainly because of Internet and the World Wide Web technologies. Most digital libraries were developed in the past by taking up projects based on specific disciplines and then developed into full-fledged digital libraries. The inter-networking communication links, low cost storage solutions, powerful desktops, workstations, servers and multimedia hardware and software technologies are now available for initiating the Digital Library projects in India. Development in ICT (Information Communication technology) have brought about the merger of the computing, information, Communication, entertainment, mass media industries thereby providing a means of exchanging information in the digital format used by computers.

What is ICT?

ICT are the hardware and software that enable society to create, collect, consolidate, and communicate information in multimedia formats and for various purposes.

National Agricultural Innovation Project (NAIP)

NAIP is world's second biggest World Bank assisted agriculture project being executed by NARS with a lifespan of seven years, started from July 24, 2006 to 2014 and it has been extended up to March 2014 with 26 New Partner Libraries. The objective of the NAIP is to facilitate an accelerated and sustainable transformation of the Indian agriculture, so that it can support poverty alleviation and income generation through collaborative development and application of agricultural innovations by the public organizations in partnership with farmers, the private sector and other stakeholders. Among the 4 components of NAIP, the component- I aim at bringing in the organizational changes in the NARS so that it becomes a dynamic innovation system, capable of responding to the present as well as the future needs of Indian agricultural research development. The emphasis inter alia is on:

1. Strengthening of the ICAR NET
2. Digitized content creation and knowledge management
3. Strengthening of libraries of SAUs and ICAR institutes into the fully electronic libraries connected over the ICAR Net
4. Formation of an ICAR e-journal Consortium for centralized subscription of eresources and information sharing in the agricultural domain at national level, etc.

It is important to mention here that the current web based information systems, services, networks and library related ICT based implementations, i.e. KrishiPrabha, CeRA, eGranth, etc. being innovative things; have been supported through NAIP.

It provides digital access to library resources of different research institutes and agricultural universities which include OPAC, important institutional repositories, rare books and old journals and makes them publically accessible over internet under NARS with Online Computer Library Center (OCLC) partnership.

Overview of eGranth Consortium

NARS has a very large collection of repositories in agriculture and allied sciences, spread all over the country in different libraries, academic institutions, museums, and in authors' collections. This invaluable heritage has to be documented, preserved and made easily accessible to end users, for which digitization is the solution. "Strengthening of Digital Library and Information Management" under NARS (e-GRANTH)' is a subproject under component-1 of National Agricultural Innovation Project (NAIP), Indian Council of Agricultural Research (ICAR). National Agricultural Research System (NARS) in India comprises of Agricultural Research Institutions and Agricultural Universities.

It provides digital access to library resources of 38 different research institutes and agricultural universities which include OPAC, important institutional repositories, rare books and old journals, etc. and makes them publically accessible over Internet under NARS with Online Computer Library Center (OCLC) partnership. AgriCat is the major activity of the eGranth Consortium Project and responsible for the Union Catalogue of partner libraries and making the resources accessible to each other with the help of OCLC, USA. So it is necessary to comprehensively cover the eGranth Consortium Project.

Objective

Library management includes automation of Acquisition, Serials Management, Circulation and Online Public Access Catalogue (OPAC). Open source software like Koha, NewGenLib are fairly powerful software comparable or even better than some the commercial software. One of the experts has recommended adopting KOHA as it is Indian origin and is compliant to local requirements. In addition, technical support which includes legacy data migration, annual maintenance etc., is offered by third party organizations.

1. To create OPAC under "Indian Agricultural Research Group Catalogue" of all partner library resources with OCLC partnership.
2. To digitize important institutional repositories (limited to IARI, New Delhi; IVRI, Izatnagar; ANGRAU, Hyderabad, UAS, Bangalore and shortly considering Madras Agricultural University, Chennai) including rare books and old journals and make them open access under NARS.

3. To strengthen capacity building for Library and Information Management System (open to all libraries of NARS).
4. Implementation of KOHA (Library Management Software) among all new Partner's Libraries of eGranth Project.

Following are the major tasks:

1. To make all records created in other software so far in the MARC 21 files formats and upload them to WorldCat.
2. To catalogue the unfinished items in the libraries meeting world standards and upload them to WorldCat.
3. To create the "local interfaces" for displaying the Indian Agricultural Library Group India catalogue.

Types of Digital Resources under e-Granth

Digital material can be taken as computer readable material in general.

1. Theses, annual reports, newsletters, success stories, special bulletins, convocation addresses, endowment lectures, faculty/scientists' profiles.
2. Pre-prints, authors' collections, monographs, handbooks, course curricula, lecture schedules, lecture notes, proceedings of trainings, ppts.
3. Important reports of committees, notifications, projects, statistical reports.
4. Archives of heritage value such as awards, certificates, visitors' handbooks, rare photos.
5. Digital objects of plant varieties, insects, nematodes, microbes, audio/video recordings, etc.

The major tasks:

- Identification of documents for Digitization based on the central catalogue.
- Scanning and OCR of the documents prior to conversion to search able PDF documents.
- Storage of e-Documents in Digital Repository Software at centralized facility.

The following Strategy in the digitization process under eGranth

1. Digitization of M.Sc, M.V.Sc, M.F.Sc, and Ph.D theses would be done under Krishi Prabha project. Syllabi, postgraduate records, lecture notes, class schedule etc. are being included under AGROWEB and another NAIP project, and these are not included here.
2. A local-level committee appointed by the Director of institute/ VC of the university would be solely responsible for the selection of digitization resources, outsourcing of the job, ensuring the quality of production, OCR, digital preservation, appointment of consultants and uploading in the website for online access by end-users of NARS etc. A common standard protocol would be developed for all the institutes for strict compliance.
3. The priority has been given to repositories in the public domain and our own institutional repositories for which we need not seek permission for copyright.
4. It is likely that digital copies of 60% of rare books and old journals may be available due to multiple projects being undertaken or completed globally including by the publishers. Some of our libraries may be having multiple print holdings of same resources. With the above assumption, only 40% of the resources under this category are included in deriving the cost of digitization. The copyright issues need to be addressed before digitization. Consultation with other digital library projects would be availed in the form of consultancy.
5. Training to both library staff and temporary employees engaged in this project would be imparted in digitization work so that the skills and knowledge in continuing to execute the job are upgraded.
6. Need-based outsourcing of this job to reputed and experienced vendors would be allowed.
7. The job of metadata creation can be partly done under in-house arrangement and partly by the vendors.
8. Group training to those involved in library management including tenurial staff appointed under this consortium would be given.

9. Hands-on training on maintenance of digital library and repositories will be additionally given by the vendors.

For example: scanning a page producing a computer readable (digital) image of the paper within the computer. The computer only recognizes a digital picture of the page. The second stage is to have the computer extract information from the digitized image. For text, it is done by Optical Character Recognition (OCR) software to convert the text image into ASCII format for editing and manipulation of information and to store in textual format.

Digital Library: A digital library is a library in which all collections of a library are stored in digital formats, and anyone can access to this collections without any barrier. The digital content may be stored locally, or accessed remotely via computer networks. A digital library is a highly organized collection of electronic resources.

Purposes of Digitization: There are three major reasons for digitization endeavours: (i) there is a need to preserve endangered library resources, (ii) improvement of the efficiency of information search mechanisms, and (iii) digitization improves access to library resources. Most libraries are digitizing materials which might be lost in the future, such as old manuscripts, research projects, photo images, analogue maps, non-live musical recordings, government official gazettes and several other historical records.

Institutional Repository: An institutional repository (IR) is a web-based database (repository) of any institute's scholarly materials. Include works of various stages in the process of scholarly inquiry. In addition to published works, an IR may include preprints, theses & dissertations, images, data sets, working papers, course materials, or anything else a contributor deposits. The main task of institutional repository is to collect the scholarly materials to store and disseminate in digital format for widely used.

Implementation of KOHA

Under e-Granth sub-project of NAIP project of ICAR, all ICAR and SAUs libraries are moving from their respective commercial LMS (Library Management Software) to uniform Open source software KOHA, without any compromising of quality of services. Koha has been successfully implemented in all the 12 old partner libraries and further, issued guidelines for 26 new partner libraries for the implementations.

It facilitates

1. To import bibliographic information from agricultural and other libraries at national and international level.
2. Auto reminders to user for returning the borrowed books.
3. Online feedback of users.
4. Online reservation of books required by users and auto-intimation as whenever book is returned in library.

Available Technologies

Under e-Granth sub-project of NAIP project has already taken care of Hardware and software for digitization of the documents. Digitizing and converting the images to information are very difficult tasks. The computer hardware and particularly the software that performs these functions are good and practical but less than perfect. Optical scanners have high resolution, but are mechanical devices. They need single sheets of paper, which means photocopying the material first. Now there are efficient book scanners to fill this gap. Optical Character Recognition (OCR) may result in errors, which have to be manually corrected. This is particularly true if the material is old and in mixed languages, faded etc. Even after digitization the problem of searching and finding information is often difficult. The bandwidth connections, compatible browsers etc. also should take in to consideration.

Copyright (eGranth)

Ownership of the Material

Under e-Granth sub-project of NAIP project of ICAR taken care of copyrights and having a copy of the material does not mean ownership in terms of copyright laws. There is only one copyright owner even though many copies are made. This is true of computer copies, digitized or physical copies apart from the conventional print form. Further, right to re-distribute material usually is not acquired when a copy of the material is bought. Many allow material for copying for research purpose by individuals, under the fair use clause of the copyright laws. However, making copies for re-sale or re-distribution is a matter that comes under the copyright law.

Like the physical material, the digital material of the library is valuable. Access to it must be guarded. Security for the digital material should be provided in the form of restricted access to the computers that hold the digital material. Unlike the physical stock, the digital material must be copied and secured. This protects it from natural disaster, damage and software errors. Access security must be allowed for in the digital library. There is need to evolve a method of authorization for persons to access the digital library.

Standards, Formats and Protocols (eGranth)

These are the rules by which objects are described, their data are stored and the systems communicate. In all these cases, the function is to try to unify the representation, manipulation or transmission of some piece of information so that two or more different systems can understand it in the same way. The standards are the basis of interoperability, portability, modularity and building blocks, etc. The standards fall into three major areas: material description, user access and system architecture. Under the material description, we need to look at two forms - the abstracted information (Metadata) which constitutes the bibliographic description in a library system. The other form is the material itself. Description standards include SGML and HTML from the web and PDF, etc.

i. Bibliographic standards are: MARC II, Dublin Core, Metadata, AACR, URL etc.

ii. Record structures are: ISO 2709, Extensible Markup Language (XML) and Hypertext Markup Language (HTML).

iii. Encoding standards are: Unicode, ASCII.

Capacity Building (eGranth)

Digitization is complex process good staff training at an early stage is important. Training in project management is valuable for those engaged in digitization projects where many partners and providers are involved in collaborative programs. Some of the young library professionals who were short-listed for training abroad under INDO-US Knowledge Initiative can be accommodated under this project. A select list of Co-PIs may be deputed to National Agricultural Library, USA. and FAO, Rome for orientation training on digital library. Annual conference will be held to sensitize users on library information management systems and digital libraries.

Training of library professionals and other staff associated with the project includes:

The national trainings can be arranged at ICRISAT, Hyderabad or IARI, New Delhi.

1. Digital library software & OAI-PMH.
2. Library automation and WorldCat.
3. Digital library Content Management Standards.
4. Capacity building of librarians and other professionals on library management with reference to union catalogue.
5. Creation, organization and management of online digital libraries and institutional repositories.

Technical Issues Involved (eGranth)

- High bandwidth computer networks supporting efficient multimedia document transfer. The infrastructure is critical in a digital library setup. A fiber optic backbone connecting the computers in the university with at least 2Mb Internet connectivity.
- Open communication protocols (client-server, Z39.50 for IR). This will enable the servers in the network to get connected and query and retrieve data without knowing the environment of the other library.
- Information access tools (browsers, display and search tools). The Netscape Navigator and Internet Explorer etc.
- Meta databases (databases that describe and provide links to other databases). Cataloguing the web resources with description, access, retrieval etc.
- Electronic publishing tools. Necessary for creating the resources to make available on the Net.
- Data compression for data transfer electronically and achieving the digital resources.
- Digital storage devices like CD / DVD media and the large Hard disk storage solutions now available.
- Scanning and conversion technologies. The issues and methods for scanning and OCR technology are critical in converting the printed texts, photographs, audio etc.

- Media integration technology (multimedia) to make the digital resources more powerful in delivering the material integrating the text with multimedia.
- Advanced retrieval, indexing, routing and filtering etc. This is essential as the digital data needs a better controlling mechanism for accurate retrieval from the user end.
- Document description and representation standards (SGML). The standard description and representation in electronic format is essential for network access to the digital resources.
- Inter-operability over the network. Any information stored in any server in any platform should be built for access over the complicated network environment.
- Privacy, authentication and security of information. The information stored needs security and access needs proper authentication. Building firewalls to protect the data from hacking etc.
- Location dependent naming of digital source.

Conclusion

The recent scenario of world's libraries are changing very fast by ICT based products & services. The change enforced by ICT, to adoption of products and services of ICT in libraries are robust indicator of this response. It provides a means for overcoming historically intractable problems of isolation and lack of access to information and knowledge, crucial impediments to libraries development. The eGranth is a fast developing project of the NAIP and one of the most important web based agricultural information systems and services for the NARS users, Libraries and Librarians and have so far been most successful, starting with the NATP (National Agricultural Technology Project) model. The mission and objectives of the eGranth and its AgriCat component are being achieved especially as far as libraries, librarians, web based systems and services under NARS are concerned. The practical outcomes have started coming from all the point of views of the project and it has given new directions to the access facilities of NARS libraries and will achieve its goals and new heights as per its mandate in the time to come.

References

http://www.ukoln.ac.uk Accessed July 12, 2013

http://www.naip.icar.org.inAccessed July 16, 2013.

http://connexion.oclc.org. - Accessed July 16, 2013

http// www.oclc.org. - Accessed July 12, 2013.

http//www.worldcat.org.Worldcat -. Accessed July 12, 2013.

Nabi Hassan, (2011). Agricat@egranth: Consortium Access to NARS Institutional Repositories. In" International Journal of Digital Library Services", Vol.1, Nos. 2,Oct. - Dec, (2011) pp. 49-59.

OCLC Connexion Services - Accessed July 12, 2013.

29

Innovative Practices in Management of Agricultural Libraries of Chhattisgarh

Madhav Pandey
Librarian, Nehru Library
Indira Gandhi Agricultural University, Raipur 492012, Chhattisgarh
Email- raipurpandey@gmail.com

Introduction

The Indian Council of Agricultural Research is the apex body for co-coordinating, guiding and managing research and education in agriculture including horticulture, fisheries and animal sciences in the entire country with more than hundred and above ICAR libraries and fifty six state agricultural universities libraries spread across the country this is one of the largest national agricultural library network in the in the country under consortium of e-Resources in Agriculture. The Indian Council of Agricultural Research (ICAR) has contributed a lot towards strengthening of Agricultural Libraries via modern Information Technological (IT) tools. ICAR has sanctioned so many projects under National Agricultural Technology Project and National Agricultural Innovative Projects i.e e-Granth, CeRA, Krishiprabha, Krishikosh Agricat etc. for strengthening and development of agricultural libraries. These are useful to manage knowledge explosion and helpful in libraries to providing information effectively to the end user of society.

Agricultural Libraries of Chhattisgarh

The State of Chhattisgarh was formed on 1st November 2000 and represent predominate tribal area of country. Its economy is depending on agriculture. Similarly, to achieve self sufficiency in food production, Chhattisgarh Government has given priority to promote agricultural education in state. Therefore, continuously various agricultural, horticulture, agricultural engineering and fisheries colleges have been created. University like Chhattisgarh Kamdenu University, Research Institute and Krishi Vigyan Kendra and its libraries are open and ruining in this state.

Indira Gandhi Krishi Vishwavidyalaya (IGKV), Raipur was established on 20th January, 1987 after bifurcating from Jawaharlal Nehru Krishi Vishwavidyalaya, Jabalpur. From that time to this date, the University has been expanded several fold. The jurisdiction area of IGKV is the entire Chhattisgarh State situated in Eastern India consisting of 27 districts having 3 different Agro climatic Zones. Agricultural Libraries in Chhattisgarh are working under Indira Gandhi Krishi Vishwavidyalya, Raipur Nehru Library (Central Library) IGKV, Raipur, Library, College of Agriculture, Jagdalpur, Library, College of Agriculture, Ambikapur, Library, College of Agriculture, Bilaspur, Library, College of Agriculture, Kawardha, Library, College of Agriculture, Champa Janjgir, Library, College of Agriculture, Bhatapara, Library, College of Agriculture, Raigarh, Library, College of Agriculture, Koria, Library, College of Agriculture, Kanker, Library, College of Agriculture, Rajnandgaon, Library, College of Horticulture, Rajnandgaon, Library, College of Horticulture, Jagdalpur, Library Faculty of Agricultural Engineering, Raipur, Library, BRSM College of Agricultural Engineering, Mungeli, In field of Vet.& Animal Husbandry under Chhattisgarh Kamdhenu Vishwavidyalya, Anjora, Durg following Libraries are working:-Library, College of Vet. Sc. & A.H. Anjora, Durg, Library College of Dairy Technology, Raipur, Library, College of Fisheries, Kawardha. Some private college libraries are also provide innovative services inChhattisgarh i.e.Library, Shri Ram College of Agriculture, Rajnandgaon, Library, Bhartiya College of Agriculture, Durg, Library, Bhoramdev College of Agriculture, Kawardha, Library, Chhattisgarh College of Agriculture, Bhilai, Durg, Library, College of Agriculture, Ambagarh Chwoki, Library, College of Agriculture, Dantewada, Library, College of Agriculture, Raigarh, Library,

Mahamaya College of Agriculture, Dhamtari, Library, Mardarshan College of Agriculture, Ambikapur, Library, S.K. College of Agriculture, Kawardha

Nehru Library, Indira Gandhi Krishi Vishwavidyalya, Raipur

The Nehru Library established in 1987 after IGKV came in to existence by bifurcation from JNKVV Jabalpur. Before that it was the library of College of Agriculture, Raipur. The Nehru Library of IGKV has been well equipped with the modern automated tools. This was possible by the help of ICAR and Chhattisgarh Government supported for it's infra structure development and provided other facilities. The library is functioning as Central University Library for constituent and affiliated colleges of Indira Gandhi Krishi Vishwavidyalya .The library is maintaining 60 thousand collections in addition with 300 regular Indian and foreign journals, and their back volumes and various e-Resources . Library is linked with consortium for e-Resources in Agriculture and Indian thesis repository *Krishiprabha* for online journals and thesis information.

Innovative Practices in Agricultural Libraries

Under NARS (e-GRANTH)' is a sub-project under component-1 of National Agricultural Innovation Project (NAIP), Indian Council of Agricultural Research (ICAR). National Agricultural Research System (NARS) in India comprises of Agricultural Research Institutions and Agricultural Universities. It provides digital access to library resources of 27 different research institutes and agricultural universities which include OPAC, important institutional repositories, rare books and old journals and makes them publically accessible over internet under NARS with Online Computer Library Center (OCLC) partnership.

Objectives To create Online Public Access Catalog (OPAC) under "Indian Agricultural Research Group Catalogue" of all 27 library resources with Online Computer Library Center (OCLC) partnership.To digitize important institutional repositories (limited to IARI, New Delhi; IVRI, Izatnagar; ANGRAU, Hyderabad and UAS, Bangalore) including rare books and old journals and make them open access under NARS. To strengthen capacity building for library and information management system (open to all libraries of NARS).Implementation of Koha (Library

Management Software) in Partner's Libraries. The National Agenda for Governance, which is the Government's policy blueprint, has taken due note of the ICT Revolution that is sweeping the globe. Project Gutenberg, Google Book Search, Windows Live Search Books, Internet Archive, the Library of Congress World Digital Library, the digital library at the University of Michigan, and the Million Book Project completed in partnership with India. China and USA are considered leaders in the field of digital archive creation and management. Many Indian Libraries have taken up the challenge of modernization to develop the Machine Readable Catalogue (MARC) and machine readable full text documents to provide greater accessibility to full text databases of different nature, changing the focus of public libraries from providing library services to the fulfilling the long pending focus of Right To Information. The National Knowledge Commission has recently recommended an Open Access mandate for publicly funded research. Indian National Agricultural Research System (NARS) has a very large collection of institutional repositories in agriculture and allied sciences, spread over the country in different libraries of ICAR Institutes and State Agricultural Universities (SAUs). Digitization of these valuable archives would allow online access to researchers, teachers and students to which they would not otherwise have an easy access. Duplication of record creation can be avoided by pooling the efforts through common electronic protocols. Union Catalogues are useful to librarians, as they assist in locating and requesting materials from other libraries through interlibrary loan service.

AgriCat @ e-Granth

AgriCat is a union catalogue useful to all library users as well as librarians. AgriCat helps in locating and sharing materials among group of libraries. Duplication of effort in record creation (cataloguing) is avoided by pooling the efforts through common electronic protocols. Indian National Agricultural Research System (NARS) has a very large collection of printed resources in agriculture and allied sciences, spread all over the country in different libraries of ICAR institutes and State Agricultural Universities. AgriCat being a common union catalogue of these valuable archives allows sharing and online access to researchers, teachers and students and other stakeholders to which they would not otherwise have access. AgriCat has been developed using 'connexion' which is a middleware tool for cataloguing using WorldCat database. This tool has been deployed in NARS for cataloguing and creating AgriCat as a subgroup of WorldCat. Internationally accepted protocols have been used e.g., Z39.50 is a client-server protocol for searching and retrieving information from remote computer databases. It is covered by ANSI/NISO standard Z39.50, and ISO standard 23950. The standard's maintenance agency is the Library of Congress. The AgriCat group catalogue is available at http://www.egranth.ac.in/AgriCat.html or http://www.agricat.worldcat.org/ which can be accessed on 24x7 basis and provide versatile search and retrieval facilities to share library resources. The search is available at three layers global search (Libraries Worldwide), group search (AgriCat libraries) and the individual library search (Local level). A user can also register and create his own mini library using the feature like MyList, MyWatch List, MySaved Searches for further use.

Consortium for E-Resources in Agriculture (CeRA) http://www.cera.jccc.in (Online journal Portal ICAR)

More than 3000 scientific research journals are availa ble online through Consortium for e-Resources in Agriculture. To develop the existing R & D information resource base of ICAR, Institutes/universities, etc., comparable to that existing in world's leading Institutions/organizations, To subscribe e-journals and create an e-access culture among, Scientists/teachers in ICAR institutes/agricultural universities, • To develop a Science Citation Index (SCI) Facility at IARI for evaluation ofScientific publications, • To assess the impact of CeRA on the level of research publications measured through SCI.It is a customized solution for accessing and sharing journal literature subscribed by all the 142 participating libraries in the consortia , individually and collectively, through CeRA Consortium.Gives full text access to 3000 journals to all the libraries from 3 consortia subscribed publishers –Annual Reviews, CSIRO(Australia) and Springer, In addition gives access to metadata of journals from 635 publishers for those journals libraries subscribe and also Open Access Journals. The Consortium consists of the following organizations under NARS: five deemed Universities, three ICAR Headquarters and Krishi Anusandhan Bhawans, five National Bureau, fifty institutes, thirty Ntional Research Centres, nine Project Directorates, forty five State Agricultural Universities etc.

Documentary delivery systems are to be developed at IARI, NDRI, IVRI and CIFE to enable those. Consortium partners who do not have the print versions of particular scientific articles. Periodic reporting of the activities of the Consortium from time to time CeRA is Consortium of e-journals being subscribed by NAIP, ICAR and provided access to 123 libraries of Agriculture (NARS) . *IGKV Raipur is also one of the Libraries among 142*. Through this service the user can access the following three major on-line Portals and Bouquet of Journals from Publishers with full text of an articles.1. Springerlink : It is a platform of Springer and product of bouquet of e-journals on different Subjects publishing by Springer. Through this Bouquet user can access the full text of around 1100+ journals since 1996. 2. Annual Reviews : Annual Reviews are authoritative, analytic reviews in 34 focused disciplines within the Biomedical, Life, Physical, and Social Sciences etc., T hrough this product user can access the full text of an articles from 1990 onwards. 3. CSIRO (Australia) : Australia's Commonwealth Scientific and Industrial Research Organization (CSIRO) : Through this product user can access full text of complete package.4. JCCC (J-Gate Custom Content for Consortia) : It is an Contents database collected from journals being subs cribed by all 142 Libraries individually for the year 2008 (Not through Consortium) under NARS. This database is customized product of M/S Informatics, Bangalore and covers the contents of only periodical which have electronic version and also given link to approximately 4000+ open acess journals since year 2000..Jccc@cera covers in all 3000 journals.

Krishiprabha : Online Indian Agriculture Doctoral Dissertation Repository Krishiprabh http://www.totalotalit.co.in/hau/thesis.html

These doctoral dissertations are one of the very important and valuable original sources of information. There is a need to unveil this resource to the scientists across the world. This objective can be achieved if: Indian Agricultural Doctoral Dissertations Repository is set up for the preservation of information enshrined in them for the posterity and for the use of the current generation;. The Repository, s established, is used for evaluation of research findings, and the evaluation reports are used for further pursuit and generation of agricultural knowledge;3. Repository is utilized for the creation of electronic Database of Doctoral Dissertations; 4. the Database, so created, is made accessible online to the national and international users; and 5. the same Database is further utilized for the publication of an e-journal reporting abstracts of the dissertations in order to disseminate information. Access to doctoral dissertations is severely restricted due to the absence of an appropriate policy and infrastructure. Agricultural research, especially in developing countries such as India, forms an important domain of enquiry due to the vital role it plays in the economy, and in combating and eradicating hunger. A systematic effort to develop and maintain a national repository of these resources, digitize them and make them accessible online would facilitate their potential use for extracting maximum value from them. Use of modern information and communication technologies for effective data capturing, organization, storage and retrieval will enhance the value of these resources further. In this backdrop, the present project was envisioned to establish, develop and maintain a repository of Indian agricultural doctoral dissertation. More than 1800 doctoral dissertations are produced in India every year in agriculture and allied disciplines. The maintenance of the Digital Library 15000 collection in e-form Main objectives is to develop, organize and sustain knowledge base of Indian Agricultural Dissertations in digital form and make it accessible online.

Krishikosh: An Institutional Repository http://krishikosh.egranth.ac.in/

ICAR and SAUs are maintained rare documents, database, theses records etc. for sharing of such type of knowledge in users. Krishikosh is found are very useful repository for agricultural community.

Innovative Practices in Agricultural Libraries of Chhattisgarh

The impact of innovative practices can be observed in the libraries of agricultural colleges/universities in Chhattisgarh which are commendable and has created better reading environment. Innovative practices i.e. automation of library services in such a way that the information can be made available on just a single click of computer mouse and makes them available via LAN locally and via internet globally. Innovative practices in agricultural libraries include digitization, retrospective conversion, data entry, bar code generation and labeling, bar-coded circulation, OPAC, E-subscription/ online journals and various data bases CD-ROMs. e-resource, resource sharing, resources use through consortia are functioning smoothly

The libraries of Chhatisgarh are equipped with latest communication media and information technology like Internet access, CD-ROM Search of various agencies and is well connected through LAN. Library Records are digitized and available on key board developed various database, Retro conversion of rare material from physical to electronic form, Documentation services, Current Awareness and Selective Dissemination of Information Service, through, Documentation List, Library Bulletin, Current, Contents of Journals, Electronic form of user profile & document profile, Cumulative Index of Journals , Bibliography of IGKV Thesis, Abstract of IGKV Thesis, e-learning , e-class room virtual learning, teaching and training for electronic access, are the part of innovative practices in library.. In house repository is also maintained by the library.

Some other innovative practices are also useful for agricultural libraries of Chhattisgarh i.e. Web base library services, document delivery, through e-mail, online access facility, citation analysis, review literature using database, electronic resource management, creation of institutional repository, use of web technology, creation of web page, web page designing, using open source software, learning, resources, sharing, cloud computing, RFID, agricultural information through mobile technology, latest information, through web etc.

Conclusion

Today, role of library and information centers are more important compare than other system for the growth and development of society. The study concludes that innovative practices in library management of Chhattisgarh especially in agricultural libraries, such as *Union catalogue AGRICAT, e-Granth, Consortium of e Resources in Agriculture (CeRA), Krishiprabha* etc. can play a significant role in increasing library services more effectively and better cooperation. They also improve teaching and research environment with qualitative output of any organization. Systematic contribution under National Agricultural Research System in India to increase the effective usage for sharing of Agricat, e-Granth, CeRA, Krishiprabha and various e-resources should expand under ICAR umbrella. Study strongly recommends that relevant authorities must provide the necessary and relevant support such as connectivity, equipments, funds, technical support to all libraries related to agriculture. Such innovative practices in libraries will definitely helpful to improve library services in digital era.

References

AgriCat@eGranth http://www.egranth.ac.in/AgriCat.html

Consortium for e resources in Agriculture JCCC@CERA http://www.cera.jccc.in/

Indira Gandhi Krishi Vishwavidyalaya Raipur http://www.igau.edu.in

Krishiprabha http://14.139.232.167:8080/equestthesis/

Nehru library, IGKV Raipur http:/igkvkohaopac.firstray.in/

Pandey, Madhav 2012. Problems and prospects in managing e-resources in agricultural library system in proceeding National Conference of Agricultural Librarians and user community NCALUC-2011, Transformation of Agricultural Library in Collaborative Era at Solan 17-11 Nov. 2011, Organized by Association of Agricultural Librarians and Document lists of India in association with Dr, Y.P.S. Parmar University of Horticulture and Forestry, Nauni Solan (H.P.) . edited by M.S. Pathania, K. Veeranjaneyulu, Indveir Mohan, Prem Singh and P. Visakhi pub. by BSP Publication Hyderabad. Theme paper:191-198.

Pandey, Madhav. 2011. Study of usefulness of e-resources in agricultural research and teaching Paper presented and published in National Conference on Agricultural Libraries and user community 2011 on "Agricultural Libraries in the knowledge web" 24-25 February 2011. Organized by Indian Agricultural Research Institute Library, New Delhi. :5

Pandey, Madhav, 2010. Impact of Automation in Agricultural Libraries and Information System. Paper presented and published in National Conference on Knowledge Management in the Globalized Era. 21-23 April 2010. Organized by Association of Agricultural Librarians and Documentalists of India in association with Indian Council of Agricultural Research Library and Indian Agricultural Statistics Research Institute Library, New Delhi. Lead paper:501-506

30

Harnessing Access to Information and Knowledge in Digital Libraries

Rabindra K. Mahapatra
Chief Librarian, Orissa University of Agriculture & Technology, Bhubaneswar Odisha.
and
Yadunath Prasad
Assistant Librarian, U.P. Pt. DDU Veterinary University, Mathura-281001

Introduction

As we all know that the 21st century has witnessed the changing phenomenon of information and its communication resulting a dynamic transformation not only in the social structure but also in the perception of human mind. Exchange of information and knowledge has empowered the human being and enabled them to achieve sustainable development. From paper- based society to paperless society, information has remained the most valuable commodity. In the traditional paper based society, information is being largely used in traditional libraries. But in the present era information is communicated in soft form through networked environment. The paperless society was conceived by Lancaster in 1978 which has become a reality. It is due to the advent of ICTs that has enabled access to vast resources of information at a single place within a short time. The users have changed their information seeking behavior and demand resources and services from the libraries electronically. The emergence of digital technology using digital media has accelerated the growth and development of information in soft form and made the communication process more vibrant and dynamic. The proliferation of information in different formats creates problem of access. In case of traditional library where paper-based information and communication system is confined to library and information centers, instant access appears to be limited. But, in a vibrant system of communication where everybody can access to information located in remote library and information centers through a network is termed digital information. The resultant phenomenon is the emergence of digital libraries where instant and easy access to scholarly information is guaranteed. Since the publication process of all types of materials is made electronically, the formation of digital library is inevitable.

Digital Libraries: Concept and Definitions

The concept of digital library is based on the system where facility has been developed to have instant and easy access to contents of a document available in a library through the help of ICTs. The library scientists face the access problem and question themselves how can we ensure that our faculty and students will have the access they need to the world's scientific, technological and other literature. The collaboration of library scientists and information technologists resulted in the development of digital libraries. When a library converts its documentary resources into electronic formats and makes those available in a network for easy access and use, it is digital library. A library, desiring to make its resources digital, should develop its collection of digital objects such as texts, video and audio and organize in such a manner for larger dissemination though a network.

A new paradigm for the digital library has been developed (Berring 1993) through the creation of bibliographic, factual and full text databases, the application of powerful inquiry technologies, and their linkage through complex communications networks. The model is referred to as the 'digital library', 'virtual library' or even 'cybrary'. In its narrowest sense the digital or virtual library can be considered to be merely an "online repository of electronic texts" (Ince 2001) or "electronic stock of information which can be accessed via databases" (Dictionary of Library and Information Management 1997). Both of these definitions focus on storage and access to content but miss the other dimensions of a library. "A system providing the services of a library in digital form" (Johnston, Gregory et al. 2000) offers an alternative definition which better describes a library operating electronically.

Borgman (1999) is of the same opinion with Digital Library Federation (1998) which states that digital libraries have unique characteristics that differ from traditional libraries and their approaches to information provision. From a traditional librarian's point of view, digital libraries present a transformative model of a large-scale, user-centric organization that is moving towards an integrated form with various components. However, the main purpose of digital libraries remains consistent with that of traditional libraries in that the purpose of digital libraries is to organize, distribute, and preserve information resources just as it is for traditional libraries. Lynch (1994) says that, "digital Libraries provide users with coherent success to a very large, organized repository of information and knowledge."

Digital libraries ascertain the instant information provision irrespective of time and space. One is elimination of the time and space constraints of traditional "bricks-and-mortar libraries". Unlike libraries that occupy buildings accessible only to those who walk through their doors, digital libraries reside on inter-networked data storage and computing systems that can be accessed by people located anywhere in the world. When the full potential of a digital library is realized for a particular community, people shall be able to access all human knowledge hosted in that digital database from any location. Digital libraries that are accessible over the Internet provide opportunities to advance knowledge and improve the possibility of required scholarly information at hand.

According to Unesco, a digital library is an online collection of digital objects, of assured quality, that are created or collected and managed according to internationally accepted principles for collection development and made accessible in a coherent and sustainable manner, supported by services necessary to allow users to retrieve and exploit the resources.

According to Leiner (1998), the digital library is a collection of services and collection of information objects that supports users in dealing with information objects available directly or indirectly via electronic/digital means. In other words, a digital library is based on the process of converting very useful resources in electronic form and making them available online in a searchable and browsable form to achieve universal access to information and knowledge.

A modern library must include the concept of digital library as an integral part of its infrastructure and services. The most useful collection should be converted into digital formats which are required to be effectively managed and made accessible to a large number of users. Some digital libraries develop networks to meet the information needs of specific group of users. This is a collaborative effort of those partner libraries forming a consortium who share and exchange their digital collection through a system of interoperability. The long run benefit of a digital library is developing digital archives for longer preservation of information resources.

Web Technology for Digital Libraries

The web technology has made tremendous changes in dissemination of scholarly information and knowledge. The growth and usage of Internet is so enormous that huge number of organizations and institutions and large number of people have adopted the medium as their common platform in regular manner not only for official work but also for information exchange and dissemination. As per one study, there are more than 15 million web sites and 10 billion web pages. It can be said that internet has become the most sought after tool without which it is very difficult to develop the practice of information dissemination system. Day by day the demand for Internet increases and its accessibility in remote areas is improving. The most vibrant role played by the Internet is to harness the wider access to information and knowledge through digital technology. The exchange of knowledge in digital form is effectively possible through the web based technology and services. Hence the web technology is the basic requirement of successful digital libraries.

Uses of Digital Library

The purpose of digital library is to facilitate direct access to information resources available in a particular library and to develop the links among the partner libraries for wider access to information. According to Trivedi (2010), the purpose of a digital library includes:

- To expedite the systematic development of procedures to collect, store, and organize information in digital form.
- To promote efficient delivery of information economically to all users.
- To encourage co-operative efforts in research resource, computing, and communication networks.

- To strengthen communication and collaboration between and among educational institutions.
- To take leadership role in the generation and dissemination of knowledge.

The basic objective of digital library is to develop a system in which a library can rejuvenate the decaying cultural and scientific information and make it accessible in readable format for further use and preservation for posterity. All the valuable documents of historical importance need to be preserved through developing digital archives. Libraries practicing to develop digitization of its information resources should make the facility of access for a wider audience so that the purpose of the law of library science 'information for use' is fulfilled. Another most important consideration is that intellectual property rights are not violated in developing digitization. It is the role of the library to create interoperability of digital library system through open standard. During the present era when scholarly communication of information is the order of the day digital library plays a pivotal role in linking to research and development networks. Hence creating digital contents and its effective dissemination globally is the basic tenet of a digital library. Another significant responsibility of a library in its digitization effort is to create the institutional repository of its intellectual property. Digital library is the panacea to such a situation. Hence taking advantage of the ICTs, the libraries are successfully developing digital contents of their own collection.

Creation of Digital Contents

The onerous task before the library authority is to take a decision for conversion of print collection into electronic. Normally two types of digital collection are available in libraries, such as 'born digital' and 'turn digital'. Those contents already available in soft copy format are termed as born digital and those collections are to be converted into electronic formats for which it is called turn digital. The library authority must take a decision of selection of documents for digitization. In this process it allows the creation of virtual collection bringing together material across continents. Irrespective of the place of publication and origin of content a library must decide the usefulness factor of the materials to be digitized.

Libraries used to create contents in different manner and most information services are contents created from the library collection and repackaged to tailor the needs of the users. But here in digitization process, it is different types of content creation where information selected should have the quality of the scholarly uses. Before creating contents, the information specialists have to design the strategy of developing the contents in digital formats. One should emphasize the factors such as, type of contents, method of creation cost involved, and needs of the users and sustainability of content creation for a longer time. In these circumstances, what type of contents are to be created is a matter to be decided by the library authority. How the nature of content will attract the user groups is to be taken into consideration. A long term budget will be needed for the creation and effective management of such contents is often required to be serviceable for a longer period. The contents created must serve the users community so that they must derive proper uses and utmost satisfaction with such contents (Mahapatra, 2012).

Digitization is basically done for the documents which are of research use and needs archival preservation. The institutions desiring to preserve their research outputs are to develop institutional repositories for which digital library is the only answer. Some libraries have fragile documents which are required to be preserved for the future. Such types of documents are old manuscripts, old music recordings, newspapers, cultural artifacts, etc need preservation. Other important documents are local history collections of a library which are decaying day by day need to be preserved through electronically. Most university and public libraries have very old books, annual reports, research reports convocation speeches which are also very useful publications in specific subjects which do not come under copyright restrictions may be digitized. Other types of documents need digitization are endangered/ threatened species of plants and animals, collection for disabled and children. Content creation of all those materials may be taken up by the libraries so that the digitization effort will be a successful.

Developing Networks

Internet has been developed as a global network of networks in which information can be browsed by any one and accessible at any point. The global Internet using population grew 444.8% from

2000 to 2010 (MMG, 2010). Through such a network, it is not only possible to develop a digital library, but also form other types of metropolitan networks or country wide networks for developing a digital library. In most subject based networking consortia are developed among similar organizations for effective dissemination of specific subject based information such as engineering, medicine, agriculture, etc. In India, subject based consortia have been developed through networks, such as UGC Infonet, INDEST, CeRA, Forsa, etc. Such networks are primarily designed for dissemination of e-journals among specific disciplines. However, such other digital libraries in India have been developed are: Muktabodh digital Library, Vidyanidhi, KrishiPrabha, eGranth, Open Med, ePrint@iisc and J-Gate to name a few. They have developed their own networks in subject based approaches to scholarly dissemination of knowledge. It is imperative on the part of the library to either develop its own network, or become the partner of a larger network for effective dissemination of information.

Requirement for Accessing Digital Library

Traditional libraries developing digital contents in its ambit face a number of problems. In order to develop comprehensive access to digital scholarly information, certain pre-condition are to be fulfilled. The first and foremost requirement is developing a sound infrastructure comprising communication network, computer hardware and software. Telecommunication network is obviously a pre-requirement. It is normally accepted that Internet is the most favourable network which can be used for developing a network for the digital library. The adoption of a broad band connection of Internet helps develop the sound network for which the use of digital library is feasible.

Procurement of computers and other hardware constitutes the next level which is essential to enable use of the digital library. Internet facility with high speed broadband capacity is essential. Without enough computers, it is impossible to get sufficient access time. Without adequate memory, speed and storage, it is impossible to open, download or use electronic scholarly information. These problems can be compounded by ageing hardware and lack of technical support.

Up to date and efficient software is equally important. Proprietary software may be too expensive and lack compatibility with other systems. Open source software appears to be very useful, but it needs thorough knowledge and expertise for developing a system so that such free software can be made useful in digitization of library resources.

Since designing and implementing digital library primarily depends upon knowledge and skill of the library professionals, there is a greater need for training and skill development of the professionals working in the library. Use of scholarly information demands high levels of literacy and the development of information literacy. Those who do not have the opportunities to develop the necessary skills are unable to use digital scholarly information effectively. They lack the codes to open the digital library. Advanced skills are required to manage systems and to be able to develop digitization. Without those abilities, scholars remain idle and their creations are locked out of contemporary scholarly communication. Language is the most important ability. Other languages are catching up to English and are doing so at a faster rate than was predicted (Pastore 1999).

Conclusion

Digital libraries are the neo form of electronic libraries that are designed to accelerate the flow of scholarly information. Technology has already reached the stage where traditional libraries can be converted into digital libraries provided the librarians take the initiative and the library authority supports the decision to develop digital libraries. Internet and other web based technologies, system and services will be effectively used to expand the horizon of digital libraries. Developing digital libraries involves huge cost and strong technological knowledge and expertise. However, necessary infrastructure, computer hardware and software, telecommunication networks, adequate skill and expertise and after all positive attitude can be the sources through which a digital library can be developed in a sound footing. Moreover, digital library is the answer to the right dissemination of scholarly information for research use.

References

Berring, RC 1993, 'Future librarians', in Future libraries, RH Bloch and C Hesse, eds., Berkeley, University of California Press pp. 94-115.

Borgman, C.L. (1999). What are digital libraries? Competing visions. Information Processing & Management, 35: 227-243.

http://cyberatlas.internet.com.

Ince, D 2001 A dictionary of the Internet, Oxford Reference Online, Oxford, Oxford University Press. http://www.oxfordreference.com/

Johnston, R, Gregory, D, et al. 2000 The dictionary of human geography, xreferplus, Oxford, Blackwell. http://www.xreferplus.com/entry/734102.

Lynch, C.A. (1994). The integrity of digital information: Mechanism and definitional issues. Silver Spring, MD: ASIS.

Mahapatra, R.K. (2012). Digital content creation and management in agricultural libraries in India; Trends and Issues. DESIDOC Journal of Information Technology. V.32 No1.

Miniwatt Marketing Group (2010).World Internet Usage Statistics. www.informworldststs. com/stop.htm.

Pastore, M 1999, 'The language of the web', in Cyber Atlas, 6 July 1999.

Trivcdi, M. (2010) Digital libraries: functionality, usability, and accessibility. Library Philosophy and Practice. Available: http://unllib.unl.edu/LPP/trivedi-diglib.htm

UNESCO (2009). Digital Library Manifesto. www.unesco.digital

WSIS 2003, 'World Summit on the Information Society', International Telecommunications Union. http://www.itu.int/wsis.

Author Index

a

Arvind Mittal 197

b

B.P. Singh 67
B.R. Yadav 67
Balwan Singh 1
Barsha Gupta 139
Bhanu Partap 145
Bharat Praveen Sonker 187
Brajesh Tiwari 15, 207

c

Chandresh A. Shah 247

d

D. Ravinder 25
Dev Walia 33
Devraj 169

f

Faheem Khan 39

j

Jadhav U.S. 255

k

K. N. Kandpal 39
Kamal Lochan Jena 237
Khaisar Muncebulla Khan 47

m

M. Papegowda 81
Madhav Pandey 267
Manoj Tiwari 73, 117
Minhaj Fatima 59

n

N.S. Rohila 67
Nidhi S Tiwari 117
Nidhi Srivastava 73

p

Prem Lata 93

r

R. H. Walmiki 81
R.D. Dabhi 99
R.M. Shivakumar 81
Rabindra K. Mahapatra 247, 277
Rajive Pateria 145

Rajkumar Singh 107
Ramnivas Sharma 73, 117
Rishabh Kumar Jain 129

s

S.S. Rawat 39
Saurabh Nagariya 139
Seema Parmar 145
Stanley Madan Kumar 161, 169
Subarna K. Das 177
Subramani, M.K 161
Sudhir Gupta vi, 93
Sunil Kumar Satpathy 227
Surendra Kumar Pal 187

t

Tarvinder Singh Handa 197

u

Uaday Kumar Watti 15, 207
Ushabala 99

v

V. Srinivasa 81

y

Y. Ch. Venkateswarlu 217
Yadunath Prasad 277
Yashodha Negi vi, 93

FSC
www.fsc.org
MIX
Papier | Fördert gute Waldnutzung
FSC® C083411

Zeitfracht Medien GmbH
Ferdinand-Jühlke-Straße 7
99095 Erfurt, Deutschland
produktsicherheit@kolibri360.de